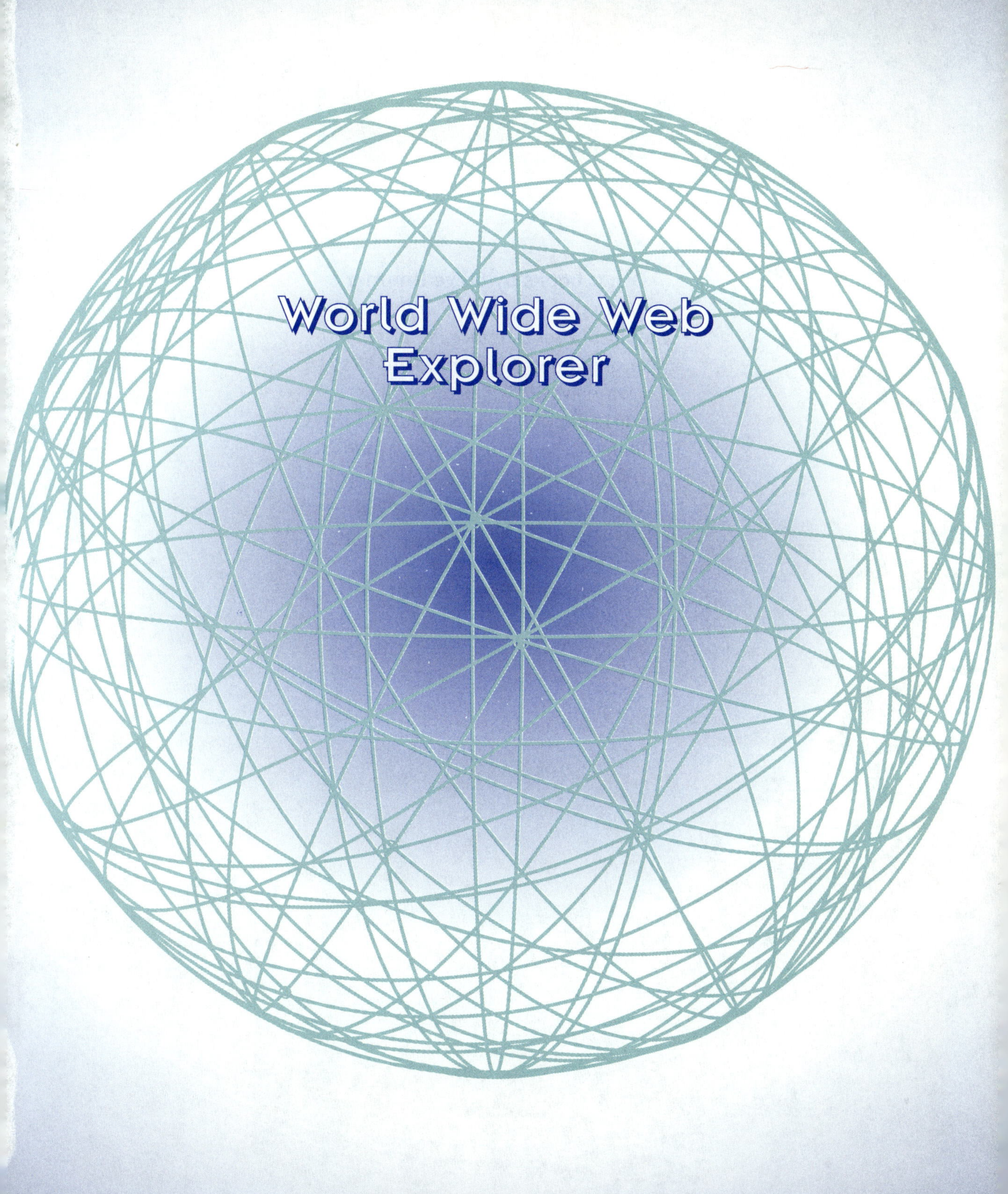
World Wide Web
Explorer

Other books by Steve Rimmer

Bit-Mapped Graphics — 2nd Edition
Graphical User Interface Programming
Supercharged Bitmapped Graphics
Windows Bit-Mapped Graphics
Super VGA Graphics: Programming Secrets
Multimedia Programming for Windows
Canned Code for DOS and Windows
Constructing Windows Dialogs
Advanced Multimedia Programming
Planet Internet
Return to Planet Return

World Wide Web Explorer

Steve Rimmer

McGraw-Hill
New York San Francisco Washington, D.C. Auckland Bogotá Caracas Lisbon London Madrid
Mexico City Milan Montreal New Delhi San Juan Singapore Sydney Tokyo Toronto

McGraw-Hill
A Division of The ***McGraw-Hill*** *Companies*

The classic graphics in this book are courtesy of Planet Art, 505 S. Beverly Drive, Suite 242, Beverly Hills, CA 90212, (213)-651-3405

The gargoyle art in the "Incredible Collectibles" is courtesy of John Bottomley, Gargoyle Renaissance.

The illlustrations in the topic "The Mother of All Humor Archives" are courtesy of Nigel Sussman.

The photographs in the "World Wide Glide" are courtesy of Lisa A. Doyle.

pbk 1 2 3 4 5 6 7 8 9 FGR/FGR 9 0 0 9 8 7 6 5
hc 1 2 3 4 5 6 7 8 9 FGR/FGR 9 0 0 9 8 7 6 5

Library of Congress Cataloging-in-Publication Data
Rimmer, Steve
World Wide Web explorer / by Steve Rimmer.
p. cm.
Includes index.
ISBN 0-07-053027-0 (p)
1. World Wide Web (Information retrieval system) I. Title.
TK5105.888.R56 1995
025.04—dc20 95-39235
CIP

McGraw-Hill books are available at special quantity discounts to use as premimums and sales promotions, or for use in corporate training programs. For more information, please write to the Director of Special Sales, McGraw-Hill, 11 West 19th Street, New York, NY 10011. Or contact your local bookstore.

Acquisitions Editor: Brad Schepp
Editorial team: Kellie Hagan, Book Editor
Robert E. Ostrander, Executive Editor
Production team: Katherine G. Brown, Director
Ollie Harmon, Coding
J. M. Hall, Computer Artist
Wanda S. Ditch, Desktop Operator
Joann Woy, Indexer
Design team: Jaclyn J. Boone, Designer
Katherine Lukaszewicz, Associate Designer
0530270
PI2

About the author*

Sir Steven William Rimmer, knighted in secret ceremony by Queen Elizabeth of England, awarded the Order of Lenin, Marquis of Brandenberg, titular king of Rwanda, Viscount of Prague, initiate of the 47th degree of the Most Noble and Ancient Brotherhood of Parrotmongers, Earl of Glen Fiddich, special envoy to Her Majesty the Duchess of Bohemia, President of the United States in absentia, discoverer of Australia, court astrologer to Edward I (1272–1307), present holder of the Americas Cup, inventor of the first practical interstellar faster-than-light propulsion system, holder of the Medal for Meritorious Service to the People of Albania, Duke of Tuscany, Anubis the Egyptian god of the afterlife, Tahitian Minister for Alpine Development, cofounder of the Institute for Hyperintelligent Penguin Research on Pitcairn's Island, recipient of the Gold Star with a Severed Monkey's Foot from the Grateful Government and People of Burundi, High Privy Chancellor of East Anglia, Father-Confessor to Catherine de Medici, Prince Bob of Hungary, and composer of the Himalayan national anthem is a reclusive person, and very little is known of him. He lives with his wife Megan and a Bengal tiger named Fluffy somewhere in the western hemisphere. He has written 10^{11} books on subjects ranging from *Sumerian Macroeconomics in a Context of Neo-platonic Oligarchy Extrapolated Through a Continuum of Uncertainty* to *Pet Recycling: A Growth Industry for the 21st Century*. His current projects include directing the remake of D.W. Griffith's classic silent film *Birth of a Nation* as a slapstick musical.

* Mostly lies

Contents

Introduction

Don't read this book if you're easily offended. This is the girl your mother warned you about going out with, or the boy your dad immediately knew was bad news. It's the car that got really bad safety ratings that you bought anyway, the movie that required two separate screens to display all its warnings, the dog that ate all the other dogs at the pet shop an hour before you took it home, all the erotic underwear your friends were sure you'd never have the nerve to wear, Mother Theresa on drugs, half-price bungee jumping because the cord's a bit frayed, the President of the United States directing traffic in a clown suit, microwaving eggs on high and leaving the room, sending a live scorpion to Billy Graham by Federal Express, all the great paintings of the Louvre sorted by ascending breast size, and finding out that the AT&T long-distance ads say "I am an unclean spirit of the netherworld" if you play their soundtracks backwards.

Actually, it's even worse than that. This book will introduce you to a place where people all over the world do whatever they want, all the time. With thirty million people on the case as I write this, a lot of things happen there that would make the foregoing look pretty tame by comparison. Government types, social theorists, and religious leaders call this sort of thing *anarchy*, and it scares the hell out of them. Most of the rest of us would call it *freedom*. That scares the hell out of them even more.

This book is an entry visa and universal green card for the World Wide Web, a facet of the Internet that's bounded only by the collective imagination of the people who use it. While it will walk you through connecting to the Web and give you a tour of an impressive gallery of Web pages, it won't even begin to describe the real diversity of the universe you're about to enter. This is something you can experience only first-hand.

There are two issues to contend with if you want to start navigating the Web. Specifically, you must:

1. Figure out how to connect to the physical hardware of the Internet, choose some suitably intelligent software, get a Net account, and remember where you wrote down your password.
2. Find out where to go once you accomplish step 1.

Step 1 will take you an afternoon; step 2 can occupy the rest of your life if you like.

The first part of this book addresses the issue of getting connected to the Internet with an eye to accessing the World Wide Web. This is neither as easy as it could be nor as difficult as most introductions to the Internet would have you believe. It's a bit perilous, however, because making the wrong choice might leave you with a larger access bill than you really deserve, or with access that's less flexible than it should be. If you read only one chapter of this book, make it the first one.

The second part of this book is a list of over 125 Web pages you can browse to begin your exploration. Because most Web pages include links to still other pages—and those pages have links as well, and so on—this initial library of links will get you to an unending universe of places to click and things to check out. Several hundred new pages come online in the average week—it's a rapidly expanding, unending universe.

Unlike other aspects of the Internet, the World Wide Web is user-friendly, not really very technical, and dead easy to operate. While this book discusses the tricks and nuances of Web access, you'll probably find the whole effort so intuitive as to require no explanation. You can be on the Web an hour after you get connected to the Net, and completely lost in hyperspace an hour after that.

The Web is gratification so instant as to make Polaroids and nukeable popcorn seem tedious by comparison.

Parental guidance is advised

The tricky thing about freedom is that it works only if everyone has it. Limited freedom is a lot like partial tyranny. You'll experience this if you go into a bookshop looking for a book the government doesn't think you should read, or try to get answers to questions the government doesn't think you should know about. At least at the moment, the Internet embodies real freedom—and all the consequences thereof.

The freedom to read whatever you want on the Internet has a lot to do with everyone else's freedom to write whatever they want. This is especially true of the creators of the World Wide Web pages you'll be browsing in a little while. Some of them are pretty extreme.

Most users of the Internet find the freedom it represents exhilarating, especially compared to the suffocating restrictions of the "real" world that most of us are used to. However, there's a catch of sorts to this freedom. From time to time you'll encounter things on the World Wide Web you might think are inappropriate, offensive, vulgar, disgusting, contemptible, and grounds for attacking their creators with small tactical nuclear missiles. You won't be able to do much about it, however, save for going somewhere else and trying to forget about them.

There's no one on the Internet to complain to, and no one with any authority to suppress even the really ugly aspects of the Net. However, this also applies to things that you might really enjoy, however ugly others might find them.

It seems fair to point out that if any of this makes you feel a bit uneasy about connecting to the Internet, the commercial online services are much less likely to offend you. America Online, CompuServe, and Prodigy, for example, are so rigorously policed and sanitized that you can spend your life on one of them and never see so much as a bare breast or read a single expletive. Stories of bondage and discipline, drug abuse, and extreme politics need never trouble you . . . even if you want them to from time to time.

When the sort of things that turn up quite regularly on the Internet appear on the desks of politicians, most of them start drafting laws to regulate the Net and its content. It's beyond the scope of this book to discuss the wisdom or even the practicality of such restrictions—hopefully in the time between my writing this and your reading it the proposed "decency in communications" act before the United States Congress will have gone the way of other forms of prohibition, perhaps this time before it becomes law.

The matter that most proponents of regulating the Internet cite as just cause for doing so is the possibility of children being exposed to the sort of things the Net is becoming infamous for. If you have kids, this is an issue you should probably resolve for yourself.

If you think that children shouldn't be exposed to erotic graphics, really foul language, and frank discussions about sexuality, drugs, racism, violence, and other extreme topics, you really don't want to give them access to the Internet. It's an adult environment, and while the great majority of the resources on the Net wouldn't trouble anyone, there are certainly a few things that kids shouldn't see.

If you choose to introduce your kids to the Net, plan to be around to supervise their use of it. The same holds for this book. Just keep in mind that the Internet isn't a public-access bulletin board. As will be discussed in detail in chapter 1, it takes money to access the Net, usually plastic. Few indeed are the banks willing to issue a Visa card to a ten-year-old. You can easily prevent your children from using your Internet account, and they'll have a pretty hard time getting one of their own.

Mother Theresa on drugs

If you've never explored the World Wide Web, you can't imagine the time you're about to have. Forget all the dogma about the information superhighway, cyberspace, and hypereality. You'll find your own words to describe the experience in a while. They'll be pretty exciting words, too. The Web is the most fun you can have with your clothes on.

Thanks in advance for reading this book—I hope your explorations of the Web are at least as much fun as mine were while I was writing it. You're about to go where everyone has gone before, and they're all waiting to buy you a pint when you get there.

Steve Rimmer
alchemy@accesspt.north.net

Part 1

Tutorial

1

Introducing the World Wide Web

The thing that makes the Internet so fascinating and much beloved of the people who write magazine articles about new technology is that it's impressively vast. What it lacks in user-friendliness it more than makes up for in content. Until very recently, the lack of user-friendliness exhibited by the Internet was sufficient to make Microsoft's technical support services seem almost obsequious by comparison. The Internet, created by people who knew what they were doing for a lot of other people who knew what they were doing, didn't really care much about the rest of the world.

A few years ago the Internet was the embodiment of the aphorism "if software is hard to create, it ought to be hard to use as well." At the same time, the Internet was also an almost closed society—you had to be attending a college or university with Internet access, be working for a large corporation that had lots of money it didn't like the look of or be employed by the U.S. government to access the Internet. Under these circumstances it didn't really have to be user-friendly. There was always someone around to ask questions of if the Net did something untoward.

The real revolution in the way the Internet behaves took place to a large extent when everyone else started obtaining access to it. A number of companies were created to sell access to the Net through dial-up phone connections. Rather than requiring a $50,000 minicomputer in your basement and a $2,000-a-month hardwired connection to an Internet backbone, these dial-up service providers allow anyone with a modem and a PC to connect to the Net for less than a dollar an hour.

Just as computers themselves got a lot friendlier and more sophisticated once they started being sold to people who shopped at Sears, so too has the Internet found itself evolving—some would say mutating—as a result of all the new, nontechnical users flooding its streets and alleys. A lot of things that long-time dwellers of the Net have never really had trouble with turned out to be a bit taxing for first-time Net users. In addition, the Internet's traditional media aren't as graphical and interactive as computer software in general has become.

Figure 1-1 illustrates two pages with much the same content. This text actually came from the Internet, by the way, although having been written in 1749 its original presentation predates personal computers by a few years. Which one of these documents would you prefer to read?

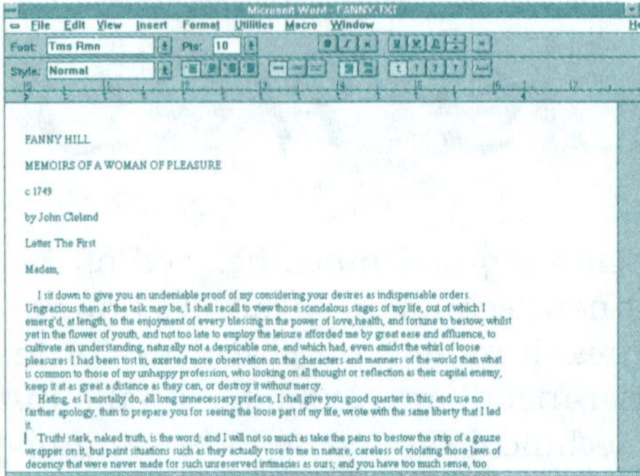

B

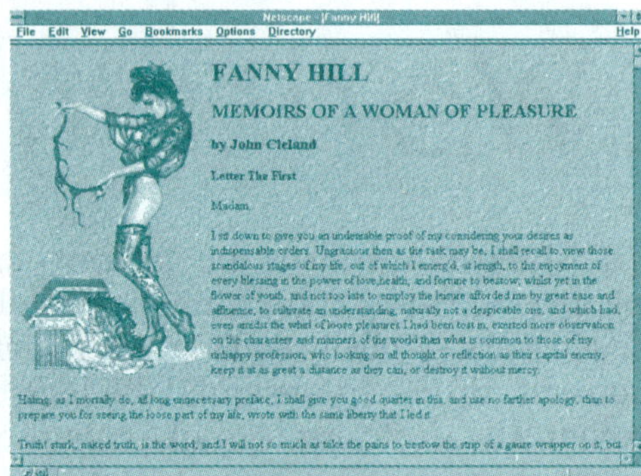

1-1 Fanny Hill on the Internet. 1-1A is a simple text file and 1-1B is a World Wide Web page.

This excerpt from *Fanny Hill* illustrates some of the underlying superficiality of the Western mindset, to be sure. The text-only version of the story requires a lot less space to deal with a lot more information than the graphic version does. Nonetheless, the graphic version is a lot more readable.

The salient point in all this is that you have to read several pages into *Fanny Hill* before you get to the bit where Fanny loses her virginity and the book starts to get interesting. If the presentation of the book is so unexciting and generally unreadable as to make this a labor you're reluctant to get around to, you'll probably never bother with this seminal work of English literature. *Fanny Hill*—as with all sorts of other things to be found on the Net—is meant to be read and enjoyed. The presentation of the book in Fig. 1-1B, which is formatted and occasionally dotted with graphics, is a lot more readable.

There's not a lot of point in producing exciting resources on the Internet if they don't look any better than Fig. 1-1A, and no one bothers to read them as a result.

If you don't like this justification for pages that have been infested with boldface text, periodic italics, and pictures, you might want to consider that the advent of word processing, desktop publishing, and laser printers has meant that most people express themselves with typography, rather than merely with text. Being able to include italics and bold headlines in writing has become part of the way we convey what we really mean when we write. Just plain words don't cut it like they did back in 1749.

The engine that makes simple text look like Fig. 1-1B is something called HTML, or *hypertext markup language*. It's actually a very simple way of coding text so it includes definitions for things like font changes, text formatting, graphics, clickable links, and all sorts of other phenomena. Better still, you'll never have to learn anything more about it than I've explained in this paragraph in order to use it as it appears on the Internet. The best thing about HTML is that it stays out of your face when it's at work.

Think of HTML as a sort of word-processing document format you can readily send over the Internet that's understood by software on a variety of computers. Several things make it really useful as a way to communicate expressively over the Internet:

- HTML documents are typically very small.
- They can include hypertext links to other documents.
- They don't define specific text effects, only specifications.
- They can include other media.

This requires some additional explanation, but once you understand what HTML really is, you'll be a long way toward understanding the World Wide Web, which is presumably why you bought this book to begin with.

Figure 1-2 will be familiar to anyone who has worked with a Microsoft Windows application, and probably not unfamiliar to Macintosh or OS/2 users. It's a help file, and most operating systems allow for something along these lines to be embedded in applications running under them. A help file is one of the most common implementations of hypertext.

The underlined bits in Fig. 1-2 are hypertext links. If you click on one, the current page of text and graphic will be replaced with a new page, possibly having further links. Click on one of these new links and you'll find yourself looking at yet another page. Each page in a hypertext document can link to dependent pages, which can link to still more dependent pages, and so on.

The original text of *Fanny Hill* is a linear document. This means that it's intended to be read from beginning to end, with no obvious digressions or jumping around. While this is how you'd properly read a novel, you might want to improve on it. Being well over a quarter of a millennium old, some of the language and many of the colloquial references—and a lot of the more interesting sexual innuendos—aren't as easily understood as they might have been when the book was written.

In a paper book, this sort of situation is usually handled with footnotes or references at the back of the book. In a hypertext document, however, you could deal with it by using links. You could set up the words or phrases that might require further explanation as links to dependent pages. If you wanted to see the explanation for a specific obscure phrase, you could click on it and call up its page.

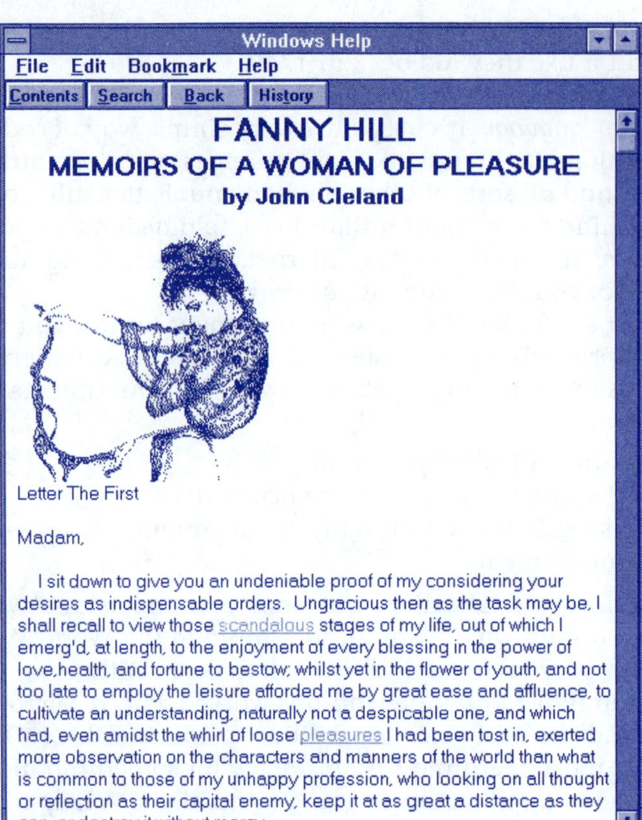

1-2
Fanny Hill meets Windows help.

Hypertext documents are hierarchical. A diagram of the links in a typical hypertext document would resemble an inverted tree—a root page with lots of dependent branches.

In a help file like the one in Fig. 1-2, the dependent pages accessible through links must be physically located in the same file as the first page. In an HTML document, links can point to part of the same document as the home page, different documents on the same server as the home page, or different documents on a wholly different server located in the back room of a semiretired fishmonger's warehouse in east Sussex. Whenever you click on a link, the software displaying the HTML document in question will figure out where the link points and fetch the page for you, even if the page in question is halfway around the world.

Here's a bit of "netspeak" having to do with HTML. The software that displays HTML documents and lets you click all over the world is properly called a *mosaic client*. More commonly, it's called a *Web browser*.

Styles, graphics, and sounds

Web browsers exist for pretty well anything that has a microprocessor and is more complex than a toaster. This includes PC, Macintosh, and UNIX-based systems, among many other things. Figure 1-3 illustrates a Web browser displaying a typical HTML document from the Internet. This is actually the home page for my company.

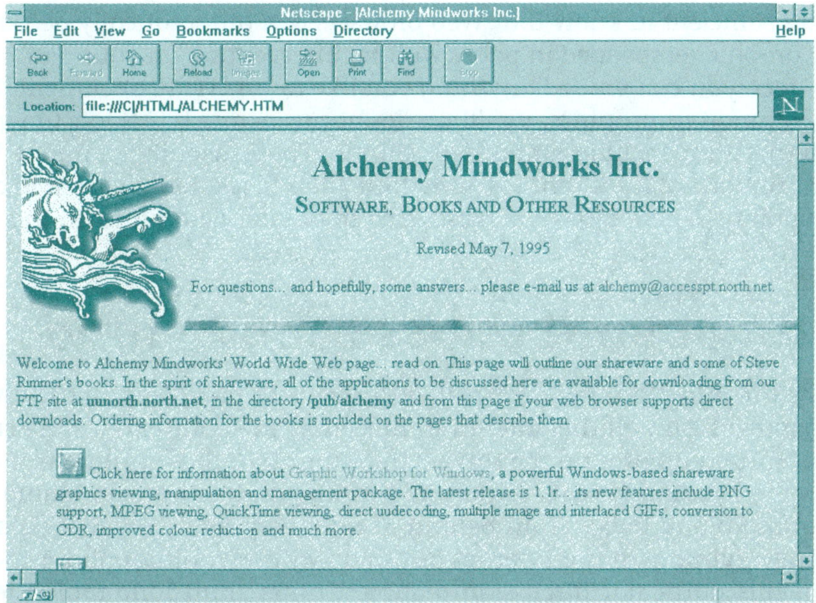

1-3 Netscape (a Web browser) revealed.

The important thing about the document in Fig. 1-3 is that, while I created it and subsequently displayed it on a PC running Windows, it would have come up looking more or less the same on a Macintosh or anything else running a graphical Web browser. The HTML document definition was written with this in mind. The document that defines what Fig. 1-3 looks like is unlike a conventional word-processing document because it doesn't specify anything that's specific to Windows or PC systems—or anything else that isn't readily portable. For example, those bold headlines aren't defined as 36-point Times Roman Bold in this document, but rather as something called <H1>, or a first level head. Every Web browser is free to define what the font for a first level head is, based on the fonts that really exist on the machine that's running it.

As a result, your experiences of the World Wide Web might not look cosmetically identical to the ones printed in this book, but they'll always be attractive and readable. In most cases you'll find that your Web browser allows you to define the fonts and other typography used in HTML documents to suit yourself. The collected definition of all the fonts and such to be displayed is called a *style*.

Aside from the text back in Fig. 1-3, there's a unicorn. Clearly not a text element, the unicorn is an illustration of one of the additional features of HTML: including graphics with the text on a page. Graphics are typically stored in one of two file formats when they appear in HTML documents, GIF and JPEG. I'll say a lot more about this later on—it's potentially a bit complex. For the moment, it's sufficient to know that Web browsers can automatically decode and display graphics embedded in pages with no intervention on your part.

In fact, you can embed anything you like in an HTML document. While not as common as graphics, you'll no doubt run across HTML documents on the Internet that include embedded sounds. These usually manifest themselves as buttons or links that say something like "click here to listen to a poodle exploding." These too will be discussed in greater detail later in this book.

Boffing blond babes from behind

Actually, the thing that makes HTML documents so prevalent on the Internet at the moment isn't all this interest in links and such. Rather, it's the culture that has sprung up around the servers that maintain the documents in question. As the heading for this section might suggest, this has something to do with boffing blond babes from behind, if only very obliquely. I should note that not everything on the Internet has to do with sex, although for the purposes of this particular discussion a subject other than long-molecule synthetic polymers in stress-related industrial applications is probably called for.

On the Internet as it existed a few years ago, if you wanted to create some sort of a resource to discuss boffing blond babes from behind—or some other matter that might not have met with the unconditional approval of the society of the Internet as a whole—you would have been faced with a bit of a quandary. The most commonly encountered public forum of the Internet was that of Usenet, or newsgroups. You could have attempted to create a newsgroup along the lines of alt.boffing.blond.babes.from.behind, but Usenet is a service that must be explicitly carried by all the servers people will be using to access it. The administrators of specific servers are free to carry individual newsgroups or not, as they see fit. If a significant number of administrators decided that alt.boffing.blond.babes.from.behind was in bad taste, frivolous, or otherwise beneath their consideration, it probably would not have achieved wide enough exposure to really work as a newsgroup. (Of course, it arguably *is* frivolous and in bad taste, but this isn't the issue here.)

Another approach to this problem—and, incidentally, one more analogous to what an HTML document would ultimately provide for such a resource—would have been to create a gopher server for the subject. This, however, requires a substantial bit of software and, if you wanted your gopher to be registered with the University of Minnesota, the "central gopher hole," you'd also require their consent and probably the exchange of some cash. People looking for gopher servers usually start with the central gopher at the University of Minnesota—not being registered there would severely limit the number of potential users of your resource.

The really restrictive thing about both of these examples is that they entail your resource having the approval of other parties. In this case, the parties in question might object to the project on the grounds of it being politically incorrect. In the case of Fig. 1-3 a while back, some old-time Internet puritans might complain that a page for my software company represents a commercial use of the Internet, something traditionally frowned upon in certain circles. We'll touch on this matter a little later, too.

An HTML document living on a server connected to the Internet doesn't need anyone's approval for its being there. It's just a publicly accessible file. If someone comes along with a Web browser, they can view it. It need not be linked into any formal structure, like Usenet or Gopher. The only problem with it is getting people to come and look at it. This is where all that cultural flotsam mentioned at the beginning of this section turns up.

Traditionally, an HTML document in this context will have, in addition to whatever it's set up to do, a list of links to other interesting HTML documents elsewhere on the Internet. Recall that links can call up pages from other servers. If you go to the set of links on my page back in Fig. 1-3 and click on one of them, you'll find yourself at a wholly different page dealing with a completely different subject.

The tradition that has seen a number of links to other resources at my HTML document means that there will also be some links at whatever documents you link to from my page. Those links will point you to still more links, and so on. You can click all over the world this way, spanning a breathtaking variety of subjects. This structure is what's called the World Wide Web. It's constantly growing—as I write this there are about 25,000 pages, with perhaps 500 new ones coming on line every week.

Anyone can create a Web page, about any topic imaginable. The cost of doing so is negligible—two or three dollars a month will usually cover the cost of the space on the server where a Web page exists, and in some cases you can have the storage for free. All that's required to link a new page into the Web is for the owners of a few existing pages to add it to their list of links.

There are, in fact, a number of repositories of links to most of the Web pages on earth—or some reasonable fraction thereof. There's also a Web page that lists announcements of new pages, updated every few days. I'll deal with these resources in detail later in this book. For the most part, though, the World Wide Web is a fantastic universe of scattered resources that you can explore 'til your monitor burns out.

To date, nothing has turned up specifically to deal with boffing blond babes from behind, by the way, but there are countless reasonable substitutes.

Getting online: a quick look at the options

Accessing the Internet used to be easy, as there were relatively few ways to do it. It has become a great deal more complex because everyone wants to provide you with access—for a price. The magnitude of that price and the exact nature of the access in question varies a lot; more to the point, they're not always quite what they seem. This section deals specifically with some options for dial-up Internet access.

At least in terms of dealing with the World Wide Web, most Internet access allows you to handle what I'll be discussing in this book. However, you'll find that the cost of doing so and the overall flexibility with which you can manage the Internet is worthy of a bit of forethought.

To begin with, there are two basic sorts of dial-up connections. You can deal with either a dedicated Internet access provider or a large dial-up service that provides Internet connectivity as one of its features. Among the latter services as I write this are Prodigy and America OnLine. As a rule, the former are considerably less expensive and the latter are generally easier to get started with.

You can access the World Wide Web using nothing but plain text if you want to—there's a Web browser called Lynx to handle this—but almost no one wants to; the graphical nature of the Web is one of the things that makes it so interesting. With this in mind, you'll probably want to deal with the Internet, and from there with the Web, in a graphical environment such as Windows, OS/2 Warp, or Macintosh. Some of the software discussed in this chapter exists for all these platforms—the computer you use won't actually make much of a difference in how you work with the Web, or what Web pages will look like to you.

Dedicated Internet access providers were the first avenues to the Internet for users without hardwired connections to it. In the simplest sense, an Internet access provider consists of a server—a computer to deal with the Net—and a number of phone lines and modems. Typically there's also some accounting software in there somewhere to keep track of how much each user of the service owes the owner of the server.

For the purposes of this discussion, Internet access providers allow you to connect directly to the Internet through their servers. In fact, what really happens is that the software on your computer that wants to deal with the Internet talks through several intermediate stages of communication between your system and an actual Internet backbone. The effect, however, is the same as a direct hardwired link from your computer to the Net, save that it's significantly slower. You also have to establish the link each time you want to access the Net by dialing the server.

These dial-up connections are governed by a fairly rigid communications protocol. Two protocols are typically supported by Internet access providers: SLIP and PPP. These stand for *serial line Internet protocol* and *point-to-point protocol*, respectively. As a rough guideline, SLIP is a bit faster and PPP is somewhat easier to set up and, in theory, a bit more reliable. In practice, either one will suffice for a dial-up Internet connection.

If you decide to access the Internet through a dedicated access provider, then, you'll need someone to provide you with a SLIP or PPP connection—most of them do. You'll also probably want someone to help you configure some of the software you'll be using—this is discussed in greater detail later in this chapter in the section about the dark and grisly reality of Trumpet WinSock.

There's a lot to be said for dealing with the Internet through a dedicated access provider. One of the first things you'll probably say about it if you decide to use one is that it's a very inexpensive way to access the Internet. As a rough guide, plan on spending about 50 cents an hour to access the Net this way. The commercial services, such as Prodigy, offer you a lot of user-friendliness that dedicated access providers typically don't, but those 24-hour toll-free help lines and menus springing out at you from every direction have a cost associated with them.

It's probably worth noting that, while dedicated Internet access providers typically don't offer you the sort of seamless interface to the Web that CompuServe or Prodigy do, they'll often provide you with another sort of very useful help. Most of these companies are run by old Internet hands—people who've been using the Net since pure text was state of the art. They can advise you about matters of *netiquette*, that is, how to behave on the Net so as not to be regarded as a barbarian from the ugly side of town looking to buy souvenirs.

Of course, a few weeks after you get started with the Web you probably won't require much help of any sort. At this point, a dedicated Internet access provider won't be charging you for any.

Another consideration in using a dedicated Internet access provider to browse the Web is that doing so gives you the flexibility to choose the software you'll be using. Later on in this chapter I'll deal with World Wide Web software called Netscape, which is the package I use. However, if you use a dedicated Internet access provider you don't have to agree with my choice—there are over half a dozen popular Web packages available to run under Windows and several other operating systems as I write this, and you can choose the one that best suits your needs.

There are also a lot of Internet access providers, with more appearing all the time. Appendix A lists several of them, with information about finding the current list.

WinSock, Windows, and Netscape

While you might well access the Web through something other than Windows-based software, you should read this section just the same. It deals with several basic elements of the Web and Web access that are common to all platforms.

As was touched on earlier, the window through which you can view the Web is an application called a *Web browser*. There are a lot of Web browsers about, for a variety of computers. While some of them are more functional than others, they have a common basic structure. They're also pretty easy to understand. Operating a Web browser is almost as complicated as operating a pencil.

This discussion deals with the Web browser I use, a Windows application called Netscape. Because the structure of the Web suggests a pretty obvious approach to writing Web browsers, however, you'll find that the features and operation of Netscape are reflected in most other Web browser packages. This is also true of the Web as it appears through America Online, Prodigy, and other large dial-up services. Figure 1-3, earlier in the chapter, illustrates Netscape and its various elements.

Let's begin with the most basic consideration of the Web, to wit, how pages are located. With your Web browser running and connected to the Internet, you need to tell it where to find the first page you want to look at. Web pages are addressed through what are called URLs, or *uniform resource locators*. They're a bit cumbersome to work with, but you might well have to type only one in. You can thereafter just click from one page to the next as you explore the World Wide Web. This is the URL for my Web page:

```
http://www.north.net/alchemy/alchemy.html
```

A URL that specifies an HTML document always begins with http. As I'll discuss later in this book, URLs can point to other things on the Net, such as FTP sites. Following the definition of the type of resource to be browsed there are always a colon and two forward slashes. The next part of the URL specifies the name of the server that the Web page about to be browsed lives on, in this case uunorth.north.net. Finally, there's a path to the page itself: 8000/alchemy/html/alchemy.html.

Some Web browsers allow you to enter the URL of a page you want to browse through a dialog box. In the case of Netscape, you can do so by typing the URL into the Location field near the top of the Netscape window and hitting Enter. Netscape will fetch the page in question and display it for you.

Most Web pages are too long to be displayed in their entirety. Netscape provides a scroll bar to pan over the pages it displays. Figure 1-4 illustrates some of the salient landmarks of my Web page. These are elements you'll encounter in virtually all the pages you browse through on the Web.

The most important objects in Fig. 1-4 are the page links. Netscape, by default, displays these as underlined blue text if you haven't linked to them recently and as underlined purple text if you have. You can, of course, revisit linked pages as often as you like—the purple links are useful in keeping track of where you've previously been.

In addition to text links, Web pages can include graphic links. A graphic link is a clickable graphic element. They work the same way text links do, and are wholly cosmetic. Nonetheless, you'll find them used extensively in Web pages. Most civilized Web pages have text links that correspond to their graphic links for use by Web browsers that can't display graphics or that have had their graphics switched off. I'll get to the latter situation in a moment. It's worth noting that this is by no means always the case—some pages are very graphics-intensive, so you can't use them properly without the graphics.

In the page in Fig. 1-4, the square stones beside the various items on the page are graphic links. For example, clicking on either the first square stone or the underlined text *Graphic Workshop for Windows* will get you to the Graphic Workshop for Windows page.

You'll notice a link at the very top of the page, under the title. This is my e-mail address. You'll usually find links like this in Web pages. In most cases, when an e-mail address appears as a link it calls up a Mail To box rather than another Web page. A Mail To box is a very tiny e-mail editor. It allows you to compose a message and send it to the owner of the e-mail address in question, all without having to run your own mail software. Not all Web browsers support Mail To, but most do.

Here's something else to keep in mind about Web pages in general, and about the page in Fig. 1-4 in particular. Netscape is among the most popular of Web browsers. In fact, it's so popular that its author has defined some minor extensions to the basic HTML language definition, and these extensions have become widely accepted among the people who create and maintain Web pages. There are a few of them visible in my Web page, including the textured background and the text to the right of the unicorn graphic—pure HTML doesn't allow for these—as well as the variable size fonts in the second line of the heading at the top.

A Web browser other than Netscape—that is, one that doesn't recognize the Netscape HTML extensions—would still display my page, but it wouldn't

Alchemy Mindworks Inc.

SOFTWARE, BOOKS AND OTHER RESOURCES

Revised January 5, 1995

For questions ... and hopefully, some answers ... please e-mail us at alchemy@accesspt.north.net.

Welcome to Alchemy Mindworks' World Wide Web page... read on. This page will outline our shareware and some of Steve Rimmer's books. In the spirit of shareware, all of the applications to be discussed here are available for downloading from our FTP site at **uunorth.north.net**, in the directory **/pub/alchemy** and from this page if your web browser supports direct downloads. Ordering information for the books is included on the pages that describe them.

- Click here for information about Graphic Workshop for Windows, a powerful Windows-based shareware graphics viewing, manipulation and management package. The latest release is 1.1o... its new features include direct uudecoding, multiple image GIFs, conversion to CDR, improved colour reduction and much more.
- Click here for information about Graphic Workshop for DOS, a powerful DOS-based shareware graphics viewing, manipulation and management package. The latest release is 7.0e... its new features include direct uudecoding
- Click here for information about Desktop Paint, a powerful DOS-based shareware paint package.
- Click here for information about Pagan Daybook for DOS and Windows, a calendar to keep track of the festivals and observances of the pagan year. Pagan Daybook is being distributed as bookware.
- Click here for information about QuickShow Light for Windows, a powerful Windows multimedia slide show package. QuickShow Light is being distributed as bookware.

If you don't wish to download these files directly, you can order a disk set with shareware versions of all our applications for $10.00. Call 1-800-268-1138 or 1-905-936-9500 to order it by credit card, or click here.

The following are books by Steven William Rimmer.

- Click here for information about DOS Programming books, including **Bitmapped Graphics** and **Super VGA Graphic Programming Secrets**.
- Click here for information about Windows Programming books, including **Windows Bitmapped Graphics** and **Windows Multimedia Programming**.
- Click here for information about Professional Graphics books, including **Corel Draw It** and **Graphic File Toolkit**.
- Click here for information about Internet books, including **Planet Internet**.
- Click here for information about Steve's novels, including **The Order** and **Wyrcad**.

The following are our low cost graphic and clip art collections, and other features.

- Click here for information about the Graphic and Sound CD-ROM, a collection of over a thousand hand-chosen public domain graphics.
- Click here for information about our Monochrome Clip Art Library, a collection of black and white public domain images.
- Click here for a list of other interesting World Wide Web pages.

If you have any questions about our shareware, Steve's books, any of our other products or why so few dolphins can expect a rewarding career in the field of dental prosthetics, click here to send us some e-mail.

Click here for information about contacting Alchemy Mindworks through other media... there are a lot of other media.

All the information on our Word Wide Web page is as accurate as we can make it. Alchemy Mindworks Inc. accepts no responsibility for any loss, damage or expense caused by your use of these pages, however it happens. If you can figure out a way for any of this to cause you loss, damage or expense you have a sneakier mind than any of us. This page and all dependent pages are copyright (c) 1994 Alchemy Mindworks Inc.

Should you fail to register any of the shareware listed in this page and continue to use it, be advised that a leather winged demon of the night will tear itself, shrieking blood and fury, from the endless caverns of the nether world, hurl itself into the darkness with a thirst for blood on its slavering fangs and search the very threads of time for the throbbing of your heartbeat. Alchemy Mindworks Inc. accepts no responsibility for any loss, damage or expense caused by this, either.

1-4
Some common elements of Web pages.

look quite the way I designed it. Some elements of it might look decidedly incorrect. If you're using a Web browser other than Netscape you'll probably encounter pages that look really odd from time to time for this reason. Figure 1-5 illustrates the top of my Web page as seen by a different Web browser.

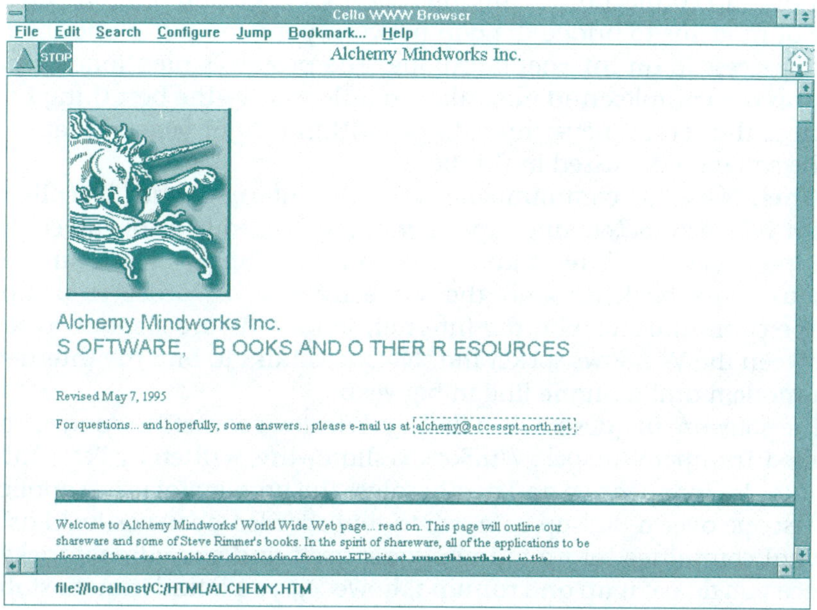

1-5 My Web page as seen through the Cello Web browser.

There's one other important element in a basic Web browser. As you navigate the Web, you'll probably encounter pages you like and want to return to. Most Web browsers have a bookmark facility to keep a running list of the interesting pages you come across. Under Netscape, you can add the URL of the current page Netscape is looking at to its list of bookmarks by selecting Add Bookmark from the Bookmark menu. Bookmarks turn up as additional items in the Bookmark menu, and as items in a list of bookmarks you can call up as a separate window. Selecting a bookmark from the list will cause Netscape to fetch the page in question. After a while your bookmark list will probably start getting a bit full.

WinSock—Netscape's dark side

Thus far nothing has been said about how Netscape actually communicates with the Internet. In fact, the interface can vary a bit—this section deals specifically with communication through a dial-up interface. If you enjoy the luxury of a hardwired connection to the Net, a lot of this discussion won't apply to you. You should be grateful if this is the case, as a lot of the following has all the elegant simplicity and seamless perfection of two freight trains colliding.

A dial-up connection to the Internet involves using a phone line and a couple of modems to bridge the gap between your computer and the nearest physical access to an Internet backbone. The protocols mentioned earlier for doing this are complex and more than a little weird—the best thing I can say of them is that you'll never have to get within a light year of them to work with the software discussed in this book.

When Netscape communicates with the Internet, what it really does is talk to a *Windows socket*. Once again, you don't need to know precisely what a Windows socket is, save that Netscape sends things to one and expects things to come back through the same avenue. In order to actually let Netscape communicate with the Internet, some software is required to mediate between the Windows socket that Netscape talks to and the Internet itself, with a modem and a phone line in between.

The software in question is a dial-up Windows socket "manager," a package called Trumpet WinSock. WinSock is shareware, written by Peter Tattam of Tasmania. It's inexpensive and neatly solves the problem of using applications like Netscape over a dial-up connection, but it's also about as lucid as a congressional committee set up to investigate itself and exceedingly tricky to set up. Once you do get it up and running, however, you'll find that it's stable and relatively easy to use.

Most Internet access providers will help you around the bulk of WinSock's problems by providing you with two key files, to wit, TRUMPWSK.INI and LOGIN.CMD. The former will set up WinSock with all the weird numbers pertinent to your specific Internet access provider, and the latter will automatically dial the appropriate phone number and handle all the initial formalities, usually including entering your user name and password.

In fact, you should be able to have your Internet access provider send you a disk with WinSock, several other shareware and freeware Internet access packages—Netscape, for example—and all the configuration files you require to get up and running. With this level of preinstallation, a dedicated Internet access provider is no more difficult to get up to speed with than is Prodigy or America Online.

If you do have to install WinSock yourself, you'll need several bits of information from your Internet access provider in order to complete the WinSock Setup dialog. Figure 1-6 illustrates this. Specifically, you must know the following information about the server for your Internet access provider. I've included example values here—these won't work unless you use the same access provider I do:

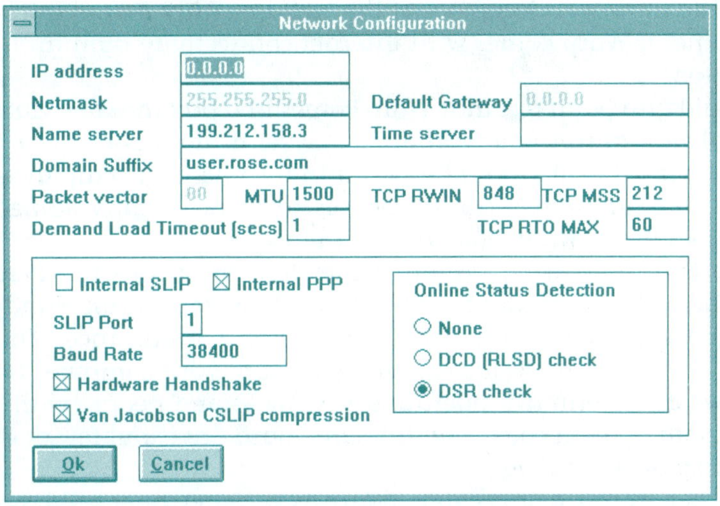

1-6 The Trumpet WinSock setup dialog. Not a pretty sight, and every bit as venomous as it appears.

IP address 198.52.32.165
Default gateway address 198.52.32.14
Net mask 255.255.255.0
Name server addresses 198.52.32.1 198.52.32.3
Domain suffix north.net
Packet vector 00
MTU value 1500
RWIN value 4096
MSS value 1460

You also have to know whether you'll be using a SLIP or PPP connection—Trumpet WinSock supports both.

As a final note, the WinSock package is shareware. Considering that it works quite well once it gets running and is the fundamental element in connecting you to the Net through Windows, it's well worth what it costs. If you use it, be sure to register it.

Warp

Warp is the latest incarnation of IBM's OS/2 operating system. It's a vast improvement over previous releases—and it has been the recipient of a lot of high-power advertising of late, including the memorable television ads with subtitles. The nuns who long to surf the Net are easily my favorite. As I'll get to in a moment, Warp comes with Internet connectivity built in. It's quite respectable, too.

I should also point out that Warp comes in a box that describes it as "the totally cool way to run your computer." Several months before I wrote this, IBM announced that it would be permitting some of its employees to retire their gray suits and wear casual clothes to work. Clearly someone's been putting vodka in the water coolers over there.

Warp is an operating system, somewhat analogous to Microsoft Windows. In fact, Warp includes facilities that allow you to run Windows applications as well, albeit with less than stellar performance. For practical purposes, you'll have to decide whether you want your computer to run Warp or Windows as its primary operating system—some people with 16 fingers can make both of them coexist on the same hard drive, but few of them speak any recognizable language.

All other things being equal, Warp is a better operating system than Windows 3, and arguably even a bit slicker than Windows 95. Its drawback is that there's much less software available for it than for Windows, a situation which isn't likely to change any time soon. Warp is much more difficult to develop applications for than is Windows, something which has slowed the growth in availability of Warp software.

None of this will directly affect your use of Warp to access the Internet, and specifically the World Wide Web. The Warp package includes software to handle interfacing to the Net through a dial-up connection and a Web browser to run with it. It also features the Net itself, as I'll get to in a moment.

The Warp Internet software includes a dialer and connection manager that calls a dedicated Internet access provider, handles all the handshaking for a SLIP or PPP connection, and then deals with communication for the specific Internet tasks the package provides. Unlike WinSock, this package could be successfully set up by a liberal politician with half his brain in his coat pocket. You'll still require a number of weird addresses and other fragments of information to load into the dialer the first time you call your Internet access provider, but the dialer does a fair bit of sanity checking and is about as helpful as anything can be when it's confronted with Internet server address information.

I use Warp with a PPP connection to a local Internet access provider—it's exceedingly solid.

The Warp World Wide Web browser is surprisingly good for software designed primarily to be usable by nuns. It's not the equal of Netscape and some of the other really sophisticated Windows WinSock-compatible Web applications, but it's more than adequate for modest Web browsing. Its chief failing is that it insists on downloading an entire Web page before it returns control of itself to whoever's running it. You can't, for example, scroll around the downloaded section while you're waiting for the rest of it to show up. It also lacks the Netscape HTML extensions—this is purely cosmetic, and doesn't affect its functionality.

The Warp browser also doesn't handle graphics as well as some other browsers—they don't appear particularly quickly, and they're surrounded by three-dimensional frames, which often interferes with the way graphics are used in Web pages. Once again, this is unlikely to affect how you use the Web, but it's a noticeable cosmetic problem.

In addition to simply selling you software to access the Internet, IBM would like to sell you Internet connectivity as well. While you can certainly use the Warp software to access a dedicated Internet access provider, you can also use it to access IBM's own dial-up Net server. This is a pretty conventional dial-up provider, save that all the weird addresses and such are preconfigured in the Warp Internet dialer software. You can set up an account in seconds with a credit card, and be online before the shrink wrap from the Warp box has finished uncrumpling itself on the floor behind your desk.

The IBM Internet access package isn't particularly expensive—while there are various pricing plans to suit the amount of Internet access you require per month, the basic package cost was about three dollars an hour (Canadian) as I was writing this. This makes it significantly cheaper than America Online or Prodigy, with somewhat faster access and more resources.

While it doesn't directly apply to the applications discussed in this book, I should point out that Warp's Internet software also includes a mail reader, Usenet newsgroup reader, Telnet client, FTP manager, and several other Internet tools. They're all pretty respectable, although, as I write this, not without a few bugs.

Finally, if you decide to spring for Warp you'll find the following disclaimer in the box—those gray suits are still hanging in closets somewhere:

> *You are about to embark on an adventure that spans the globe. Information can be accessed across countries and cultures. These sources of information belong to many different organizations, companies, governments, and people around the world.*
>
> *Certain Internet services may contain language or pictures that some individuals may find offensive, inflammatory, or of an adult nature. Such contents are the sole responsibility of the Internet service provider. We do not endorse such material and disclaim any and all liability for their contents.*

Someone's lawyer clearly got a bit nervous.

Local bulletin boards

Here's a weird little secret of the Internet, one you might well want to investigate. If it proves to be workable for you, you'll probably find that it's the cheapest way to get connected to the Net.

A long time ago, local computer bulletin boards were pretty simple affairs consisting of a few PCs networked together with a stack of modems and some phone lines to connect the whole works to the outside world. As with most things having to do with computers, however, the parties running some of the bulletin boards made them into commercial enterprises and became increasingly competitive. In order to attract more users, many of them expanded their services beyond simply exchanging messages and downloading files.

Quite a few of the larger bulletin boards introduced limited Internet access a few years ago. Initially, this involved being able to send Internet e-mail and access Usenet newsgroups, and wasn't all that exciting. However, in order to do this, the companies that ran the bulletin boards in question needed hardwired Internet connections of some sort. Of late, several of them seem to have realized that they had everything it takes to be a dedicated access provider.

One of the Internet access providers I use, Rose Media in Toronto, is actually a computer bulletin board that decided to sell its Internet connection directly. While Rose offers various pricing plans, access starts at about 40 cents (Canadian) per hour. The Rose facility offers a text-based interface and SLIP and PPP connections.

This arrangement sounds like it ought to have a hidden catch somewhere, but it doesn't. This is the absolutely lowest cost dial-up Internet access available, and it's as close to anything can get to free without coming with a cat at no extra charge. The only potentially troublesome aspect of accessing the Internet this way is in locating a bulletin board that offers this facility—by no means all of them do, and you typically won't find them in the yellow pages under B.

Should you be local to Toronto, you can contact Rose Media at 1-905-731-8805.

Prodigy

A joint effort of IBM and Sears, Prodigy is one of several large commercial dial-up services to have bolted Internet access to its other features of late. It's beyond the scope of this book to comment on the principal activities of Prodigy, save that if it existed in real space rather than cyberspace it would certainly be populated by entities in IBM-gray suits sitting in uncomfortable polyester furniture from Sears. Perhaps not surprisingly, Prodigy will accost you with all sorts of warnings and disclaimers about the potentially nasty, loathsome, vile, debased, depraved, and obscenely biological things you're likely to encounter when first you attempt to access the World Wide Web through its auspices.

Like America Online, Prodigy will happily send you a starter kit to explore its service. This includes special software to handle Prodigy's user interface and initial account information. As of this writing, you can order one by calling 1-800-776-3449, or if you're into vanity phone numbers, 1-800-PRODIGY.

The first thing you'll notice when you connect to Prodigy is its user interface, and this probably deserves some mention here if you're thinking about using Prodigy primarily to access the World Wide Web. Never before in the history of civilized society has anything had a user interface as mind-numbingly ugly as that of Prodigy, as I write this. Most accounting software is more attractive. All its text is drawn in unreadable NAPLPS stick-figure characters, its controls are antediluvian, and its general organization seems almost deliberately unintuitive. Even in the Windows implementation of its access software, nothing behaves as you would expect a Windows application to.

I mention this not to heap derision on Prodigy—however richly it might deserve it—but rather to enjoin you not to have one look at it and immediately reformat its disk. Prodigy's weird little interface appears throughout its service—with the exception of its World Wide Web functions. Once you get past all the warning screens, Prodigy's Web access software turns out to be a normal Windows application. Figure 1-7 illustrates the screens leading up to Prodigy's Web interface, and then my home page as seen by Prodigy.

The Prodigy Web software is actually remarkably good. It's not the equal of Netscape and some of the other stand-alone World Wide Web applications, but it's quite workable. It's also fairly snappy as dial-up services go. It requires virtually no complex setup to use, something you might want to keep in mind if you found your skin crawling at the discussion of WinSock, the interface for dedicated Internet access providers.

Prodigy costs somewhat more than a dedicated Internet access provider would, something to keep in mind if you plan to spend a lot of time on the Web.

Modems: too big to file, too stiff to fold

As I touched on informally earlier in this chapter, the thing that links your computer to the Internet over a dial-up connection is a box called a *modem*. Modems are really complex little monsters—there's a dedicated computer inside every one of them just itching to get out and cause some trouble. Fortunately, the things that modems are really good at causing trouble over aren't aspects of modem technology you need ever get involved with for simple Net access.

Modems come in various strata of quality, ranging from exceedingly cheap and nasty to excruciatingly expensive and slightly less nasty. Unless

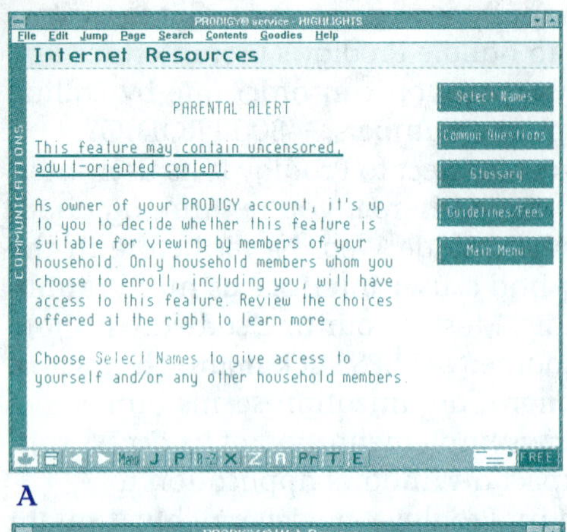

A

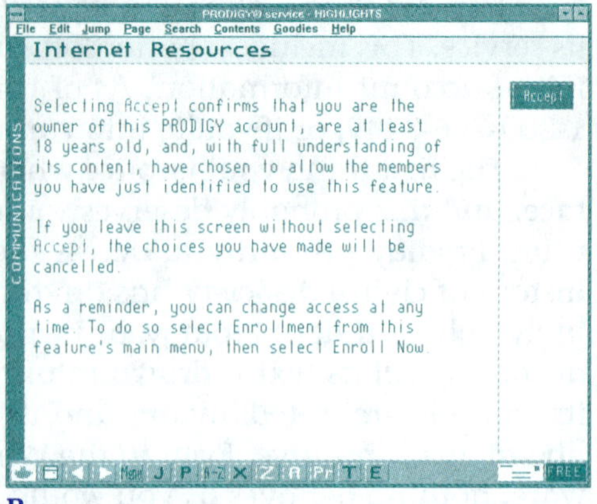

B

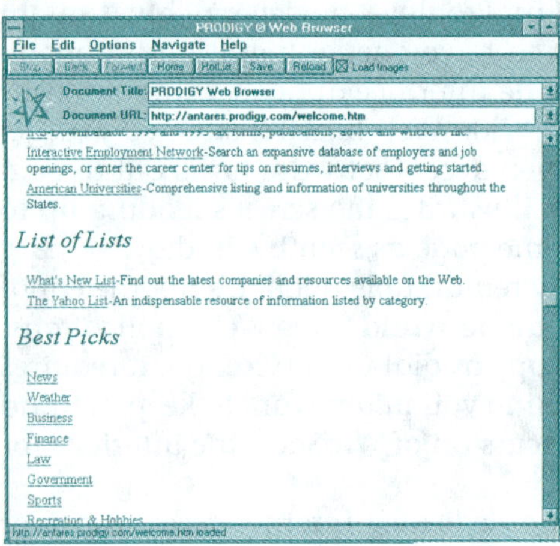

C

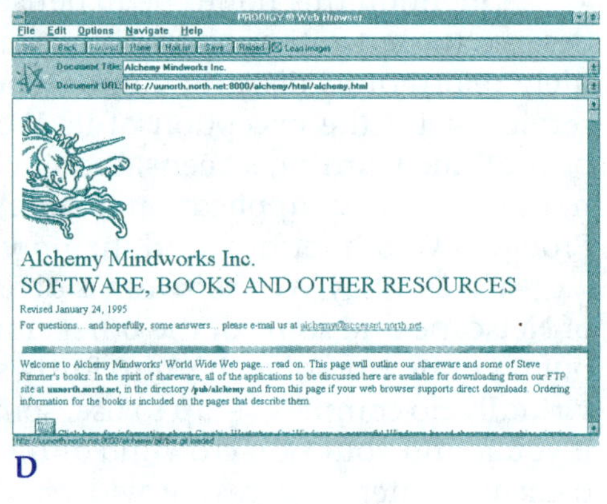

D

1-7 Attack of the killer disclaimers. 1-7A and 1-7B show two Prodigy warning screens, 1-7C is an intermediary screen, and 1-7D is, finally, my home page.

you have a bare spot on your office wall reserved for banging your head, you'll do well to avoid the really cheap ones.

The most salient aspect of modems is how quickly they can move data. The speed of a modem is measured in bps, though the outdated term *baud* is often used. As far as Internet access for realist Web browsing goes, here's how bps rates stack up:

300 bps These are garage-sale modems. The only possibility of them ever being useful again is if one of your great-great grandchildren finds a box of them one day and cleans up at an antique shop. The ones with the rubber cups to hold an old-style phone handset will probably fetch the best price.

1200 bps These are also garage-sale modems, but you can use them to call local bulletin boards in a pinch.

2400 bps You can still buy these things at Sears—but then, you can still buy Miracle Brushes and patent leather shoes at Sears, too. Don't plan on surfing the Web with one unless your idea of conventional surfing takes place in a dry lake bed.

9600 bps This is the bottom of the heap for realistic World Wide Web access. You can do a lot with one of these modems, and they're not particularly expensive.

14,400 bps These are the sorts of modems most people access dial-up connections to the Net with as of this writing.

28,800 bps These modems are very fast, and still pretty costly as I write this.

There are a few other catches involved in modems—but then, if you've used a computer for more than a week you probably already know this. To begin with, before you turn your Visa card into a shapeless puddle of molten plastic for a 28,800-bps modem, make sure your Internet access provider either supports 28,800 bps or expects to some time in the future.

Note that modems are very clever about speed. If you use a 28,800-bps modem to call a modem that only supports a lower bps rate, the two modems will scream at each other until they find a rate they can agree on. You might decide to buy a fast modem even if your access provider doesn't support its maximum bps rate right now. It will work properly at lower speeds 'til it does.

The other catch about 28,800-bps modems is that they require pretty clean phone lines to work at 28,800 bps. If two modems communicating at a high speed decide that the phone line between them is too noisy to realistically get data over the connection, they'll negotiate a lower bps rate. For example, the phone lines out where I live are connected to a switching system that appears to have been personally hand-wired by Alexander Graham Bell himself and not touched since. I can use any modem I like over these lines, but they all switch down to 14,400 or 9600 bps after a few minutes.

High-speed modems—that is, ones that communicate at 9600 bps or better—do so through a protocol that takes care of how to deal with the restrictions of conventional phone lines. The basic protocol is v.32 for 9600- and 14,400-bps modems, and v.34 for 28,800-bps modems. A v.34 modem also knows how to handle v.32, for those times when it negotiates a lower speed.

You don't want to know what those *v* numbers really mean—it's technical enough to make some quantum physicists leap out of fifth-floor windows rather than listen when it's explained.

The important aspect of high-speed modem protocols is that the two I've mentioned here are available to anyone who wants to make modems, and almost all high-speed modems work this way. This means that your v.32 or v.34 modem can communicate with anyone else's v.32 or v.34 modem, even if different companies make them.

There are several other proprietary high-speed modem protocols, most notably the U.S. Robotics USR protocol and the Telebit Trailblazer protocols. Modems that support only these protocols can talk only to other modems by the same manufacturer. You're unlikely to find these things except in the discount bins of some of the less reputable computer shops.

Note that several of the companies that used to make these proprietary-protocol modems now make modems that handle the v.32 and v.34 protocols. For example, U.S. Robotics makes very good modems that use the common protocols and will communicate with anything else you want to call.

The modems I use are made by Intel and Zoom—there are certainly all sorts of other good modems available as well, but these have proven to be pretty reliable.

Web tales and spider stories

As with many aspects of the Internet, things on the Web don't always work as flawlessly as books like this one might lead you to believe. Perhaps it would be fairer to say that real-world applications of the Internet in general—and the Web in particular—entail some compromises. This is especially true if you'll be using the Web through a dial-up connection.

This is where a bit of understanding of what HTML is really up to behind your back will prove useful. This section won't get into the grotty details of creating pages, but it will introduce you to some of the characters behind the scenery.

My Web page, back in Fig. 1-4, consists of some text and numerous graphic elements. The text for this page is one long file called alchemy.html. The graphics are stored in separate .GIF files: unicorn.gif, bar.gif, bullet.gif, and so on. When Netscape connects to my home page, alchemy.html, it begins to read the text and display it. Eventually it encounters a reference to a graphic image. This is, in effect, a bit of text that says "don't display this text directly—replace it with the graphic file unicorn.gif."

Graphics files are a lot larger than text files, even when they consist of only very small elements like the ones in my Web page. In the simplest sorts of Web browsers, when a reference to a graphic is encountered, the browser fetches the whole graphic and displays it before it carries on with the text. In the case of my Web page, you'd have to wait for the whole unicorn to be displayed before you got to see any of the text that follows it. This isn't much of a hardship for users of the Internet who have "fat" hardwired connections to the Net, but it can represent a serious wait for dial-up users.

Netscape has been designed to get around this problem. When it encounters a reference to a graphic, it downloads only enough to determine how much area it will occupy on the page being created. It draws a frame for the graphic to live in and carries on fetching text. When all the text has been downloaded, it goes back and fetches the graphics, replacing the empty frames with images. Meanwhile, you can read the text. The whole works is abortable—just click on the Stop button at the top of the Netscape window to abort the current page, or click on a link to jump somewhere else. Since graphical elements are usually decorative, Netscape offers you the option of not waiting to see them if you're in a hurry to get somewhere.

Netscape also allows you to disable the downloading of graphics entirely. You can toggle graphics on and off through the Auto Load Images item of the Options menu. Web pages will load a lot faster with Netscape's graphics turned off, but you'll probably encounter a fair number of pages with graphic elements as an integral part of their design that you can't really use without them.

If you find that you like browsing the Web with your browser's graphics switched off, you'll probably want to know about another of Netscape's many features, the Reload button. It's visible in the tool bar at the top of the Netscape window. If you find a page that contains graphics you'd like to look at, switch the graphic feature of Netscape back on and click on Reload to fetch the page and its graphics.

There's actually quite a lot to say about graphics as they pertain to the Web—I'll get back to them in detail later in this book. You'll probably want to know one more thing about them before you go venturing out onto the Web in search of adventure and glory, though. Some Web pages contain graphics that will appear to be doing something a bit peculiar when they turn up on your screen. Specifically, rather than being painted from the top down, they'll show up in what seem to be random lines. Such pictures do eventually appear in their entirety, but the process is decidedly odd. These graphics are referred to as being *interlaced*. One of them is illustrated in Fig. 1-8.

Interlaced graphics actually appear one line at a time in a specific order—it's just not the usual order for scanned images. They're handled this way because it can take a while for pictures to be sent over the Net, and you might want to be able to abort a graphic before it's complete if it turns out to be something you're not interested in looking at. You can get a better idea of what a picture's about before it's complete if it's sent interlaced.

There's a catch to interlaced graphics as well, as least as they pertain to Netscape and other Windows-based Web browsers. Every time Netscape has to paint one or more lines of a graphic to your screen, it has to enter into a fairly complex bit of negotiation with Windows. This takes some time to complete. Noninterlaced graphics are displayed in bands, with each band comprising several lines of the original image. Netscape has to negotiate with Windows only once for each band. By comparison, interlaced graphics are displayed one line at time, which increases the amount of negotiation Netscape must

1-8 An interlaced graphic forming in a Web browser.

undertake to display the image. All other things being equal, an interlaced graphic requires much more time to download to Netscape and be displayed than a noninterlaced one will.

You can overcome this to some extent by opening the Preferences dialog from the Options menu of Netscape and switching to the Network and Images page. Set the Display Images field to After Loading. Doing so will prevent Netscape from displaying an image until the whole file has been downloaded. Depending on the sort of Web pages you like to browse, this might improve the apparent performance of Netscape. It will reduce the overall time required to download graphic-intensive pages, especially if they contain a lot of interlaced images. However, as you won't be able to see the graphics 'til they're completely downloaded, you won't have the option of aborting them partway through transmission if you don't want to look at them.

I've mentioned aborting the downloading of pages and graphics in Netscape throughout this section. The feature that handles this is the Stop button in Netscape's button bar. You might want to keep in mind how Netscape downloads pages, and how the Stop button actually works as a result of this. It calls for the whole page of text you've selected, and then goes back and fills in the graphics. As such, clicking on Stop when it's off looking for graphics will usually get you all the text of your page.

If you use Stop to abort a page, you can click on Reload to fetch it again.

Clicking on a link will effectively stop the current page, as will clicking on the Back button in Netscape's tool bar. The Back button steps back through the recent history of your hypertext links. You can also select previous pages in the current hierarchy of your Web session through the Go menu of Netscape. Various items are added to it as you browse Web pages, and selecting one of these will step you back to an earlier page.

Note that this "recent history" feature of the Go menu is smarter than it looks. World Wide Web links are always hierarchical—you typically link from page to page as you move through the Web. The history of links maintained in the Go menu reflects this. If you select an item representing a previous link, the Go menu will step back through the links between your current page and your selected page, discarding each as it goes.

You can also use the View History item of the Go menu to review the links you've visited during your current session, and to jump back to them if you like.

The Bookmark menu of Netscape allows you to add links to a permanent list of places you might want to go again. It also provides a list of bookmarks to jump to. To add the link for your current Web page to the Netscape bookmark list, select Add from the Bookmark menu when you're linked to the page in question. To select a previous link, open the Bookmark menu—your current list of bookmarks will be appended to the end of the menu.

Actually, Netscape's use of the Bookmark menu as a tool for selecting individual bookmark links will probably become a bit of a problem if you add a lot of links to the bookmark list. When the menu starts getting full, it can take a noticeable amount of time to appear. Furthermore, Windows menus have a finite capacity, while the Netscape bookmark list can be added to indefinitely. To this end, you might want to introduce yourself to the Bookmark List dialog, accessible through the View Bookmarks item of the Bookmarks menu. It allows you to select items from your bookmark list without having to deal with the limitations of the Bookmark menu. You can search your current bookmark list and delete items if you like. Selecting an item from this dialog and clicking on Go To—or just double-clicking on the item name—will link you to the page in question.

2 Graphics

Being able to see what things look like in Web pages, rather than merely reading descriptions of them, is one of the things that makes the World Wide Web a great deal more fun than newsgroups and long typewritten documents about Carolingian pottery-making. In theory, graphics should be a pretty seamless element of the Web; in practice, they're a bit more complex than they might appear.

In addition to seeing what things look like, Web pages often let you hear things. You can have some Web pages play sounds for you. These, too, aren't quite as easy to get along with as they probably should be.

This chapter deals with some of the less-frequently mentioned elements of graphics as they appear on the World Wide Web. While it might seem a bit daunting at first, most of it makes a perverse sort of sense with time. Make it through this chapter and you'll never be terrorized by a bitmap again.

Pictures they never dare mention

One of the first things you're likely to remark on in this chapter is that the whole thing is about as well organized as a spaghetti dinner, but not quite as appetizing. Even the graphic elements of the Web that seem to be reasonably well integrated into it are a bit funky, and some of the loose ends that surround the whole dog-and-pony show could probably be used to knit a whole other dog. Not all of this is by design, exactly—it just happened that way.

As I'll get to in a moment, storing pictures in a form that a computer can read isn't a simple matter. In the past, whenever people came up with a new computer operating system or a major application to work with graphics, they traditionally devised a new way of storing pictures to go along with it. In the literature that typically accompanies new software, these would be described as "new and improved," but most of the users of the applications in question typically found that they were more along the lines of "new and incompatible."

The World Wide Web addresses this issue by deliberately *not* defining a new graphic format, but rather adopting several existing ones. In making use of graphic files that already existed prior to the introduction of the Web, it's a great deal simpler for Web page creators to put together pages without having to scare up a lot of brand-new software.

This is one of the reasons why you can look at complex, graphical Web pages today in unprecedented numbers, rather than reading an exciting press release about the capabilities planned for the World Wide Web when it finally gets off the ground in the spring of 2010. However, it also has a few catches—the graphic file "formats" being used by Web pages were never really designed for this application, and embody a few aspects that might get in your way.

To properly understand graphics on the Web, you'll probably have to plunge into the following fairly lengthy digression about graphics in general. It's not as terrifying as it seems.

Most people are used to looking at the world in a very nondigital sense—everything before us simply is, and if we look somewhere else all that will be too. In fact, there's a fantastic biological camera and image-processing computer in your head, but it's a pretty well-integrated machine and you never have to bother trying to understand how it works just to use it.

In allowing a computer to visualize things, human beings were forced to invent an equivalent to human vision in a form that computers could deal with. Not having had a few million years and a massive research and development budget to apply to the task, computer-based image perception isn't anywhere near as good as human image perception. It takes a lot less memory, however. Figure 2-1 illustrates what computer-based imaging is really all about.

Figure 2-1A is a digitized image that looks like something you might have seen with your own eyes. In fact, it's actually a mosaic of tiny dots of light, something that's a bit easier to spot in the enlarged portion shown in Fig. 2-1B. The tiny dots of light are called *pixels* (a contraction of the term *picture element*). If the world had been based on a well thought-out plan, such images would be called "pixel maps." In fact, they're called *bitmaps*. If you have software written by IBM, pixels are referred to as *pels* (also from *picture element*). There's no obvious reason for this.

If the pixels in a bitmap are small enough and numerous enough, the result is an image that looks pretty much like a real photograph as long as you don't scrutinize it too carefully. At least it can be—there are a few more things to keep in mind about bitmaps.

Had this been a coffee-table book about migratory sea birds in southwestern Namibia, Fig. 2-1A would have been printed in color. In this case, each pixel in the image could have been a unique color, potentially different from all the other colors in the image. On a computer, a color is represented

A

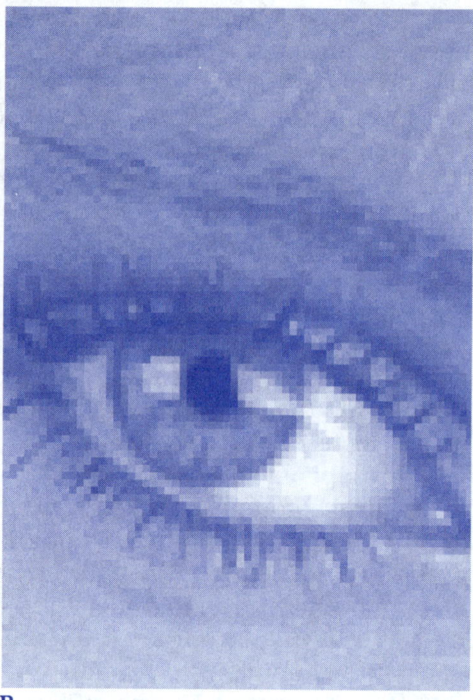

B

2-1A is how a computer sees reality, and 2-1B how a computer really *sees reality.*

as three numbers that define the amount of red, green, and blue light required to define the color in question, called *RGB*.

In a color image, then, each point of light would be defined by three numbers. Each number would be stored in one byte, which is the smallest thing a computer has to store a single number in.

The dimensions of a bitmap are defined by the number of pixels across the image and the number of pixels down. Your computer's monitor is a bitmap—most people run Windows or OS/2 warp using a screen resolution of 640 × 480 or 800 × 600 pixels. If Fig. 2-1A were reproduced at, say 800 × 600 pixels using RGB color, the results would look fairly reasonable, even for a coffee-table book.

If you allow your fingers to dance across the keys of a calculator for a moment, you'll find that such a picture requires rather a lot of bytes. The total would be 800 × 600 × 3, that is, the image dimensions multiplied by the number of bytes required to store one pixel. The total, should you not have a calculator handy, is 1,440,000 bytes, or slightly more than twice the amount of storage required to contain the entire text of this book. Such a picture could require anything up to half an hour to download over the Internet through a moderately fast dial-up connection. Using such graphics as casual decorations in a Web page could have certain shortcomings.

Bitmaps tend toward obesity in much the way that liberal politicians tend toward fact-finding junkets to the Caribbean several times a year. This being the case, there's a vast realm of science, research, and cheating concentrated on the vexing problem of making bitmaps live in smaller files than they ought to. I'm going to only touch on this subject here, because most of it's monumentally dull and uses the sorts of equations written on blackboards that can also be used, with subtle modifications, to predict the outcomes of horse races.

One of the most important things to keep in mind about a World Wide Web page is that no one will ever mistake one for a coffee-table book about migratory sea birds in south-western Namibia. Vacuous though they might be, coffee table books are superb examples of very high-resolution lithography. By comparison, the resolution of a Web page is about that of your monitor—something like 75 dots per inch on a good day—which is exceedingly coarse. Most of the fantastic color available in RGB graphics would be wasted in a Web page even if you wanted to wait for half an hour for such a graphic to download.

Some of the aforementioned monumentally dull science involved in graphic files deals with how to reduce the number of colors in a file so it no longer requires three bytes to hold each pixel. In fact, through some fairly basic trickery and internal witchcraft, it's possible to reduce the number of colors in a graphic from the 16 million possible colors supported by RGB color down to 256 colors, and reduce the resulting file down to a third of its original size. A pixel that's one of only 256 colors can be stored in one byte, rather than three.

The results of "color reduction" aren't indistinguishable from the original RGB graphics that fathered them, but they're pretty close. Unless you're a serious image purist, the distinction won't matter much for graphics on a Web page.

In fact, you can achieve even further space savings by using still fewer colors. Reducing a photorealistic image down to 16 colors will usually leave you with a pretty loathsome graphic—at least, it certainly won't fool anyone into thinking they're looking at the original. Other sorts of pictures, however—symbols, line drawings, and decorations—can get by with 16 colors quite admirably.

The second approach to making graphic files smaller is called *compression*. This is where the prematurely bald 14-year-old kids in white lab coats really get a chance to illustrate how incomprehensible mathematics can get when it wants to. Data compression theory has the potential for being really tedious if you let it—which I won't in this example.

Here's how it works in simple terms. Figure 2-2 illustrates the unicorn from my Web page back in chapter 1 of this book. Allowing that every dot in the image in Fig. 2-2 is a pixel, you'll probably notice that a lot of the pixels aren't doing much of anything. They're just sequential white dots. Compression works by finding areas in a graphic that have sequential pixels and re-

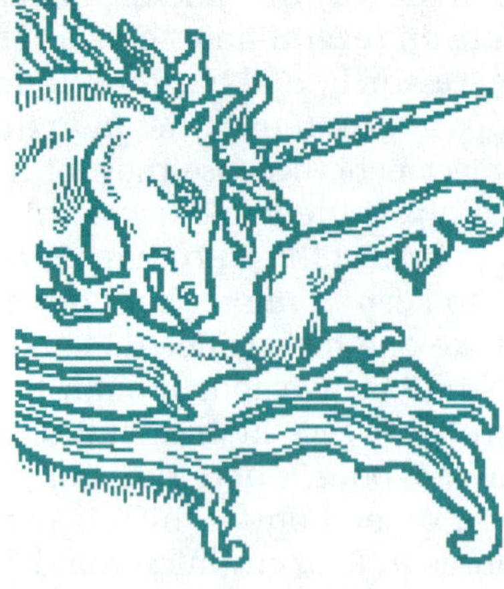

2-2
The return of the wood-cut unicorn.

placing them with "tokens" when the picture is stored in a disk file. A token is some sort of marker than says "there used to be 192 consecutive white pixels here." Software that subsequently reads a compressed file would see these tokens and replace them with the actual pixels they represented.

In fact, image compression can be a lot sneakier than this, but it all works under essentially the same principles.

Image compression works very well on simple graphics, like the unicorn in Fig. 2-2, and progressively less well on more complicated images. As a rule, increasing the maximum number of colors in an image increases its complexity, and hence reduces the amount by which it can be compressed. Images with 256 colors compress somewhat, while RGB color images hardly compress at all in most cases. Drawn images, like the unicorn, usually compress a lot better than scanned photographs.

Thus far, I've been discussing what's called *lossless* image compression, which means that, no matter how effectively an image is compressed and how small its disk file gets, what went into the file is identical to what comes out of the file when it's uncompressed, down to the last pixel. This is how most applications for graphics would prefer images to be handled.

As I noted a moment ago, photographic images don't compress well, and it's scanned photographs that most imaging applications want to work with. As such, a few years ago someone came up with the idea of *lossy* compression. Here's what it's up to.

Imagine an image of a black cat on a black tar roof at night. Such a picture would be largely black and very dark gray. The software that attempted to compress such a graphic would go looking for consecutive identical pixels to reduce to tokens. What it would probably encounter would be a lot of nearly identical almost-black pixels, each one just minutely different from the one beside it. This would fox the compression, and produce a very large file.

You might well look at such a picture and decide that the minute details represented by those almost-black pixels could easily be done away with, and replaced with pure black. This would result in a much more compressible graphic, and ultimately a smaller file to transmit over the Internet or save to your hard drive.

Lossy compression attempts to do just that. Presented with a graphic and a "quality factor," that is, the amount of detail it's allowed to discard in the interest of better compression, it simplifies your graphics to make them occupy less space. Lossy compression lets you retain almost all the details of your graphics and have relatively large files, or discard almost all the details, resulting in relatively small files. In most cases you'll choose something in between, that is, a quality factor that doesn't introduce an objectionable amount of image degradation into your graphics, but that will allow for reasonable compression.

The real world (head for the hills)

There are all sorts of *graphics file formats*, that is, predetermined structures for storing and compressing graphics into files. Each one has been designed for a particular set of objectives. These objectives usually include things like:

- Creating the smallest possible files, a laudable sentiment.
- Creating files that can be read quickly, a laudable sentiment that unfortunately doesn't usually work with small file sizes.
- Being able to store other information in the same file as an image in a flexible and structured way.
- Creating files that no one else can read, so you'll have to buy software from the company that invented the files. This is a loathsome sentiment, but it's by no means uncommon.
- Creating files in a format no one is likely to face legal action for using. I'll talk more about this later in the chapter.

There are several dozen image file formats commonly used among PC applications, but the two that turn up on the Web most of the time are GIF and JPEG, which stand for *Graphic Interchange Format* and *Joint Picture Experts Group*, respectively. You might find that a third format, called PNG, has largely replaced GIF by the time you read this. Once again, I'll discuss this in detail later in the chapter.

It's important to understand what these file types are really up to in order to avoid the sort of problems most people encounter with graphics on the Web. They're not particularly contentious, but they aren't precisely what they seem to be.

The GIF format was created by CompuServe in 1987 with the intention of introducing a standardized graphic file format so people could download pictures from CompuServe's dial-up server and, in so doing, rack up connect charges. This worked pretty well, and over the next few years GIF became the most widely used graphic file format on the planet. It probably would still be, save for some perfidy on the part of CompuServe, which I'll discuss later.

The GIF format is lossless, that is, whatever goes into it is what you see when you decode the file. In fact, at the moment the compression process used by GIF files offers the most effective compression for images with 256 or fewer colors. In addition, GIF files have two very important facilities for World Wide Web pages: transparency and interlacing.

A transparent image—at least as one might pertain to a Web page—is one in which a particular color in the graphic is defined as transparent, rather than as a solid area. In painting a transparent GIF file on your screen as part of a Web page, a Web browser allows the area beneath the GIF file to show through anywhere the transparent color appears. Figure 2-3 illustrates both a conventional and a transparent GIF file in a Web page.

A

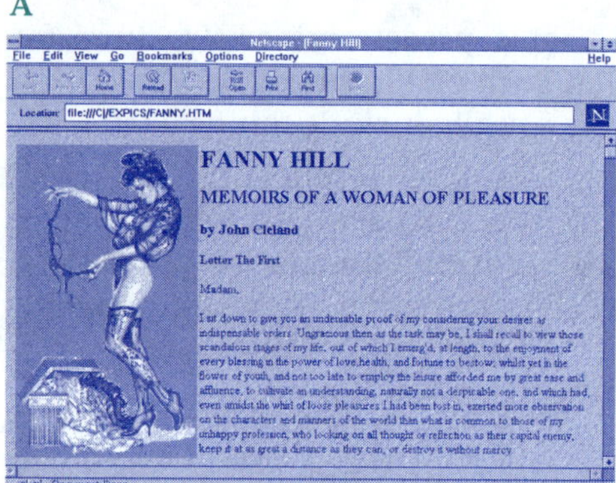

B

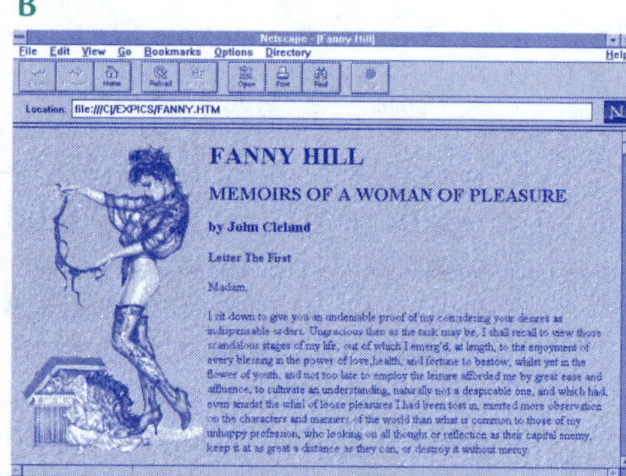

2-3 A conventional image (2-3A) and transparent image (2-3B) in a Web page.

Transparent GIF files are very popular on Web pages, as they allow non-rectangular images and symbols to be presented as if they were part of the page itself, rather than as pictures pasted on after the fact. In fact, all a transparent GIF file really consists of is a bit of information associated with the image in the file to tell your Web browser which of the colors in the image to regard as being transparent. However, GIF is one of the few graphic file formats to include this sort of transparency information.

Secondly, as was touched on in the first chapter of this book, GIF files allow for interlaced images. An interlaced image is structured so its lines of image data appear in an irregular order. If the individual lines are being sent to your computer relatively slowly—as will be the case over a dial-up connection to the Internet—having them appear interlaced will give you a better idea of the content of a graphic earlier in the transmission. The process by which Windows and most other graphical operating systems display graphics, however, substantially increases the amount of time it takes an interlaced GIF file to be displayed in a Web page.

The primary limitation inherent in GIF files at the moment is that they can support only a maximum of 256 colors. You can't store RGB images in a GIF file directly. This is of little matter for those Web pages, like mine, that use GIF files to provide small incidental graphics and decorations, but it's something to think about for more complex imaging applications. These unquestionably do turn up on the Web.

The quest for more color

In order to better understand the limitations inherent in GIF files and their maximum of 256 colors, you'll probably have to plunge into another digression—it probably seems like you just crawled out of the first one. Graphics are like that, too. Consider that graphics, albeit in a somewhat more primitive form, have been the longest-standing form of self expression on earth. (Getting 20,000 years of human experience into a single chapter does entail a bit of jumping about.)

An RGB graphic—or what the serious graphic people call a *true-color graphic*—can contain 16 million unique colors. Admittedly, it would have to contain 16 million pixels to do this, and few true-color graphics actually get this large. For the sake of this discussion, however, let's allow that such a graphic could have 16 million distinct colors.

You might be wondering how the number 16 million got into all this. The actual number is 16,777,216, or 2^{24}. This in turn derives from each color in a true-color graphic being stored in three bytes, with each byte having eight bits. The maximum number of colors in any graphic can by figured out as two to the power of however many bits are required to store one pixel. In addition to being called RGB and true-color graphics, these sorts of pictures are also referred to as *24-bit graphics* for this reason.

A 256-color image requires one byte to store each pixel, so the maximum number of colors is calculated as 2^8, or 256. These graphics are also called *8-bit graphics* for this reason.

If you scan a color image with a scanner, the result will be a true-color, or 24-bit, graphic. The problem of reducing the colors in such an image down to 256, so the whole works will fit in a GIF file, requires a degree of ingenuity that would make locating a lawyer's conscience trivial by comparison.

Without getting into a lot of technical explanations about color theory, after all sorts of head-scratching and enough equations drawn on enough blackboards to reduce the entire white cliffs of Dover to so much chalk dust, the people who really know what all this is about came up with a process to handle this sort of conversion. It's called *quantization* and *dithering*.

The problem in reducing a true-color graphic to 256 colors is that 256 colors aren't anywhere near enough to actually make a photograph look realistic. To create the illusion of there being more colors in such a picture than there really are, the images being converted are *dithered*, that is, alternating dots of color are used to create the illusion of colors that aren't really there.

Here's a very simple example of dithering, one that turns up in Windows and most other graphical operating systems all the time. Suppose your computer wanted to paint a green area on your screen, but none of the colors available to it were, in fact, anything like green. It could achieve a pretty convincing simulation of green by painting every even numbered pixel yellow and every odd numbered pixel blue. From a few inches away, the individual pixels wouldn't be visible as such, and you'd think the color you were seeing was green.

Dithered graphics are more complex than this, but they work the same way. Figure 2-4 illustrates a picture before and after dithering.

Dithering creates the illusion of a full range of colors, but because of those alternating colored dots, it does so at the expense of some of the sharpness of detail, or resolution, of the original image. In most cases it's an acceptable compromise for the sort of imaging applications that appear on the Web—but not always.

There's another catch to dithering. I mentioned earlier in this chapter that more complex images compress relatively poorly. Those alternating pixels in a dithered image serve to make the graphics themselves more complex, and less readily compressed.

Here's a final consideration in working with photorealistic images and dithering. The display cards in personal computers also have a finite number of colors they can display. While a growing number of systems are being shipped with cards that will handle 16 million colors—and a few old relics from Sears still come with cards that can handle only 16 colors—the most commonly seen configuration is 256 colors. For this reason, most Web pages limit the number of colors in their graphics to 256. At least, they do if you want them to. I'll get to this next, in the discussion of JPEG files.

JPEG: the quest for smallness

As I mentioned earlier, GIF files are limited to 256 colors. While this can be used to create pretty convincing photorealistic images, the resulting graphics are noticeably less detailed than the true-color images they started off as. However, true-color graphics don't compress well enough to be downloaded in

A

B

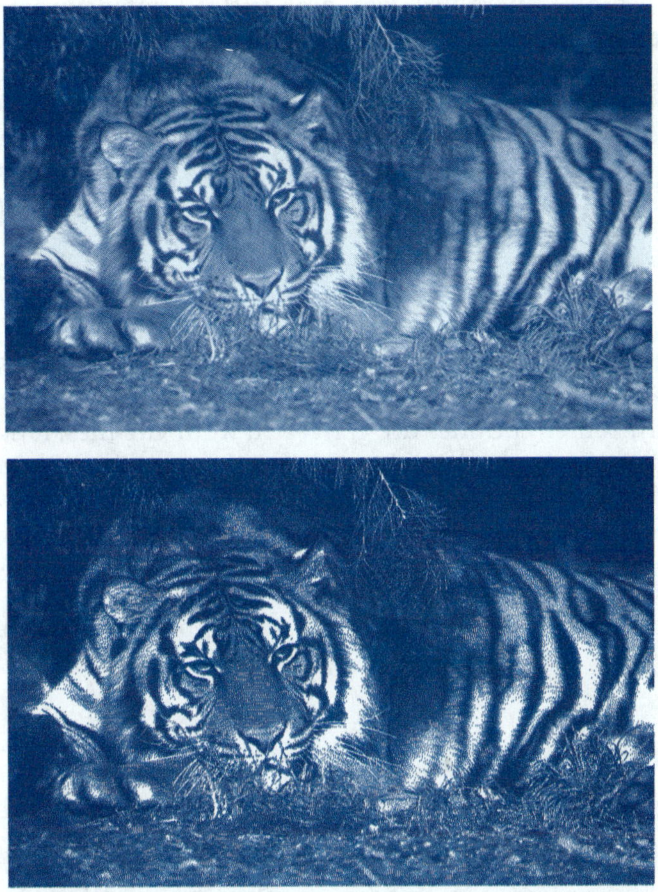

2-4 2-4A is a graphic as it appears in true color—or true gray, in this case—and 2-4B shows how it would look dithered.

a short enough time to make them workable for a World Wide Web page, especially if you're accessing the Net through a dial-up connection.

The way around this problem, for applications that require true-color images in Web pages, is to use JPEG files. The JPEG format achieves high levels of compression by throwing away some of the details in an image; it's lossy compression, as was discussed earlier.

Unlike GIF files, the JPEG standard allows for images with up to 24 bits of color. In fact, it insists on them. Any image with less color "depth" is promoted to a 24-bit image when it's stored in a JPEG file. This doesn't magically undo the resolution loss of a dithered 256-color image—it just affects how images are stored internally by JPEG, and how they appear when they're unpacked later on.

This is actually where JPEG gets a bit tricky. I noted earlier that most PC display systems can presently handle a maximum of 256 colors. A JPEG file that presents itself as a true-color image with 16 million colors would confront your computer with something of a problem. To get around this, the part of a Web browser or other reader that actually deals with the image information in a JPEG file can be told to automatically dither JPEG files being read down to 256 colors. In a sense, they can be treated just like conventional 256-color GIF files.

As you might expect, having read thus far, there are a few catches to this, too. The first one is that the dithering procedure used to reduce a JPEG image from 24 to 8 bits has been designed to be fast, rather than optimally attractive. You'll probably find that JPEG images displayed in a 256-color environment aren't all that pretty.

Secondly, some JPEG files are converted from GIF files. Since GIF files of photorealistic images must be dithered to get them down to 256 colors, a JPEG file from such a source will get dithered twice if it's displayed in a 256-color environment. The results are often markedly ugly.

The important thing to keep in mind about JPEG is that it's a compromise; it makes true-color images available over Web pages and other media for which size is a concern, but it doesn't always provide particularly faithful imaging.

PNG, CompuServe, Unisys, and the surprise GIF tax

I mentioned earlier in this chapter that there's a third graphic file format you'll probably encounter in growing numbers on the World Wide Web. It's called PNG, or Portable Network Graphics, pronounced "ping." It has come about very recently, for reasons that probably deserve some elaboration.

The GIF graphic file format is one of the most common image file standards in use as I write this because it compresses pictures relatively well, allowing them to be downloaded more readily and to be stored in less disk space. The GIF format was originated by CompuServe, the large online service, in 1987. At that time, CompuServe explicitly gave software developers license to use GIF without paying any royalties on it, as long as they acknowledged that it was the property of CompuServe.

It turns out that in 1985 Unisys, an also-ran mainframe computer manufacturer, had obtained a patent on some aspects of LZW compression, which is the algorithm that the GIF format uses to store graphics. CompuServe apparently failed to do a proper search to ascertain whether it actually had the right to grant royalty-free use of the GIF format, which as it turns out it didn't.

Unisys said nothing about the ongoing "infringement" of its LZW patent by developers of software that supported GIF files until GIF was a well-established standard and widely in use. It appears to have contacted CompuServe in January of 1993 and concluded a licensing agreement for the use of LZW compression in the summer of 1994. CompuServe itself maintained that it had the right to license GIF without the payment of royalties right up until the end of December, 1994, never mentioning its negotiations with Unisys.

As developers have since learned, neither Unisys' failure to enforce its patent until it was widely in use as an ostensibly public-domain entity nor CompuServe's deception as to its rights to grant a free license for the GIF format can be used as grounds not to pay Unisys its royalties—at least, not without a lengthy court battle. Both Unisys and CompuServe have deeper pockets than most software developers.

In the aftermath of this somewhat deplorable situation, users of GIF files might be a bit uncomfortable about their legality. As of this writing, here's the situation:

- No patent applies to GIF files—it applies only to software that reads and writes GIF. Some authorities question whether the patent can be applied to software that reads GIF files but does not write them.
- Unisys has stated that it does not expect royalties to be paid for freeware or unregistered shareware.
- Royalties are paid by the developer of software that handles GIF files, not directly by the end users—although the cost of the royalty and the cost of administering it is built into the registration fees of applications that support GIF.

Your use of GIF files within the scope of this book should not subject you to any liability to Unisys or CompuServe. If you use freeware applications to access GIF files or World Wide Web pages that include them, your software will have been explicitly exempted from the payment of royalties by Unisys. If you use shareware or commercial software that reads or writes GIF files, you will be paying a royalty to Unisys through the registration fee or purchase price of the software, and as such again aren't liable to any legal action.

By the way, I'm thinking of copyrighting the letter A and demanding one percent of the purchase price of every document that's ever used it, retroactive to the late Middle Ages.

In fact, many software developers have chosen not to pay Unisys its royalty, but rather to discontinue support for the GIF format and hence the use of Unisys' patented code. CompuServe did announce that it would release a revised version of GIF, called GIF 95a, which would embody an alternate compression technology, but the mood of the software community at the time was that they would rather have trusted an Elvis sighting by an employee of the National Enquirer than CompuServe.

With the departure of GIF, there arose something of a vacuum of file formats, to wit, something that allowed for good compression, interlacing, transparent colors, lossless graphics, and no strings attached. A new format was devised by a group of developers, this one based on a well-researched compression standard that was genuinely in the public domain. The PNG format is similar to GIF in that it does very effective lossless compression. In addition, it compresses true-color images directly. This latter feature probably won't see much application on the Web, as lossless true-color compression doesn't work very well—the resulting files are usually still pretty huge.

Embedded objects and helpers

When a World Wide Web page includes a graphic, it actually specifies an *embedded object*, that is, something other than text that's referenced by code in the HTML file that defines the page in question. There are several ways a Web page can specify embedded objects, and the technical aspects of it can be safely left beyond the scope of this chapter. The nature of these objects, on the other hand, will certainly affect how you use the Web.

Web browsers, such as Netscape, know how to handle certain types of files. The GIF and JPEG files discussed thus far are examples of these objects. When a GIF file is referenced by a Web page, your Web browser can decode and display it as part of the page that appears on your screen.

A Web page could include a graphic in another format, such as Windows BMP, but Web browsers don't normally know how to work with these formats, and thus can't display them as part of the Web page.

The nature of Web browsers is that they seek to be as extensible and flexible as possible. Netscape would rather not refuse to handle an embedded object in a Web page. It's much happier if it can call another application to take care of file types it doesn't recognize. These other applications are referred to as *helpers*. Figure 2-5 illustrates the Helper Application dialog of Netscape.

You can configure Netscape to call helper applications for any file type—it bases its decisions about the nature of a file on the file's extension. In order to handle a particular sort of file, a helper application must have been written to deal with it.

Helper applications are typically used to view graphic files that Netscape doesn't recognize, but there are also files on the Web of another sort, such as sounds. You can configure helper applications for these, too.

Whenever Netscape encounters a file it doesn't recognize either embedded in or referenced by a Web page, it looks through its list of helper applications to see if there's a helper to handle the file. If one exists, it downloads the

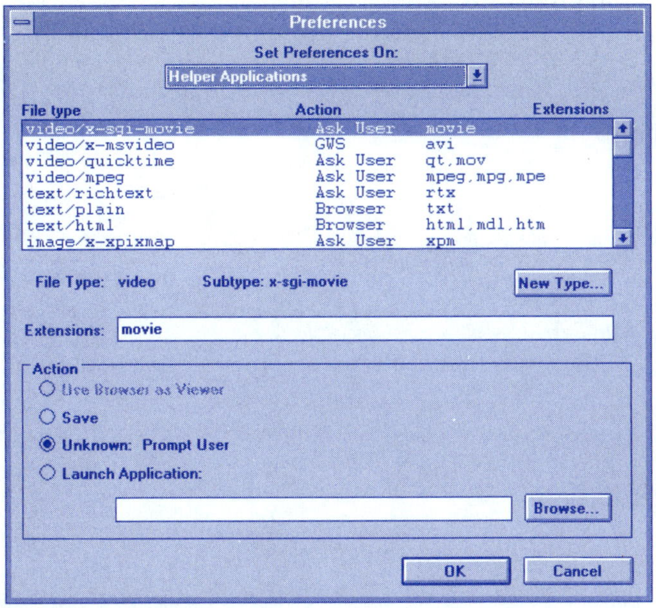

2-5
The Netscape Helper Application dialog.

file, runs the helper, and passes it a path to the file. If no helpers exist for the file type in question, Netscape will prompt you to save the file to disk.

I should note that even if you configure a helper application to handle GIF and JPEG files, Netscape will still display embedded GIF and JPEG graphics as elements of your pages, rather than calling a helper for each one. I'll explain this distinction in the next chapter when discussing FTP sites.

Using Graphic Workshop as a Netscape helper

Graphic Workshop for Windows is a large graphic application from Alchemy Mindworks, my company. It's distributed as shareware—you can download it over the Internet and try it out. While it serves a variety of functions, one of the things it's particularly good at is being a helper application for any Windows-based World Wide Web browser application, such as Netscape. Graphic Workshop supports the following file types:

- PNG
- MacPaint
- GEM/IMG
- PC Paintbrush PCX
- CompuServe GIF
- TIFF
- WordPerfect Graphics WPG

- Deluxe Paint/Amiga IFF/LBM
- PC Paint Pictor PIC
- Pegasus PIC
- Truevision Targa
- Windows 3 BMP/DIB
- Windows 3 RLE
- Microsoft Paint MSP
- Self-displaying EXE
- Text files
- Halo CUT
- PFS:First Publisher ART
- JPEG JPG
- Kodak Photo-CD
- Sun Raster RAS
- HRZ SSTV
- WMF Windows Metafiles
- CLP
- FLI animation
- ICO
- AVI
- CPT
- CDR, bitmap and preview only
- UUE UUencoded Internet graphics
- FITS
- MOV Apple QuickTime movie
- BGA
- MPEG animation
- CGM
- HPGL

You're not likely to encounter all of these as embedded objects in Web pages, and some, like MOV QuickTime animations, have a few unusual conditions associated with them. I'll discuss this later in the chapter. As of this writing you can download Graphic Workshop over the World Wide Web. Here's how:

1. Connect to the Internet and run your Web browser.
2. Enter the URL http://www.north.net/alchemy/alchemy.html.
3. When the Alchemy Mindworks home page appears, as was illustrated in chapter 1 of this book, select the link for Graphic Workshop for Windows.
4. Scroll down to the bottom of the Graphic Workshop for Windows page until you see something like Fig. 2-6.
5. Click on the GWSWIN11.EXE link. Your Web browser should prompt you for a destination for the file. Enter GWSWIN.EXE. You might also want to download QTW11.ZIP, which contains the

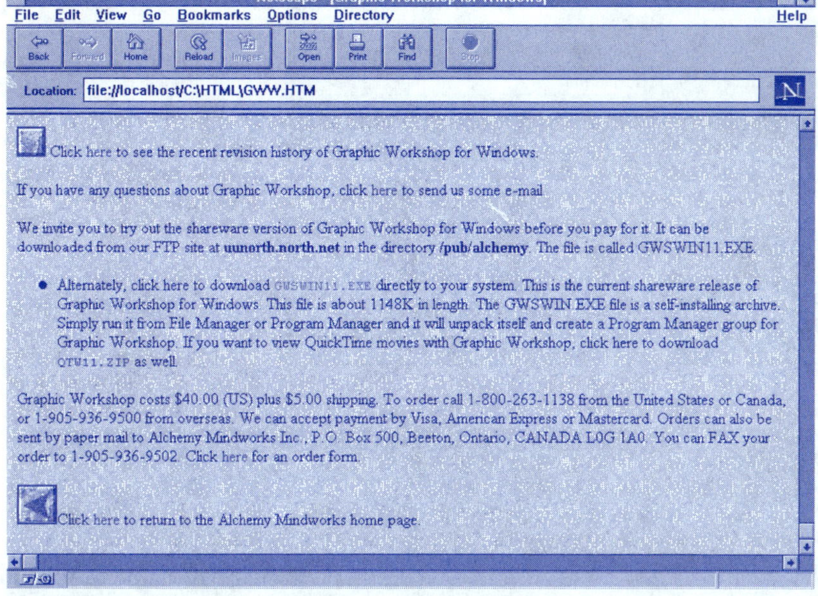

2-6 The Graphic Workshop for Windows Web page, ready for downloading.

QuickTime MCI drivers, if you anticipate viewing MOV movies from Web pages.

6. When Graphic Workshop has finished downloading, get to the Windows Program Manager and select Run from the File menu.
7. Navigate to where you downloaded GWSWIN.EXE and run it. The file you've downloaded is a self-installing Windows archive. A dialog should pop up telling you so.

Figure 2-7 illustrates the main window of the Graphic Workshop installer. Click on OK to begin installing Graphic Workshop. You must have at least five megabytes of free hard drive space to install Graphic Workshop—it doesn't require that much space once it's set up, but the installer creates some fairly large temporary files. You must also have a minimum of four megabytes of memory in your computer to run Graphic Workshop, although eight megabytes or more is preferable. If you have a 4MB system with SmartDrive, EMM386, or a RAM disk installed and configured to use a significant amount of memory, you might not have enough memory left over to run Graphic Workshop.

When Graphic Workshop has been successfully installed, you'll have a Program Manager group with several new icons. Graphic Workshop itself runs from the leftmost icon, the woman's eye.

By default, Graphic Workshop is an interactive application—it wants you to click on the names or thumbnails of files to display them. This isn't

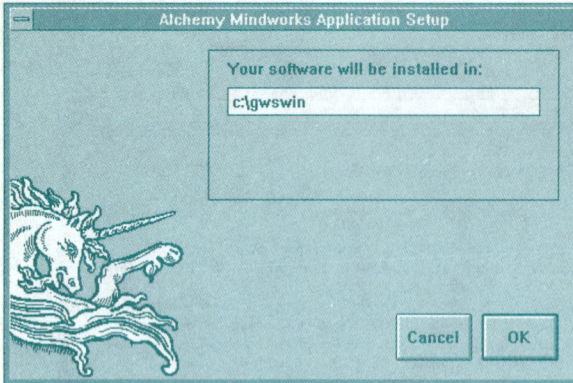

2-7
The Graphic Workshop installer.

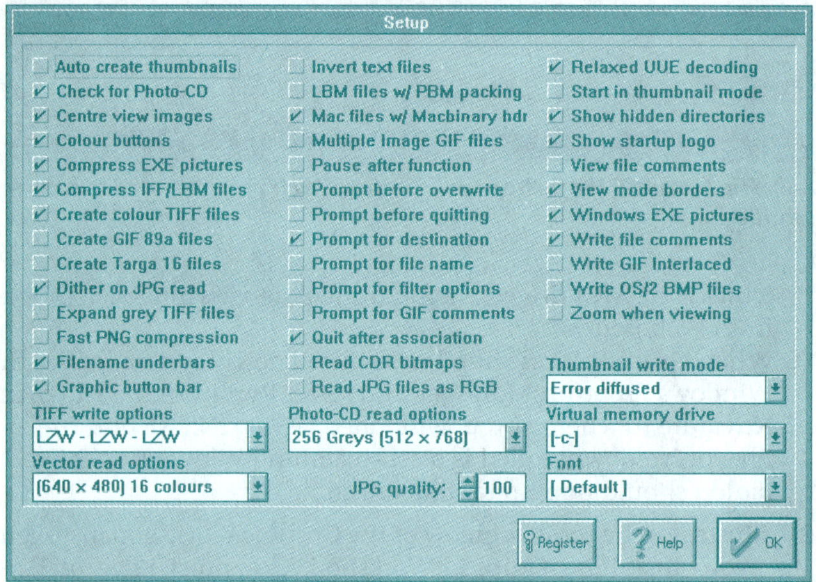

2-8 The Graphic Workshop Setup dialog.

quite what Netscape has in mind for a browser. Graphic Workshop will behave as a proper helper, but you have to make a few changes to its default configuration. To do this, Open the Setup dialog (see Fig. 2-8).

To set up Graphic Workshop to be a Netscape helper, turn on the Quit After Association item. Turn off Prompt Before Quitting. If your current Windows screen driver can display more than 256 colors, turn on Read JPEG as RGB, otherwise turn off Read JPEG as RGB and turn on Dither JPEG on Read. If you're unsure about the number of colors your Windows screen driver can handle, open the Graphic Workshop About dialog.

When you're done configuring Graphic Workshop, click on OK and then exit Graphic Workshop to save your configuration.

Once Graphic Workshop is set up, you must tell Netscape to use it as a helper for the file types it knows how to deal with. To do this, select Preferences from the Options menu and then select Helper Applications from the combo box at the top of the Preferences dialog. The Preferences dialog should look like Fig. 2-9.

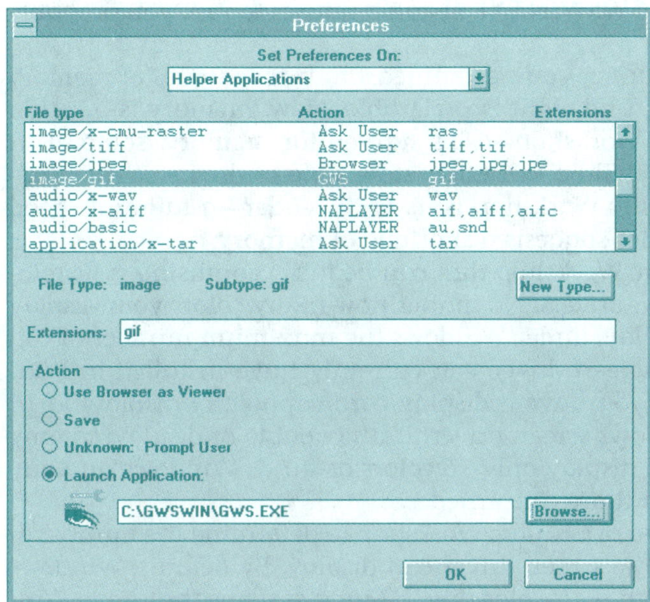

2-9 The Netscape Preferences dialog for setting helper applications.

To configure Graphic Workshop as a helper application for the supported file types Netscape has listed, select each of the appropriate file types, in turn, from the combo box in the middle of the Preferences dialog in Netscape. Click on the Launch Application radio button in the Action group toward the bottom of the dialog. Click on the Browse button and navigate over to the \GWSWIN directory. Select GWS.EXE. The Graphic Workshop icon will appear in the Action group. Use the same procedure for selecting other applications as Netscape helpers.

Dark secrets of Graphic Workshop

There are several useful things to know about Graphic Workshop as a helper application for Windows-based Web browsers. Not everything it does is immediately obvious, and in all fairness the Graphic Workshop documentation seems to run for miles.

First off, Graphic Workshop is distributed as a self-installing archive. This means that the archive is a program that, when run, creates all the Graphic Workshop application files and sets them up under Windows. If the archive is damaged, the setup procedure won't work.

Some dial-up Internet connections aren't as reliable as they could be, and the SLIP download protocol doesn't perform as much error-checking as you might imagine. If the GWSWIN.EXE installer refuses to run, you probably have a bad download.

As was touched on earlier, you need at least four megabytes of memory to run Graphic Workshop, and eight is preferable. Now, memory is a rather slippery issue. If you run Workshop so it's starved for memory, some of its functions will work but they'll be extremely slow. One of the more memory-hungry functions of Graphic Workshop is its JPEG reader—a failure to read some or all of your JPEG files suggests a shortage of memory.

One aspect of Graphic Workshop that can be fairly confusing is its relationship to Windows screen drivers. No matter how many colors your display card and monitor can display, under Windows the maximum number of colors is determined by the screen driver you currently have installed in Windows. This means that, if you have a display card capable of displaying 16 million colors and a Windows screen driver that's capable of displaying only 16 colors, your system can display only 16 colors as far as Windows and any application running under it are concerned.

Open the About dialog of Graphic Workshop to determine the number of colors your current Windows screen driver can display. By default, Windows usually comes installed with a 16-color driver. Many systems that have Windows preinstalled will have more sophisticated drivers. If your computer contains a super VGA card, consult the documentation for your card to find out how to upgrade its drivers if need be—the procedure varies from card to card.

As an aside, the standard Windows 16-color VGA screen driver is relatively slow. If your display card uses accelerated technology—most contemporary display hardware does, unless it showed up as the prize in a box of Fruit Loops—installing a driver that's been written to use the enhanced features of your card will make your graphics look more attractive. It will also speed up your computer enormously, as your processor no longer has to tie up half its resources drawing things on your screen.

Here's a quick overview of how to set up Graphic Workshop for various screen driver color depths, as found in the Graphic Workshop About dialog:

Sixteen colors Graphics with more than 16 colors will appear dithered in Graphic Workshop. Turn Read JPEG as RGB on in Setup.

256 colors True-color graphics will appear dithered and everything else will appear normal. Turn Read JPEG as RGB off and Dither JPEG on Read on in Setup.

Between 32,768 and 16,777,216 colors All graphics will appear correctly. Turn Read JPEG as RGB on in Setup.

When your Web browser calls Graphic Workshop to display an image, a gray window will appear with your graphic centered in it. You can exit the Graphic Workshop view mode by hitting Esc or Enter, or by clicking the right button of your mouse. If you've configured Graphic Workshop with the Quit After Association feature turned on, as discussed earlier, you'll find yourself back in your Web browser.

By default, a Web browser downloads a graphic to be displayed, calls Graphic Workshop to display it, and then deletes the downloaded file. If you want to keep a downloaded file that turns up in Graphic Workshop, select Save from the Picture menu and save the graphic to a new filename.

Animated graphics

In addition to single-frame still images, Web pages can include video clips and other fragments of animation. Because animation files tend toward obesity, you'll often find these set up for download rather than for direct online viewing. Downloading files will be explained in greater detail in the next chapter.

If you don't configure a helper application in Netscape for animation file formats, you'll be prompted for a filename to download animations to—in most cases, this is a really good idea.

Animated graphics work just like conventional film animation—an animation file is a sequence of small still graphic frames that, when displayed in sequence, creates the illusion of movement. If you have a calculator handy, you can probably figure out why this presents something of a problem for contemporary PCs.

At the moment, most animation files you encounter will probably have relatively small dimensions—160 by 100 pixels is common, with 320 by 200 about as big as things can become for smooth, real-time animation. As I'll get to in a moment, larger frame sizes are possible, but the animation they produce becomes decidedly unconvincing.

Here's a real-world example of the problem. Figure 2-10 illustrates the first 20 frames of a promotional video clip released for the film *Clear and Present Danger*. This animation used frames 148 × 48 pixels. There are 126 frames in the complete sequence, which runs for about 20 seconds. With the application of some image compression—and with the sound track added—this file occupies about three quarters of a megabyte.

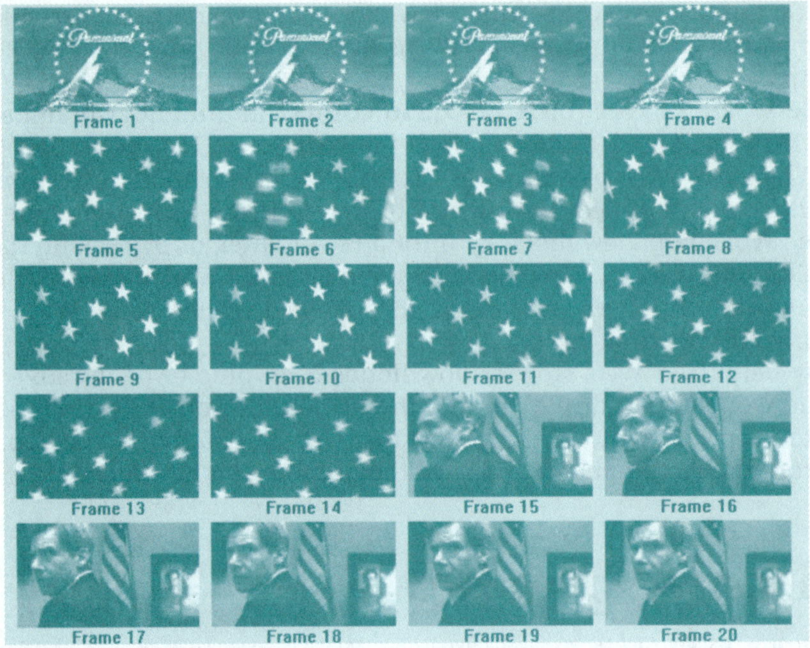

2-10 *The first 20 frames of a Clear and Present Danger disk hog (there are 126 frames in all).*

The *Clear and Present Danger* video is a very small and relatively short digital video clip. Files that run to 15 or 20 megabytes aren't uncommon, although as a rule you won't find all that many of them on the Internet. Five megabytes seems to be the upper limit as I write this.

Aside from just taking up a lot of space, digitized video files present personal computers with some serious problems. The *Clear and Present Danger* clip is a good example of this—it includes a sound track, which ideally should remain synchronized to the movements of the actors in the video. Unfortunately, the process of retrieving each frame from your disk and painting it in a window on your display takes a finite amount of time. If the video file in question is stored on a slow device, such as a CD-ROM, if it's being displayed by a slow computer or a computer with a nonaccelerated display device, or if it consists of awkwardly large frames that require a long time to paint, your computer might take longer to display a frame than the interval between frames allows for.

There are two ways to deal with this: the animation can either be allowed to slow down, in which case it will gradually slip out of synchronization with its sound track, or the software that drives the animation can skip frames. The latter is preferable, but it can result in fairly choppy animation under sufficiently unfavorable conditions.

There are four popular animation standards you're likely to encounter on the Internet. They are:

FLIC This is the oldest popular animation standard. It was created by AutoDesk, the company that makes the AutoCAD drafting software. It doesn't allow for a sound track, and exhibits relatively poor image compression. It's most often used for computer-generated animations, rather than digitized video. FLIC files have the extensions .FLI and .FLC.

Video for Windows This is Microsoft's Windows digital video format. It allows for soundtracks, and Windows includes a fairly workable protocol to display Video for Windows files. Video for Windows files can be created with variable degrees of compression and quality—the arrangement is similar to that discussed in conjunction with JPEG files. Video for Windows files have the extension .AVI.

QuickTime This is Apple's digital video format. On paper it's technically superior to Video for Windows, although in the real world both produce similar results. QuickTime has the advantage of working on both Macintosh and PC platforms, and the disadvantage of some legal encumbrances by Apple, to be discussed in a moment. QuickTime files have the extension .MOV.

MPEG This is a digital video format that wasn't created by any single manufacturer, and has to some extent evolved on the Internet. Because it can be used on virtually any platform, a growing number of MPEG movies are appearing on the net. MPEG files have the extension .MPG, or in some cases .MPE.

As of this writing, most Web browsers don't support animation directly. You have to configure a helper application to deal with these files. Graphic Workshop can handle all four types of animation files, in some cases with a bit of additional help.

Specifically, Graphic Workshop will display FLIC and MPEG animations as they stand. In order to display Video for Windows files, you must have the MCI Video for Windows drivers installed in your system. Displaying QuickTime files requires that the MCI QuickTime drivers be installed in your system. The QuickTime drivers are available at the Alchemy Mindworks FTP site at ftp.north.net in the directory /pub/alchemy as of this writing, and at the Alchemy Mindworks Web page. The Video for Windows drivers can be found at ftp.microsoft.com, Microsoft's FTP site, as of this writing. The next chapter of this book deals with FTP sites and downloading files from them.

Graphic Workshop currently requires 32-bit Windows to display MPEG files. This means that you can use it with Windows 95 or Windows NT, and with Windows 3.1 if you've installed the WIN32 package. You can't use it with Windows 3.1 as it comes out of the box.

You'll need an accelerated video card and a reasonably fast computer to make animation and video clips workable on your computer. Lesser hardware might make otherwise smooth animation look like a talking slide show. A display driver capable of handling more than 256 colors is highly desirable. In addition, you'll need a sound card to hear the sound tracks of animations that include them.

Animated graphics might seem to be a brilliant solution in search of a problem. Spending an hour downloading a file that plays for less than thirty seconds smacks of dire futility, although the images they contain are often fairly interesting. A growing number of music videos and movie promos have been appearing as digitized video clips, albeit fairly short ones. Several of the larger movie and television studios have created Web pages with video clips of their latest releases—you'll find a number of them mentioned in the second half of this book.

Two rotten apples (the legalities of digitized video)

There are two fairly minor legal considerations surrounding some of the digitized video formats discussed a moment ago. While they're unlikely to affect you directly, you'll probably hear rumors of them on the Net, and rumors are usually more destructive than reality. Both of these issues surround Apple and its QuickTime movie protocol.

The QuickTime movie format was originally developed for use on Apple's Macintosh computers. Apple seems to have decided some while later that it would be more widely accepted if it could be used with PCs as well. To this end, it developed libraries to allow Windows-based applications to create, play, and otherwise work with QuickTime movies. It also attached fairly onerous and expensive licensing terms to the libraries, so very few Windows developers have wanted to have much to do with them.

One useful exception to this is a set of Windows MCI drivers for QuickTime that Apple appears to have released with no strings attached. The MCI protocol is part of Windows—it handles all sorts of multimedia elements, including sound, music, and digitized video. With the QuickTime MCI drivers installed in your system, you can view QuickTime movies through Graphic Workshop, as touched on earlier. This is likely all you'll want to do with them in the context of this book.

The second legal issue is a bit thornier. Apple has a long tradition of suing anything with fewer than four legs, and it has recently brought its lawyers to bear on Microsoft, Intel, and Canyon Company, the latter being the firm from which Microsoft bought some of its low-level display technology for inclusion in Video for Windows. There were some early rumblings that Apple might also take legal action against software developers who use Video for Windows, and perhaps even against end users of Video for Windows software.

If this sounds unpleasantly familiar, it's worth noting that Microsoft has handled this situation quite differently from the way CompuServe dealt with the Unisys LZW patent, discussed earlier in this chapter. In February of 1995 Microsoft issued a press release stating it would defend anyone against whom Apple chose to take legal action as a result of their use of Video for Windows. As of this writing, the case is still in the preliminary stages of head-butting by the various legal councils involved.

3
FTP sites

One of the things that makes the World Wide Web so appealing is that it can insulate you from a lot of the nasty realities of the Internet. At least it can if the people who've created the Web pages you browse have provided links to the files and other resources you're interested in. As you'll probably find once you've had a chance to explore the Web a bit, this doesn't happen all the time. For any one of a number of reasons, it's very often necessary to step behind the curtain and see what's really going on.

What's really going on is a number of blindfolded polecat jugglers trying to recite all the dirty bits in Shakespeare backwards while dancing in a bathtub full of snakes—or at least a reasonable facsimile thereof. The Internet in its raw form isn't anything as user-friendly and well behaved as the World Wide Web. You might not want to spend a lot of time there, although being able to make brief forays into this perplexing little world is a very useful talent.

In its simplest sense, the World Wide Web is a very elaborate shell that mediates between you and the polecat jugglers, the real Internet. For example, when you click on a file to download from a Web page, your Web browser sends a string of barely comprehensible commands to the computer where the file lives and requests that it be sent to you. This absolves you of having to know those barely comprehensible commands. However, it limits you to accessing only files that someone has set up a World Wide Web page to deal with. Millions of files scattered about the Net can't be clicked on through Web pages—which is what this chapter will discuss.

Down in the depths of the Internet

The computers that are all linked together to form the Internet use a common operating system called UNIX. That's pronounced "eunuchs," and while the resemblance is probably coincidental, spending a lot of time working with UNIX can be like having favored bits of your anatomy lopped off.

The reason that UNIX is so hard to work with is that it was written a long, long time ago by what were then called "computer scientists." Most of these guys thought that keyboards were a passing fancy—computers back then properly communicated through a bank of switches and some flashing lights. The UNIX operating system presupposes a fantastic degree of insight about how computers work on the part of anyone using it. You've probably never aspired to this sort of insight, and if you're lucky you never will.

This chapter will discuss enough UNIX to allow you to access FTP sites through the World Wide Web, which is to say, practically none. Even though you'll be stepping out from under the protective umbrella of the Web, you won't actually have to plunge yourself into the slime and slavering creatures of UNIX.

Let's begin with a few important concepts as they pertain to FTP sites. Thus far, I've discussed the computers that maintain Web pages, called *servers*, without really getting into what they are. A server is a computer that runs UNIX and has some hardware that connects it to an Internet *backbone*, which is the actual communications system that links all the computers of the Net together. For the sake of this discussion, imagine it as a sort of virtual telephone system for packets of computer information.

All sorts of computers can run UNIX and function as servers, ranging from really big mainframe systems that occupy a large room and look like they probably require dedicated nuclear power plants to keep them online, through minicomputers about the size of a small refrigerator, right on down to desktop microcomputers. Of late, quite a few servers on the Net have appeared being run by 486 and Pentium PCs. In this case, the PCs in question have had their MS-DOS operating systems removed and replaced with Linux, a version of UNIX specifically written for PC platforms.

The distinction between these various classes of systems is the number of users the servers in question can deal with at once. A server running on a dedicated minicomputer that's doing nothing except dealing with the Net can accommodate several hundred users simultaneously. A PC running Linux can handle several dozen. When a server reaches its capacity of users, it typically denies access to any subsequent users until some of its existing users log out.

In practice, most servers start to slow down quite noticeably when they approach their capacity of users. In addition, it's worth noting that many Net servers aren't exclusively dedicated to dealing with the Net—they're also expected to do other things, which usually limits their capacity further still. I'll discuss the implications of server capacities as it affects the real world in greater detail later in this chapter.

If you don't look too closely, UNIX seems to be a bit like MS-DOS. It presents you with a command prompt where you can type commands. The commands supported by UNIX are largely different than the ones supported by DOS, and, while it's considered a bit blasphemous in most circles to say anything nice about MS-DOS, the DOS command set is a lot easier to understand.

Actually, the important thing to know about UNIX and UNIX-based servers is that they structure their directories a lot like a machine running DOS would. This is also analogous to the way OS/2 handles files and directories, or files and folders on a Mac. When you first log into a UNIX-based server, you're usually located in the root directory. Several other directories are visible from the root. These directories, in turn, probably have subdirectories, and perhaps sub-subdirectories within them. There's no finite limit to the depth of directories, and large servers with lots of files will often have nested directories several layers deep to better organize their contents.

Most of the directories available from the root of an Internet server aren't accessible unless you own the server in question. These directories contain system files for the server and personal files for the people who use the server to access the Internet. By convention, most Internet servers have a directory called pub, for public, which is accessible and contains all the other publicly accessible directories on the server. This convention isn't always followed, but you'll usually find it to be the case.

The first important thing to note about UNIX-based systems is that the names of things, such as commands, filenames, and directories, are case-sensitive. As such, pub and PUB are two distinct directories. By convention, most file and directory names on Net servers are in lowercase.

Under UNIX, the forward slash is used to indicate a directory or directory path—unlike DOS, which uses the backslash. As such, the proper designation for the pub directory from the root of a server would be /pub.

At the FTP site that my company uses to store Graphic Workshop and our other shareware, the directory where our files reside is alchemy, which is a subdirectory of pub. This is written /pub/alchemy.

Also by convention, you'll usually find that directories on an Internet server include a file called INDEX, index.txt, INDEX_00, or some variation thereof. This plain text file lists the contents of the directory in question, usually with a description of each file. These index files will turn up again in a moment.

Note that UNIX filenames aren't restricted to the same naming convention as DOS files. They can be a lot longer than eight characters with a three-character extension. So the DOS file NICEBABE.JPG could be named VeryAttractiveWomanInRedDress.Jpeg in UNIX. The latter is arguably a bit more politically correct, although it takes a lot more effort to type. When files are moved from a UNIX system to a machine running DOS—or any other environment with a more restricted naming convention—these sorts of names are truncated into fairly meaningless hieroglyphs. This one would probably become VERYATTR.JPE under DOS, for example.

The approach to handling server access that's discussed in this chapter doesn't have to deal with this.

When a computer is connected to the Net so you can access it and download files from it, it's called an *FTP site*. The acronym FTP stands for file transfer protocol, which describes the way files move from a remote server to your computer. In fact, no one has cared how this works for years—save, perhaps, for the present-day descendants of the computer scientists I mentioned a while back—and you'll never have to know anything much beyond this three-letter designation.

Actually, you might have to know a bit more about FTP access. As you might imagine, controlling who has access to computers on the Internet is an issue of considerable import in some circles. Every so often CNN finds out about someone who has "cracked" a computer on the Net and gets a good week's worth of hysteria going about the problem of security. While most FTP sites are accessible to anyone who cares to use them, this isn't always the case.

In fact, what's referred to as FTP access in this chapter is *properly called anonymous FTP*. This means that the FTP sites in question don't care who you are—the software you use to access them will tell them that your user name and password are both anonymous, and they're happy with this. The FTP access software discussed in this chapter will handle the exchange of names and passwords behind your back, and you'll never even know it's happening. I've mentioned it here only because on occasion you'll encounter an FTP site that doesn't allow for anonymous access. What they really mean is "we don't like your kind around here . . . get lost." These sites aren't for public access, and unless you have designs on being featured by CNN you won't be able to log into them.

To conclude this introductory discussion of FTP sites, it's probably worth mentioning several rules of netiquette (Net etiquette) that pertain to them. As was touched on earlier in this chapter, the server that runs an FTP site can handle only a finite number of users at one time. If the server is a large computer that does other things besides providing files for download, its resources are further required by its other functions. To this end, it's considered polite to spend as little time logged into a server as possible—log in, find what you want, download it, and log out to free the server's resources for someone else. In practice, you might want to do some browsing to see what's available. Just avoid connecting to an FTP site and then walking down the hall for a Coke and half an hour of polite conversation.

Second, keep in mind that most larger servers are a lot busier at some times than others. It's considered polite to avoid attempting to access them for protracted periods during business hours—keep in mind that business hours differ depending on where the server's located. When you first connect to a server, it will usually display a message telling you where it is and what restrictions apply to your use of it.

FTP access: what to click

Thus far I've described FTP servers without actually discussing how they're accessed. If you have a suite of applications to deal with the Internet, you'll probably have noticed some sort of FTP manager. In fact, these things exist for people who want to deal with FTP sites in something like a UNIX-based environment, or for remotely manipulating the files at a site. Browsing FTP sites can be handled by a much simpler application, to wit, your Web browser. The software that deals with World Wide Web pages also knows how to deal with FTP sites. More to the point, it can do so in a way to make FTP access almost as easy to get along with as the Web.

Figure 3-1 illustrates Netscape looking at the Alchemy Mindworks FTP site. You'll notice the absence of a unicorn. If you've previously browsed the various pages of the Alchemy World Wide Web page, you'll find that the same downloadable files appear in Fig. 3-1. All the text describing them, however, is missing.

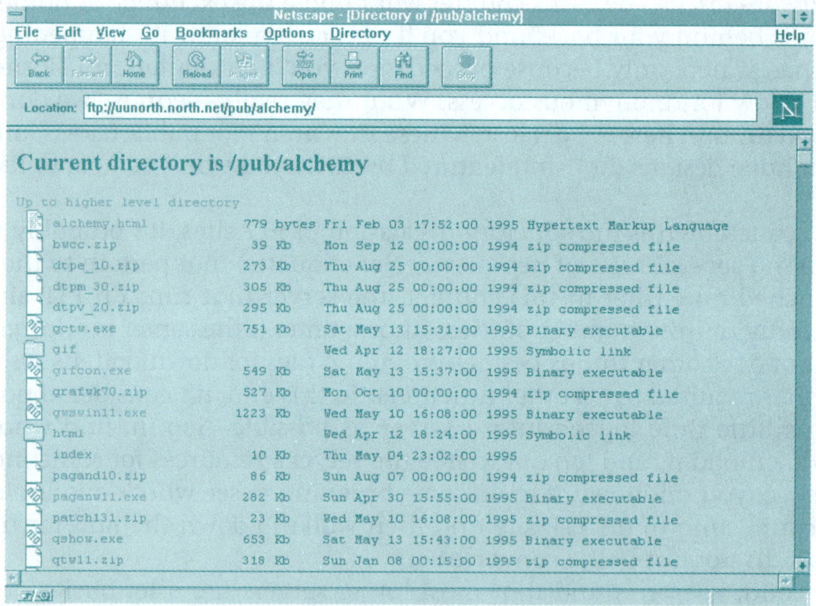

3-1 The Alchemy Mindworks FTP site as seen through Netscape.

In fact, the Alchemy Mindworks Web page and the Alchemy Mindworks FTP site consist of the same files on the same server. Only the way they're accessed is different. This isn't the case for all FTP sites, most of which don't support corresponding Web pages.

The important distinction between a Web page and an FTP site is that a Web page is created with links to specific files—it need not provide links to all the files in a directory if its author doesn't want it to. By comparison, if you use Netscape or another Web browser to access an FTP site, you'll be able to see all the files in whatever directories you log into. You'll also be able to access files from anonymous FTP sites that support no Web pages at all. There are a lot of these.

While FTP sites can't include links to other resources on the Internet, Web pages can include links to FTP sites.

You can link to FTP sites using essentially the same techniques as you would to deal with Web pages. Whereas the URL prefix for a Web page is http, the prefix for an FTP site is, perhaps predictably, ftp. To link to the Alchemy Mindworks FTP site, you'd enter ftp://www.north.net as the URL. If you're using Netscape, hit Enter after you've typed in the URL you want to link to.

Note that the URL for this FTP site and the URL for the alchemy.html home page it supports are a bit different (the latter was discussed in detail in the previous chapter). This is normal for sites that can be accessed both ways.

Also, keep in mind that FTP sites don't include links to other FTP sites. You can't navigate the Net at this level quite as effortlessly as Web pages allow. In order to access an FTP site, you must know its URL. There are some FTP sites listed in appendix B of this book, and you'll no doubt encounter mention of others as you browse the Web.

Once you've linked to the root of the FTP site you're interested in, you should see a number of directory entries. Under Netscape, they look like Fig. 3-2.

Click on the directory entry items to move down the directory tree of an FTP site and on the Back button of your browser to go back up the tree. You can also back up to the previous level of a directory tree by clicking on Up to a Higher Level Directory, the first item in the directory list of an FTP directory, if you're not presently in the root directory.

In their simplest sense, all the files at an FTP site are meaningless binary data—at least they are until an application capable of making sense of them turns up. In its ongoing effort to make the Internet friendly—even the deliberately unfriendly bits, such as FTP sites—Netscape will tell you a fair bit about the contents of files it locates. Figure 3-3 illustrates several files at the Alchemy Mindworks FTP site.

To begin with, notice that the icons to the left of each entry vary a bit from file to file. In order of their appearance in Fig. 3-3, these are icons for:

- An HTML document, that is, a Web page
- A text file
- A binary file that's probably part of an executable program
- A graphic
- A mysterious file that Netscape doesn't really understand

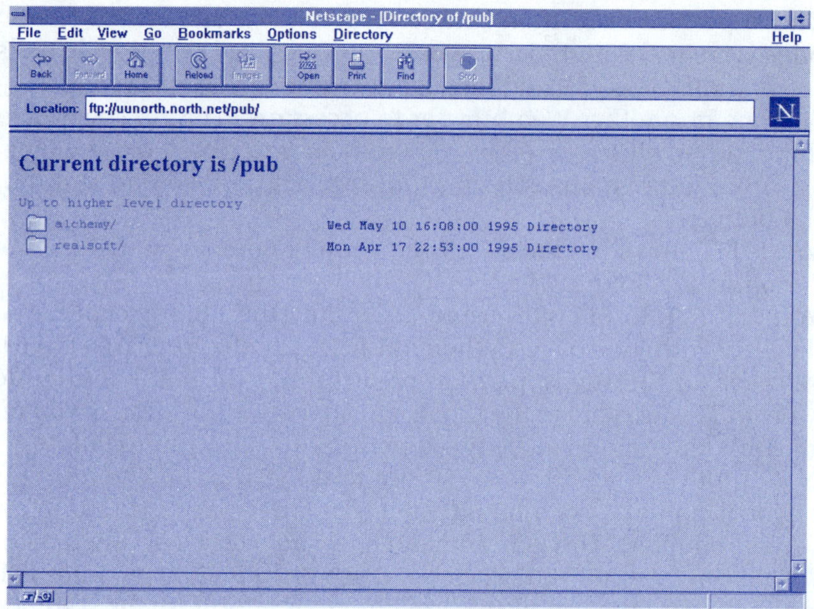

3-2 The entry for an FTP directory under Netscape. Most Web browsers use similar icons and notation.

alchemy.html	779 bytes	Fri Feb 03 17:52:00 1995	Hypertext Markup Language
theorder.txt	14 Kb	Thu Aug 11 00:00:00 1994	Plain text
gwswin11.exe	1223 Kb	Wed May 10 16:08:00 1995	Binary executable
theorder.gif	17 Kb	Sun Aug 07 00:00:00 1994	Compuserve image format
grafwk70.zip	527 Kb	Mon Oct 10 00:00:00 1994	zip compressed file

3-3 Some files seen by Netscape.

Netscape will attempt to deal with files it recognizes in a way that best suits the file in question. Here's what will happen if you click on each of the files in Fig. 3-3:

alchemy.html This is actually the file that defines a Web page. Netscape will load it as if it had been accessed through an http URL and display it as a conventional Web page, along with graphics, links, and all the other paraphernalia of the Web.

theorder.txt This is a simple text file. Netscape will download it to a temporary file on your hard drive and then call the Windows Notepad application to display it. The Notepad application has been defined as a helper application for Netscape to use when it encounters text files.

theorder.gif This is a GIF graphic. If you've configured a helper application for Netscape to display GIF files, such as Graphic Workshop, it will download the GIF file to your hard drive and call Graphic Workshop to display it.

The other two files in Fig. 3-3—paganw11.exe and grafwk70.zip—aren't objects that Netscape knows how to handle internally, nor are you likely to assign helper applications for them. If you click on these files from an FTP site, it's probably because you want to download them. As such, Netscape will call up the dialog in Fig. 3-4.

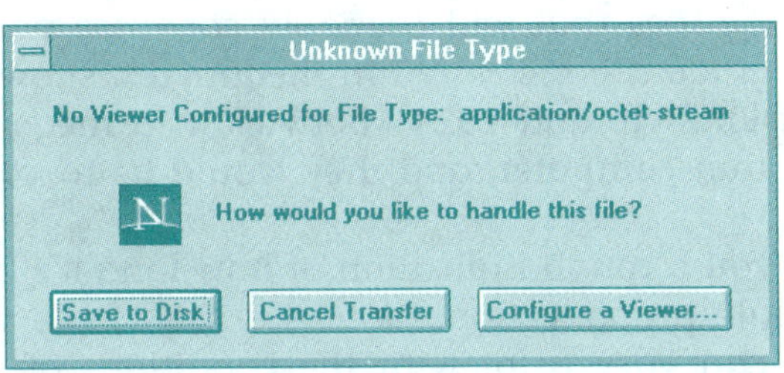

3-4
The Netscape dialog for downloading files.

If you tell Netscape to download a file, it will prompt you for a filename and begin fetching the file from the FTP site where it lives. Note that this can take a while if you've asked for a large file and you're connected to the Internet through a dial-up connection.

It's worth noting that most Web browsers—Netscape included—can be configured to view GIF and JPEG files you download directly, rather than saving them to a file and calling a helper application. You might want to enable this feature. Having it active will save you a few seconds when a file is being viewed, as your Web browser won't have to call up another application to show you your graphic. The catch to this is that most Web browsers don't let you save graphics that appear in their view modes. Specifically, they'll download a file, show it to you, and then delete it. By comparison, Graphic Workshop used as a helper will let you save the files it shows should you come across something you like.

If you're primarily interested in downloading graphics and sound files rather than viewing or hearing them online, you might want to turn off the helper applications for the common graphic files type, as discussed in the previous chapter. Having done so, graphic files will become mystery file types for your Web browser—unable to find helpers to deal with them, it will go directly to its Download dialog and prompt you to save them to disk.

The FTP handling facilities available through Web browsers are remarkably consistent—while a few of the menu items vary between Web browsers from different authors, the features I've just outlined will turn up in pretty well all of them. The default configuration of your Web browser—including what sorts of helpers it comes set up to use, how its download facilities are configured, and so on—will probably vary. Make sure you set it up to handle files the way you want them handled before you embark on an intensive download safari. There are few things more disheartening than downloading a megabyte worth of fantasy art to find that your Web browser is prepared to show it to you only once and then blow the file away.

Returning to the list of files in Fig. 3-3, there are a few more things you might want to keep an eye on in the directory lists of FTP sites. To begin with, notice that each file has a file size. Small files are measured in bytes, as indicated by the letter b after the file size. Larger files are measured in kilobytes, indicated by Kb, and really huge files that will probably convince you it's about time for a hard drive upgrade are measured in megabytes, shown as Mb. There are 1024 bytes in a kilobyte and 1024 kilobytes in a megabyte. These are nice round numbers to a computer, and they would be to you as well if you had 16 fingers.

The size of a file will offer you a rough indication of how long it's likely to take to download over a dial-up connection. Note the use of the word *rough*—file transmission times can vary a lot with the conditions of your phone line and the amount of traffic on the Internet at the time you choose to download the file in question. Other things that might increase the time it takes to download a file are the number of users on the server from which you're downloading the file, the type of modem you're using, whether it's a Tuesday in a month with an R in it, the dimensions of your cat in angstroms, the number of angels that can dance on the head of a pin, and the color of your socks.

Ignoring most of the foregoing scientific considerations, at 9600 bps a one-megabyte file takes about 12 minutes to download, so you can plan on 85 kilobytes per minute. This gets a bit better at 14,400 bps—a megabyte requires about 10 minutes to download, which is about 98 kilobytes per minute. In the event that you have a fast enough phone line to really support 28,800 bps—I'll get to the potential consequences of this in a moment—you'll be able to download a megabyte in about five minutes, which works out to about 196 kilobytes per minute. Keep in mind that, if your cat is particularly obese, all these calculations might exhibit a substantial error.

To the right of the file sizes back in Fig. 3-3, you'll find the creation date for the files. This information can be useful if you want to know whether you're about to download a file that's newer than one you already have with ostensibly the same contents. Keep in mind, however, that this date is really the date as defined by the clock of the computer on which the file in question was created. Most people don't check the clocks in their computers from one year to the next, and as such file date stamps can't always be trusted.

Things that go plump in the night

All the foregoing discussion of downloading things from FTP sites presupposes that absolutely nothing will go wrong. Most of the time, this is a fairly reasonable supposition. It's worth knowing, however, that you can't always assume the Internet will behave itself. This section will touch on a few of the shattered soda bottles, stranded but still venomous jellyfish, and topless sunbathers with cellular phones ready to speed-dial their lawyers on the otherwise idyllic beach of the World Wide Web.

The first potential problem with accessing files at an FTP site through a Web browser is that most Web browsers are a bit too well mannered for their own good. A dedicated FTP access application will connect to an FTP site and retain the connection until you explicitly log out, or until the server that's running the FTP site decides that you've overstayed your welcome and yells for a bouncer. By comparison, a Web browser accesses FTP sites like it accesses Web pages. Specifically, it makes contact with the server, downloads the file you've asked for, and then closes the connection. If you change directories, belt the Reload button of your browser, or do something else that causes your browser to ask an FTP site for information, the same procedure will take place again.

Not only is this measurably slower than a conventional FTP access package—each time your browser wants to talk to the FTP site in question, it must undertake all the handshaking required to establish contact with it—but it will probably confront you with a bit of a paradox from time to time.

If you attempt to link to an FTP site for which the server is at its maximum number of users, you'll be denied access. If you just squeak in under the limit when you first link to the server, however, you might find that actually attempting to download files will cause the server to deny you access intermittently throughout your session. Because a Web browser essentially starts a brand-new session each time you try to download a file, the server you're talking to won't know that you connected to it previously. Each time you ask for a file it will treat you as a new user. If its house is full, it will deny you access.

Users come and go pretty quickly at FTP sites—should you run into a problem like this one, try the file again in a minute or two. On those occasions when the server you're working with is really swamped, save the current directory as an HTML file and access it later—I'll discuss this in detail in chapter 5.

The other problem you might encounter is downloading files and finding that they're mangled when you finally get a chance to look at them. This might manifest itself as scrambled text, graphics that don't unpack, or archive files with corrupted entries. While corrupted files are good only for deleting if you encounter them, you might find it helpful to know a bit about how they got that way.

When you download a file from an FTP site—or indirectly through a Web page—it's sent over the Internet to your server. If you don't actually have a server of your own—that is, if you're accessing the Net through a dial-up connection—it's sent to the server of your Internet access provider and from there to your computer over a phone line.

Data sent over the Internet is reasonably secure, and gets corrupted infrequently. The same can't be said of data sent over a phone line. As was touched on in chapter 1 of this book, your choice of modems has some bearing on how well your files transfer. Both modems themselves and the protocol by which you connect to an Internet access provider do a certain amount of error correction, that is, they fix data that gets mangled in transit. Bad phone lines, or phone lines that are too noisy for the bps rate at which you're trying to communicate, can mangle your data beyond the capabilities of error correction to correct it.

Archives

Data compression was discussed earlier in this book in conjunction with graphics. In fact, much the same techniques can be applied to other forms of data, such as text files, spreadsheets, sound files, and executable software. Compressing these files will typically reduce them in size at least a bit, and allow them to move over the Net in less time.

Archives are files of files. Specifically, an archive allows you to compress multiple large files into one smaller file. An archive can be stored or sent over the Net and unpacked later, restoring the original files. Archives both save space and prevent multiple associated files from becoming accidentally separated.

As with graphics to some extent, different archive standards have appeared for the various computer platforms commonly in use. This section explains the different standards and shows you how to access them. Archive standards are typically indicated by the file extensions of the archive files they create.

ZIP ZIP is the de facto archive standard for PC-based systems. The software that reads and writes ZIP files is called PKZip, widely available as shareware. It's easy to find programs that unpack ZIP files on other platforms—unzipping tools are available as shareware or freeware for Macintosh and UNIX systems, among many others. The ZIP archive standard provides the best compression and flexibility of any of the archives to be discussed here, and turns up at most FTP sites as I write this.

ARC The ARC standard was the predecessor of the ZIP standard. It's obsolete and hardly ever encountered any longer, but you can still find PC-based shareware to unpack ARC files, most notably PKARC.

SIT SIT files are the most popular of the Macintosh archive formats. SIT is an abbreviation for StuffIt (make of this what you will). Programs to unpack SIT files on non-Macintosh systems do exist, although the slightly weird format of Macintosh files usually requires no small measure of insight into things Mac to make use of Macintosh data files on a non-Mac system.

TAR and GZIP The TAR and GZIP archive standards are native to UNIX systems, and as such can be a bit confusing. The TAR standard doesn't actually compress files—it just appends multiple files into one, along with some information to allow TAR software to subsequently split them apart. The GZIP software handles file compression. It's common to find UNIX archives with names like FannyHill.Tar.Z. This means that, in order to unpack the archive, you must first use GZIP to uncompress it and then use TAR to split it apart. Both TAR and GZIP programs are available for other platforms, but they're typically a bit inscrutable.

You might want to use Archie to explore the Net or ask your network administrator about locating archiving software for your system. If you're running on a PC platform, the PKZip software is almost essential for most of the things you're likely to download over the Web. You can mail-order a registered copy of the PKZip package from:

PKWare, Inc.
9025 N. Deerwood Drive
Brown Deer, WI 53223

It's worth noting that by no means everything you extract from archives will prove useful. To begin with, executable programs designed for computers other than yours are essentially a lot of meaningless random numbers. The same is probably the case for sound files, graphics, word-processed documents, and other application-specific files from software running on different types of computers. Unless you know how to work with the particular files found in an archive, it might not do much more than occupy hard drive space.

Viruses

If you download software from the Internet, it's worth knowing a bit about computer viruses. This will keep your computer from actually getting infected with one, and also prevent your brain from being infected with the mad, salivating fear of viruses—which is most often a lot more virulent than viruses themselves.

A computer virus is a small program that attaches itself to other programs in your system—very often the programs that make up the operating system of your computer—and subsequently does something nasty. Viruses are usually designed to travel from machine to machine—software copied from an infected machine might in turn spread viruses to previously clean systems. Most viruses are designed to remain dormant for a while to allow you to spread them around before you find out they're lurking on your hard drive. The Michaelangelo virus, for example, makes its presence known only once a year, on Michaelangelo's birthday.

Viruses range from benign and stupid to exceedingly nasty. Some do nothing more than print something from time to time that the author of the virus thought was clever, and then let you get on with your life. Others will reformat your hard drive for you.

The first really important thing to know about viruses is that only executable software can transmit them (or the boot sector of a disk, which isn't really an issue when downloading files), and the viruses are activated only when these executable files are run. This means that if you download and subsequently run software from the Internet, you could expose your computer to some risk of infection. If you download only text files, graphics, sound bites, video clips, and other sorts of data files, your computer won't be exposed to any risk.

The second really important thing to know about viruses is that the media frenzy that surrounds them is far more frightening than viruses themselves are. Viruses do exist, but they're relatively rare. You can screen any software you download before running it to make sure it doesn't include any viruses. In short, you can reduce the risk of your computer being infected by viruses to something less than the risk of being trampled to death by extinct woolly mammoths while sipping pina coladas on the slopes of Mount Everest.

Virus scanners are available for most personal computer systems. The one I use is called ViruScan, which is widely available as shareware. You can order a registered version of the program from:

McAfee, Inc.
2710 Walsh Avenue
Santa Clara, CA 95051-0963

There are two things to keep in mind about these programs. First off, new viruses turn up periodically, which means that you must keep your virus scanner up to date. Secondly, some scanners are a bit trigger-happy, and will report that viruses exist in perfectly innocent software. The Norton Anti-Virus package, for example, is legendary in this respect—one version of it decided that every copy of PKZip was actually a virus, upsetting quite a few people for a while. It's important to use some common sense when you fire up a virus scanner—if yours starts detecting viruses in files that common sense tells you couldn't possibly be infected, contact the manufacturer of the software to make sure the problem isn't an overly paranoid scanner.

If you do decide to download executable software over the Internet—shareware, for example—try to locate an FTP site or Web page maintained by the author or manufacturer of the software. This will reduce the likelihood of downloading infected software.

4

Usenet

Usenet is one of the older institutions of the Internet—while it predates the World Wide Web by several eons, many Web browsers can deal with it as an extension of the Web. This is conceptually similar to the way FTP and gopher access is offered by Web browsers, as discussed in the previous chapter.

Usenet is easily the most diverse and riotous aspect of the Internet. While it's easy to understand in an abstract sense, it's a bit like a week in Toontown when you actually get up close and personal with it.

Usenet is a collection of several thousand individual discussions of specific topics, called *newsgroups*. The easiest way to understand Usenet is to think of several thousand special-purpose computer bulletin boards, all of them instantly accessible through a common interface. In fact, the mechanics of Usenet are quite different than those of a real bulletin board, but the analogy is more or less workable—at least, it is at first.

You can leave messages, properly called *postings*, in specific newsgroups. You can also read postings from other users of the newsgroup in question, and reply to them if you like. Subsequent users might choose to reply to your replies. These are called *threaded* postings.

The thing that makes Usenet so interesting isn't actually its structure, but rather the breathtaking scope of subjects dealt with in newsgroups. You can find newsgroups that deal with things like:

- Bondage and discipline
- Jethro Tull
- New movies
- Antique cars
- The Church of the SubGenius
- Zoroastrians
- Lizards
- Devilbunnies
- Greasy pizza

This is hardly a representative list, of course—the only really representative list around has several thousand entries, with new ones being added all the time. You might well wonder what a devilbunny is, or why anyone would want to spend a lot of time talking about greasy pizza. These things defy easy explanations.

Consider that, as I write this, there are some 30 million users of the Internet. If it requires a few dozen users to keep a newsgroup agreeably lively, this amounts to something like 0.0000008 percent of the population of the Net. There are few topics for newsgroups that can't scare up this much interest.

Unlike real bulletin boards—the owners of which might fear a visit from the local thought police if they were to allow really extreme or explicit discussions on their systems—Usenet newsgroups don't really answer to anyone beyond their own users. As such, if you check out a newsgroup that purports to deal with weird, kinky sex or political views that make Vlad the Impaler seem like just another liberal, you'll probably find that the users therein say exactly what's on their mind, using whatever language they feel is appropriate.

In order to properly deal with newsgroups, it's useful to understand how they really work. The analogy of a lot of computer bulletin boards describes how Usenet appears, but it isn't particularly faithful to what it does behind your back. While knowing how the various aspects of the Internet actually function isn't always essential, in this case a bit of insight will help you avoid some of the mistakes people often make when they first get involved with newsgroups.

A computer bulletin board is typically a single computer or a single network of computers that serves as a repository for the messages the bulletin board supports. If you send a message to another user of a bulletin board, it's written to the message database and, when someone comes along to read it, it's read back from the database.

If I were to create a bulletin board to support a discussion of late post-Leyland Jaguar design or panda ranching, I'd be responsible for maintaining the system—keeping people from leaving messages on it that were off-topic, answering questions from users, and so on.

It would be really slick and leading edge if Usenet could work this way too, but a bit of calculation will indicate why it isn't the case. Millions of people access Usenet daily. If Usenet's thousands of newsgroups resided on a specific computer, it would be one of the busiest machines on Earth. In fact, the level of traffic through such a hypothetical central clearing house for Usenet groups would make the whole system unworkably slow, even if someone felt like donating a computer the size of a warehouse for the task.

Usenet runs on much smaller computers—quite a lot of them, in fact. It's based on some clever software and the sort of cooperation that usually turns up at the heart of workable enterprises on the Net. If you post something to a newsgroup, it doesn't immediately get sent to a central computer, but rather eventually makes its way to all the other servers on the Internet that support Usenet. Likewise, things posted to Usenet from other servers ultimately find their way to the repository of Usenet postings on the server through which you access the Internet. This means that, while thousands of servers must each maintain a database of postings for thousands of newsgroups—a not insubstantial amount of data—no one server is expected to deal with everyone who wants to read those postings.

The catch to this arrangement—and, incidentally, the reason why it's important to know how Usenet actually works—is that, when you post something to a newsgroup, it doesn't become instantly readable by everyone else on earth who happens to be accessing Usenet. Depending on a number of somewhat imponderable elements, it can take hours or even days for your posting to get to all the other news servers.

The time lag inherent in Usenet means that newsgroups aren't actually a very good medium for propagating news. In addition, you'll frequently encounter message threads where the replies and replies to replies seem to be slightly out of order, or whose authors have clearly ignored what would appear to be earlier postings. Neither of these things has necessarily happened—not everyone gets to read Usenet postings at the same time or in the same order.

The other aspect of the computer bulletin board analogy I mentioned earlier is that of a central administrator. Bulletin boards have them, but newsgroups usually don't. While individual newsgroups are ultimately conceived by someone, there's no requirement for the parents of a newsgroup to hang around once the little monster has been born. To be sure, newsgroups like alt.wesley.crusher.die.die.die or alt.sex.hampster.duct-tape are usually dreamt up one morning, created over lunch, and largely forgotten about by tea time. Some of the more serious newsgroups do actually have moderators to keep them on track and are more or less civil, but they represent the minority of forums on Usenet.

This probably seems like a grand, majestically conceived design for almost certain anarchy, and in a sense it is. In another sense, Usenet is one of the most orderly of social organisms that human beings have ever created. The reason for this—and, as an aside, the reason why most new users of Usenet are something less than ideally popular for a few months—is, as was briefly mentioned in chapter 3, called netiquette.

Netiquette, spamming, and flames

With no one around minding the shop in most newsgroups, you'd think that a hoard of yuppie accountants would come by and post thousands of messages about their tax shelters and money market accounts, making Usenet almost unworkable. While a very tiny amount of this sort of thing does take place, you'll probably find that it's kept down to a level that won't impair your use of the newsgroups to which you subscribe. The reason for this is *netiquette*.

As its name implies, netiquette is a sort of unwritten set of guidelines for civil behavior on the Internet, rather than a list of rules that someone comes by and tattoos on your dog the first time you connect to the Net. There are no Net police to enforce the rules of netiquette, and if you want to ignore them and behave like an inbred tourist from someplace even Californians won't go without serious provocation there's no one to stop you. You won't want to, though . . .

Here's an Internet legend. It's rather poignant because it's absolutely true and somewhat extreme, and it illustrates netiquette in a way no list of rules ever could. Future generations will read their kids to sleep with this legend—if they have slightly messed up kids. This is the story of green-card lawyers spamming the net.

Long ago and far away—in the middle of 1994—two lawyers named Canter and Siegel posted an advertisement to several thousand Usenet newsgroups offering to assist potential immigrants to the United States with the green-card lottery. This violated several tenets of netiquette, among them that it's rude to post things to newsgroups that are wildly off-topic, that it's rude to post the same message to more than a few newsgroups, and it's unspeakably rude to post overtly commercial advertising to newsgroups, save for a very few that were created to accept it.

In Usenet terms, Canter and Siegel behaved slightly more rudely than a neon-pink Honda Civic sporting green and purple stripes being driven by an overweight, middle-aged housewife with blond hair and black roots on her way downtown to spend an evening drinking light beer and watching male strippers.

Canter and Siegel "spammed" Usenet, that is, they abused its generally good nature for their own ends. Because Usenet is essentially a cooperative undertaking, most of the people who post to it take offense at this sort of thing. More people than Canter and Siegel probably knew existed took offense at their postings. They received so much nasty e-mail that their Internet access provider at the time was forced to terminate their account or get swamped. Someone found out what Canter and Siegel's fax number was and arranged to empty their fax machine every night (while it's beyond the scope of this book, there are various ways to send faxes through the Internet). A program called CancelMoose was installed by most system administrators to automatically delete further postings from Canter and Siegel.

This is, admittedly, a particularly venomous case of the Internet protecting itself—and one you need not fear unless you undertake to be even ruder than these green-card lawyers were. However, you will find that the individual users of newsgroups can get a bit caustic if you seem to be abusing the hospitality of the Net.

Here's the basis of many aspects of netiquette. It has to do with the idea of *bandwidth*, which is the amount of information that the Internet or your brain can deal with in a finite amount of time. Bandwidth is always limited, and in most cases you'll find that you have a lot less of it at your disposal than you might otherwise wish. Anything that wastes the bandwidth of other users of the Internet is considered to be rude and, as such, bad netiquette.

The green-card lawyers wasted the bandwidth of pretty well everyone who accessed Usenet at the time because they posted off-topic messages that many people actually read, not knowing they were off-topic. In addition, these messages ended up occupying a lot of space on a lot of servers, wasting the bandwidth of the individual computers that make up the Internet.

A much less extreme breach of netiquette, although a much more common one, is that of posting frequently asked questions in newsgroups. If you come upon a new newsgroup where you don't really know what's going on, the most obvious way out of your confusion is to flag down a car from the screaming traffic of the information superhighway and ask for directions. This metaphor might suggest why people regard asking obvious questions to be a breach of netiquette.

The correct approach to finding out what a new newsgroup is about is to read the frequently asked questions document, or FAQ. Most newsgroups have these—they're posted at regular intervals, and in many cases can be downloaded from an FTP site or Web page somewhere. If no frequently asked questions document appears, it's not considered impolite to post a message inquiring about where one might be found.

People who abuse Usenet by wasting everyone else's time and bandwidth usually find themselves being *flamed* by other users. Flaming is a subject of considerable depth and scope in Usenet, and one you should probably spend a minute or two getting familiar with. In its simplest sense, a flame is a posting that expresses disapproval or approbation of the postings of another user, or of some other action. Now, this is a fairly sanitized description of the situation—it's by no means uncommon to find someone expressing disapproval of another posting by suggesting that both its author's parents had the same last name, that he or she could be he or she or both at the same time, that most shag carpet has a better grasp of reality than the author in question, and so on. Profanity that would take the rust off a '78 Ford pickup at 20 yards figures prominently in flaming.

It's worth noting that really nuclear flaming is sometimes appropriate. You can, for example, subscribe to the alt.impeach.clinton newsgroup and express yourself any way you like, so long as what you have to say would go over well in a crowd of vengeful Republicans. If you can't be a bit more civil in the rec.arts.books newsgroup, however, you probably won't find yourself well liked.

A significant intensity of flaming is often seen directed at new users of the Internet. For example, there's a whole newsgroup called alt.aol-sucks which was created ostensibly for the purpose of being as unkind as possible to Internet users who access the Net through America Online.

One of the things you'll realize about Usenet within the first 20 minutes is that it's not very "nineties." Political correctness is largely regarded as an affectation of the weak and feeble, courtesy is extended only to people who are reasonably civil to begin with, and reality rather than appearance is the final arbiter.

As a final note about flaming, in addition to possibly being flamed when you post things in newsgroups, you'll no doubt eventually long to flame someone else—however well mannered you might think yourself at the moment. In some cases, flaming is justified and represents part of the way the Internet keeps itself safe from green-card lawyers and other bottom-feeders. However, what seems like a rapier-like thrust at the forces of anarchy and polyester suits when you write it might well come off reading like the output of an infinite number of monkeys locked in a room with a broken typewriter. Before you flame someone else's postings, read some flames.

The postings in newsgroups are conversations of a sort. You'll be a lot better received by the other users of a newsgroup if you consider this analogy before you post things. For example, few things are more annoying in the real world than getting embroiled in a really interesting conversation and having someone butt in and try to change the subject. While there's a tendency for posted threads to drift around a bit, it's not considered polite to deliberately hijack them.

It's also not particularly agreeable to post agreements with earlier threads that do nothing more than agree. A whole message that consists entirely of the words "ya, me too," "I wish I'd said that," or "totally awesome" and doesn't actually contribute anything to the conversation is just a waste of bandwidth.

Here's another sort of bandwidth waster in Usenet—this is one you'll have to think about for yourself. You'll unquestionably come across postings that really do seem to deserve to be flamed. These will include obvious scams, chain letters, and get-rich-quick schemes, really nasty messages from users who clearly should have been exposed at birth, and messages that obviously and deliberately do not belong in the newsgroup in question. Quite a few such postings are "flame bait"—they're posted by people who want to see how much outrage they can inspire.

If you allow yourself a bit of righteous indignation and flame these postings, you might discourage their authors from posting such things again—or you might give them the attention they're actually after. Your postings will become part of a thread perpetuating the original postings, and might draw greater attention to them. Alternately, you can e-mail flames to the authors of these things, allowing that they come with genuine e-mail addresses.

There isn't an easy answer to this question—it's something you might find you have to make up as you go along.

Subscribe and meet your fate

Usenet is structured in a way that's designed to allow you to find the things you're interested in and ignore the other newsgroups that don't really concern you. Once there, the structure of individual newsgroups makes it possible for you to quickly locate those postings you actually want to read and pass on the turkeys.

To begin with, as has been touched on informally earlier in this chapter, you must subscribe to those newsgroups in which you're interested. This is analogous to subscribing to magazines, save that no money need change hands when you subscribe to Usenet groups and you won't find yourself on a mailing list for Publisher's Clearinghouse as a result of doing so.

Subscribing to a newsgroup tells your newsreader software that you'd like to be able to access the newsgroup in question. It might seem like all that's really required is being able to select the newsgroups you want to browse from a list of all the available groups. In fact, this has a few catches in practice—not the least of which is having to choose from several thousand newsgroups every time you want to see what's happening in your favorite groups.

A second consideration is that the list of newsgroups changes frequently. You probably wouldn't want to have your newsreader download the whole works every time you boot it up, especially if you know which groups you want to browse.

Newsgroups are named using dotted hierarchical notation, which means they use a lot of periods. In theory, the first word in a newsgroup names tells you generally what sort of group is involved, with each subsequent word fine-tuning the definition a bit more.

There are lots of classes of newsgroups, but the two that you're most likely to want to check out are alt and rec. The latter indicates newsgroups that are in some way recreational. The former doesn't mean *alternate*, as you might expect—rather, it's an acronym for "anarchists, lunatics and terrorists." When CNN really gets hot and steamy about all the vile and perverse goings on around the Internet, they're usually referring to alt newsgroups.

A typical newsgroup, alt.sex, deals with a broad range of matters sexual. It has also sired numerous more specialized newsgroups—no doubt 'cause the condom broke. For example, you'll find:

- alt.sex.pictures
- alt.sex.pictures.female
- alt.sex.stories
- alt.sex.bondage
- alt.sex.bestiality
- alt.sex.bestiality.barney

There are, actually, innumerable other alt.sex newsgroups—sex is one of the more popular attractions of Usenet.

As you might imagine, having seen the previous list of alt.sex newsgroups, not everything that turns up in Usenet is necessarily all that serious. For example, the people who post things in alt.sex.bestiality are really prepared to talk about having it off with animals. The people who post to alt.sex.bestiality.barney are interested in having it off with an imaginary purple dinosaur. Taking the former prospect seriously can be unpleasant—taking the latter prospect seriously is very nearly impossible.

You'll also find quite a few newsgroups that offer no real indication of whether they hope to be taken seriously or not. For example, you'll probably have to browse around newsgroups like alt.slack, alt.alt.alt.alt.alt.alt, alt.spam, alt.devilbunnies, and so on for quite a while to get a sense of what they're about. You might want to regard these as inside jokes of the Internet.

Here's another bit of netspeak. If you browse around a newsgroup and don't post anything, you're said to be *lurking*. Despite the sinister overtones of this word, lurking is considered to be an aspect of netiquette, especially if you find yourself interested in some of the more ineffable groups. Plan to lurk for a while 'til you get a feel for the newsgroups in which you'd like to participate.

In order to subscribe to a newsgroup, it must be carried by your Internet access provider. In most cases, you should find that your access provider handles almost all the available newsgroups. There might, however, be certain exceptions:

- Some access providers get a bit uncomfortable with things like alt.sex.bondage, and some of the other really extreme groups. You might find that such groups just don't appear in the list of available newsgroups. You'll have to have this out with your access provider if you're interested in these resources.
- Some newsgroups are genuinely illegal in some areas. For example, the alt.fan.karla-homolka newsgroup, which deals with a fairly nasty murder trial, cannot legally be accessed from servers in Canada, where there's a restraining order on all publicity surrounding the trial.
- You'll encounter a whole range of newsgroups with the prefix clari. These groups are maintained by ClariNet, a commercial news provider. They're available only if the owner of your server has paid for them, which almost no one outside university campuses does.

It's worth noting that some Internet access providers don't maintain the list of newsgroups they do carry particularly well. If you find out about a newsgroup that you don't seem to be able to access, have a word with your access provider to see if it's just been omitted accidentally.

You can download a list of all the current newsgroups, along with brief descriptions of what they are, from ftp.uu.net/networking/news/config/. See the discussion of FTP sites in chapter 3 if you haven't done so previously.

Usenet through the Web

As with FTP sites and gophers, Usenet isn't strictly speaking part of the World Wide Web. However, you can access it as a function of a Web browser, and many browsers have fairly respectable news readers as part of their functionality. I'll describe accessing newsgroups through Netscape in this section—you can use roughly the same approach to handle Usenet through other browsers with newsgroup access.

Netscape wants to look at everything as a URL. While it presents you with a fairly conventional Usenet newsreader interface, it also allows you to use its bookmark facility to get right to your favorite newsgroups. It has a quick interface to a list of all the available newsgroups, too—as discussed earlier in this chapter, this may prove unworkably time-consuming if you're accessing the Internet through a dial-up connection.

To turn Netscape into a newsreader, select Go To Newsgroups from the Directory menu. An interface like the one in Fig. 4-1 will appear.

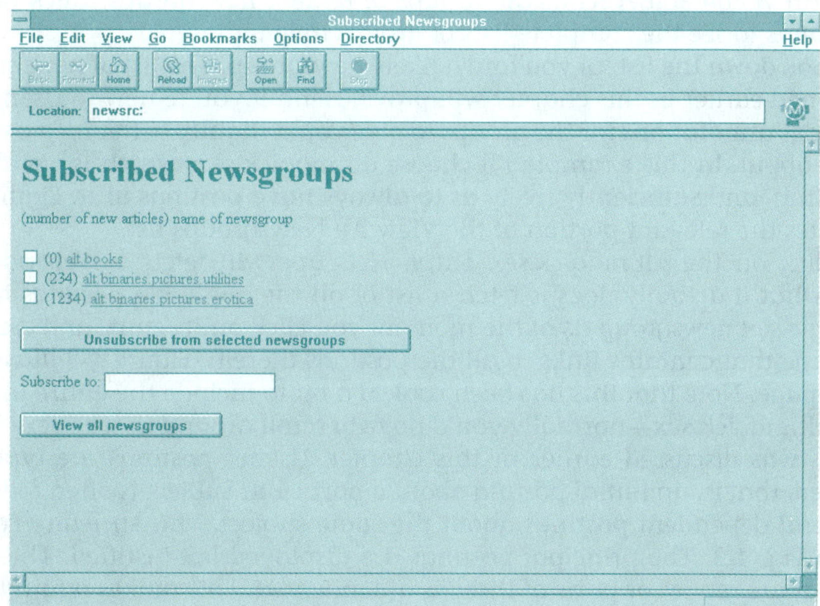

4-1 Netscape's news reader.

Initially, Netscape isn't subscribed to any newsgroups. You can add newsgroups to your list of subscribed entries by either entering the name of a specific newsgroup in the Subscribe To field and hitting Enter or clicking on the View All Newsgroups button. The latter control will download a huge list of available groups, with each group defined as a hypertext link. Click on the newsgroup you're interested in to see a list of all the articles it offers at the moment.

Note that in later releases of Netscape, the View All Newsgroups list is actually organized hierarchically. As such, you'll see a list of all the prefixes of the available newsgroups. Click on one of these, such as alt, to see all the newsgroups with this prefix, and then on specific newsgroups or groups of newsgroups.

In fact, you might find the Subscribed Newsgroups list that Netscape maintains, and its Go To Newsgroups function as a whole, to be a bit superfluous once you've selected the newsgroups you're interested in. You can use bookmarks to get to your favorite newsgroups much more conveniently.

Let's begin by subscribing to a newsgroup. Click on View All Newsgroups. After a brief wait—depending on what you consider to be brief, of course—you'll see a list of all the newsgroup prefixes. Click on alt. There'll be another pause while Netscape organizes its list of alt newsgroups, after which you should see a long list of hypertext links to newsgroups. Note that the links with white document icons beside them are actually newsgroups, while the ones with yellow folder icons are groups of related newsgroups. Click on the latter items to see the complete lists of groups they represent.

Look down the list 'til you find a likely newsgroup. The list of newsgroups mentioned earlier in this chapter will prove useful if you're new to Usenet, as it includes annotations for the groups to give you a slightly better idea of what they're about. In this example I'll choose alt.magick.sex, which is weird and interesting, and sufficiently lively as to always have postings in it. Figure 4-2 illustrates the relevant portion of the View All Newsgroups list.

Click on the alt.magick.sex entry. Netscape will fetch a Web page of sorts—what it actually does is fetch a list of all the available postings in the alt.magic.sex newsgroup as of the moment you click on its entry and create a Web page that contains links to all the postings therein. Figure 4-3 illustrates such a page. Note that this has been cooked a bit to include the entire posting list of alt.magick.sex—normally you'd have to scroll around to see everything.

As was discussed earlier in this chapter, Usenet postings are typically threaded, that is, an initial posting about a particular subject is often followed by several dependent postings about the same subject. This structure can be seen in Fig. 4-3. The principal postings are displayed left-justified. The postings that are replies or parts of threads are indented. This makes it fairly easy to read all the postings in a thread without having to skip all over the posting list looking for titles.

Each posting title also lists its author and the number of lines of text in the posting it represents, in parentheses. This latter bit is extremely useful. None of the postings in this newsgroup are particularly huge, but this is by no means always the case. Given the relatively slow download speeds for dial-up

Newsgroups list
File Edit View Go Bookmarks Options Directory Help
Back Forward Home Reload Images Open Find Stop
Location: news:*

alt.locksmithing
alt.lucid-emacs.bug
alt.lucid-emacs.help
alt.lumpkin
alt.lwaxana-troi.die.die.die
alt.lycra
alt.machines.misc
alt.mag.playboy
alt.magic
alt.magick
alt.magick.chaos
alt.magick.ethics
alt.magick.sex
alt.magick.sex.angst
alt.magnus.and.ketil
alt.magnus_and_ketil
alt.mail.cfutures
alt.make.money.fast
alt.management.tech-support
alt.managing.techsupport
alt.manga
alt.manufacturing.misc
alt.maroney

Document: Received 61488 bytes

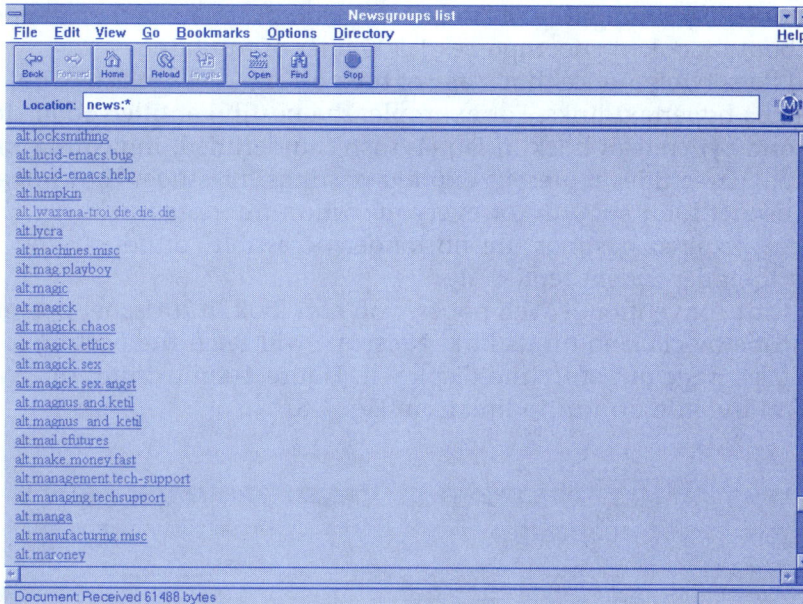

4-2 The list of newsgroup links with the alt.magick.sex newsgroup visible.

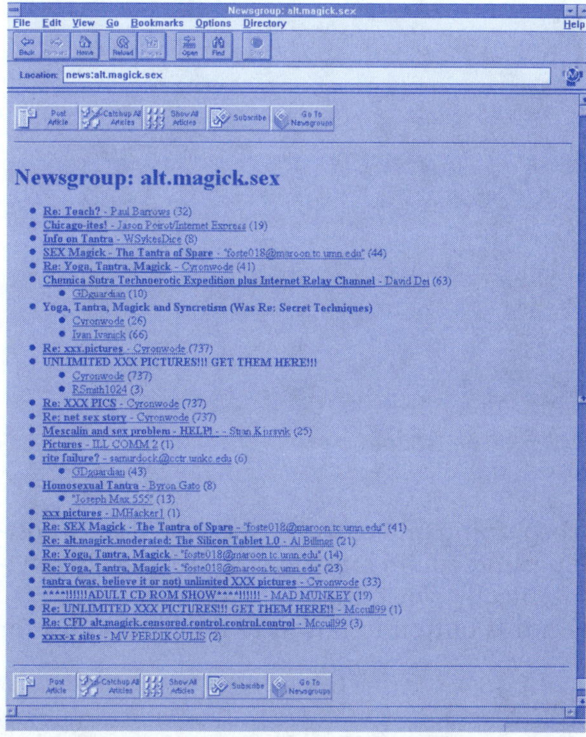

4-3
The posting list for alt.magick.sex. Erotic picture vendors seem to have taken the beaches . . .

Internet access, you might want to know ahead of time whether the posting you're about to look at encompasses 1,500 lines of rambling.

You'll probably notice that some of the posting titles are listed, but aren't available as hypertext links. For example, the posting entitled Yoga, Tantra, Magick and Syncretism back in Fig. 4-3 isn't underlined, indicating that it's not a link. These titles represent expired postings, messages that have been around Usenet long enough for everyone who's interested in them to have read them. Expired postings are no longer accessible, although you might find that their dependent replies are.

As with conventional Web pages, you can look at a Usenet posting under Netscape by clicking on its link. Netscape will fetch the posting for you, create a Web page out of it, and display it. Figure 4-4 illustrates the result of clicking on the Info on Tantra link from Fig. 4-3.

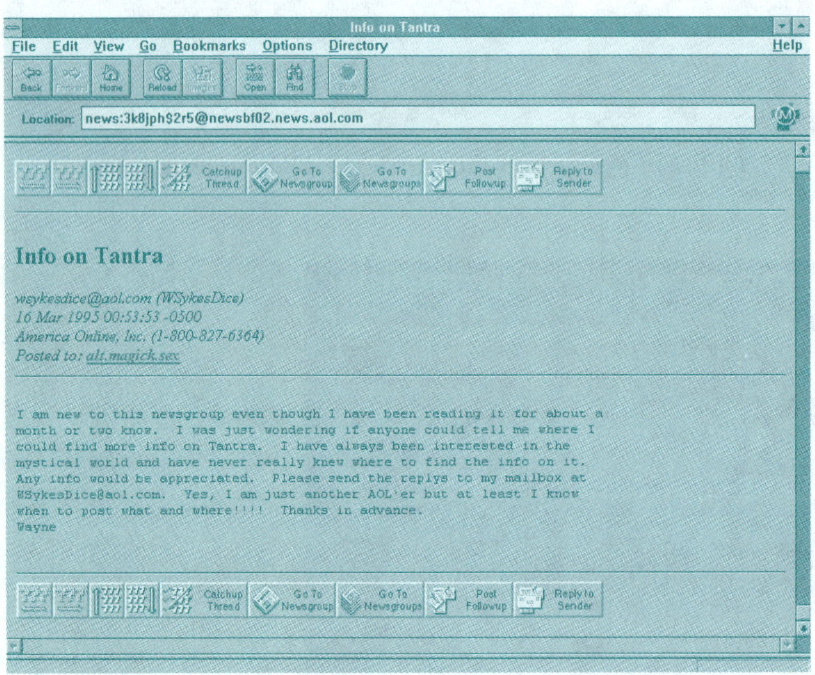

4-4 An actual posting, as seen by Netscape.

The graphic buttons at the beginning and end of a Netscape Usenet posting allow you to respond to the posting you're looking at, or to quickly navigate to other areas of Usenet. Specifically, you can:

Go to Newsgroup Click on this button to return to the posting list for this newsgroup.

Go to Newsgroups Click on this button to get back to the list of all the available newsgroups.

Post Followup Click on this button to post a reply to the message you've just read.

Reply to Sender Click on this button to send a private e-mail message to the author of the message you've just read.

Also notice the up- and down-arrow buttons to the left of the posting window. These let you to go to the previous and next postings in the newsgroup, respectively.

If you want to create a brand-new posting, one that isn't a reply to something that was previously posted to a newsgroup, click on the Post Article button at the top of the posting title list for the newsgroup in question.

Once you find a newsgroup you like the look of, you can create a permanent link to it in one of two ways. The quickest way is simply to create a bookmark for it—select Add Bookmark from the Bookmark menu when the posting list for the newsgroup question is visible. Alternately, click on the Subscribe button at the top of the newsgroup listing to add it to the list of subscribed newsgroups in the Netscape Go To Newsgroups dialog.

You'll probably find that you want to subscribe to great seething bucketfuls of newsgroups at first—the Go To Newsgroups dialog is handy for this. Creating bookmarks for your favorite newsgroups might prove a more effective way to find them once you've narrowed down your interests a bit. Most users of Usenet do after a time—there's a great deal of smoke and furor in newsgroups, and while it's fun to watch for a while you'll probably find that you get overwhelmed by it at length. When Usenet starts occupying four hours a day to keep up with all your favorite groups, it's probably time to thin your subscriber list somewhat.

Dark little secrets of Usenet

Figure 4-5 illustrates a somewhat ineffable posting from a Usenet newsgroup. In fact, if you frequent certain newsgroups, postings like this one will turn up fairly regularly. This is what's called a uuencoded file. It requires a bit of a digression to properly explain, and the implementation of some additional technology to actually use it.

Most uuencoded files are actually graphics, although you'll encounter the occasional uuencoded sound file and even some uuencoded movies from time to time. Figure 4-6 illustrates what Figure 4-5 is really a posting of. For reasons I'll get to in a moment, this is pretty well representative of what turns up in uuencoded postings.

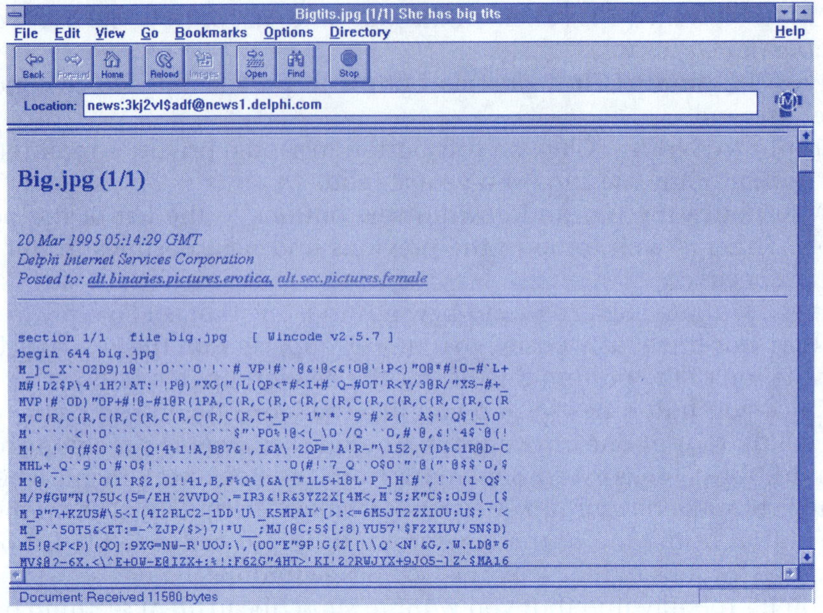

4-5 Lots of text, but very little obvious meaning.

4-6
This is what the uuencoded graphic in Fig. 4-5 actually looked like . . . or at least, what part of it looked like. One of the great things about books rather than television is that books let you exercise your imagination.

As was touched on earlier in this chapter, second perhaps only to newsgroups devoted to Star Trek, Usenet offers a lot of newsgroups having to do with sex. These newsgroups are for the most part very lively—Usenet offers anyone who feels horny or curious or just a bit raunchy the opportunity for some good clean dirty fun. There are newsgroups to discuss sex, newsgroups to exchange sexually explicit stories, and—as pertains to this discussion—

newsgroups in which to post graphics. Graphics are perhaps less involving than well-written erotic stories, but they require less imagination, too.

Now, you might consider this situation in light of the previous chapter of this book and wonder why graphics couldn't be exchanged through a medium better suited to moving files around, such as FTP sites. In fact, they can be. The reason pictures appear in Usenet postings isn't technical—it's biological. No one has yet succeeded in creating a publicly accessible FTP site offering erotic images without having it totally swamped half an hour after it came online. Because FTP sites typically serve a variety of functions, having all the capacity of an FTP server swallowed up by an endless quest for naughty pictures would render whatever else it was supposed to be up to highly impractical.

Posting graphics to Usenet spreads the huge demand for these images over all the servers on the Internet that carry the newsgroups in question. It also makes retrieving them considerably more involved than simply downloading them from an FTP site would be.

I should mention that you can find all sorts of other graphics posted to Usenet—including pictures with no naked women in them at all. They don't appear in anything like the numbers that grace the erotic picture newsgroups, but you might find them worth browsing if you like to collect less explicit images.

There are two primary collections of alt newsgroups that offer a lot of graphics, these being alt.sex.pictures and alt.binaries.pictures. Each of these categories have several dependent newsgroups. The alt.binaries.pictures newsgroups generally have more going on in them, and in addition they include a number of newsgroups that don't deal with erotic images.

The fundamental problem with posting graphics to a newsgroup is that it's impossible. Newsgroups accept only text, and then only a finite amount of text. To get around this, a graphic file must be turned into text that can later be reconstituted as the graphic it once was. This process is called *uuencoding*. If you download a uuencoded posting like the one in Fig. 4-5 and uudecode it properly, the result will be a normal, viewable graphic file of the sort discussed at length in chapter 2 of this book.

This probably sounds like a serious nuisance—well, yes, it is, but it's how the system works. As I'll get to in a moment, there are a few things you can do to make it easier to deal with.

The second catch in posting graphics to newsgroups is that a single Usenet posting has a finite upper limit as to how much text it can contain. Large graphics are typically split up over several postings, which must be reassembled into a single uuencoded file before it can be successfully decoded. I'll deal with this, too.

Figure 4-7 illustrates the newsgroup posting list from which Fig. 4-5 was actually selected. Note that some of the entries have section numbers, such as the blond cheerleader. We'll ignore these for a moment—they represent a sin-

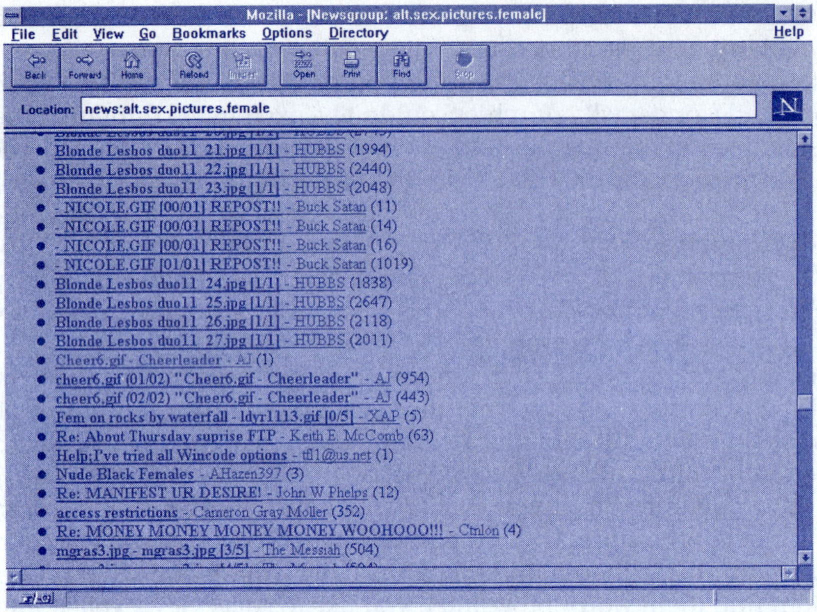

4-7 *A newsgroup with uuencoded graphics—tasteless, exploitive, politically incorrect uuencoded graphics, in this case. As I write this, the nineties are half over.*

gle graphic in multiple parts. Find a newsgroup with uuencoded graphics like these and select one that has a GIF or JPEG file in one section.

As with other things accessed by Netscape, when you click on a link to a uuencoded posting, the first part of the file is downloaded and displayed in Netscape's window. Netscape then downloads the rest of the uuencoded data. There's nothing particularly exciting about uuencoded data—you probably won't want to see the whole thing. Rather, save the posting to a disk file for further processing. Select Save from the Netscape File menu, and make sure you choose a filename with the extension .UUE.

There's a minor catch to the way Netscape saves files, and it's very important to keep this in mind when you're working with uuencoded graphics. You'd probably think that having downloaded a uuencoded posting to display in its main window, Netscape would simply save that copy of the file to disk when you ask it to. This isn't what it really does. Rather, the Save command causes it to download a second copy.

This being the case, you can click on the Stop button as soon as Netscape begins to display a uuencoded file—there's no reason to wait for the visible copy to be downloaded in its entirety. Secondly, you must wait for the copy being downloaded by the Save command to be complete before you move on to do something else. You can see what it's up to in the status bar at the bottom of the Netscape window—this field indicates the number of bytes that have been downloaded or displays "Done" when the download is complete.

Viewing Usenet graphics with Graphic Workshop

Viewing a uuencoded graphic technically requires that you decode the .UUE file you've downloaded back into whatever it was before it was originally posted and then run a graphic viewer to look at the image file your uudecoder writes. In fact, you can skip one step of this if you're viewing graphics with Graphic Workshop, discussed at length in chapter 2.

If you name downloaded uuencoded graphics with the extension .UUE, they'll appear in Graphic Workshop's file selector list. Select one and Graphic Workshop will automatically uudecode and display the image. This saves a lot of typing.

There are several minor points to keep in mind about using Graphic Workshop in this capacity. The first is that it creates a fairly large temporary file when it uudecodes a posting—make sure you have several megabytes of free hard drive space available. Secondly, it's worth noting that the JPEG format—the most commonly used format for uuencoded graphics at the moment—doesn't allow for particularly good error-checking. This means that if a JPEG file gets mangled somewhere in the uuencoding process, Graphic Workshop will probably still decode it. The picture it generates from a damaged JPEG file probably won't look like much.

Viewing Usenet graphics without Graphic Workshop

If you want to view uuencoded graphics using a viewer that can't automatically decode your UUE files, you'll need a discrete uudecoder for your system. Ask your Internet access provider or network administrator to point you to an FTP site that has one suitable for your computer.

Having downloaded a UUE file from Usenet, uudecode it to extract the graphic it contains. You can then run your image viewer to look at the resulting file.

Multiple-section files

Graphics that are too large to post to Usenet in a single section are split up into multiple postings—hopefully consecutive ones. In order to turn these things back into viewable graphics, you must download all the sections and reassemble them. It's essential that they be reassembled in the correct order.

Take, for instance, CHEERLDR.JPG, a multiple-part JPEG file (use your imagination as to what the picture it contains looks like). To download this image, you have to download each section to a separate .UUE file and then merge the separate files into a single .UUE file. This is actually easier than it would seem to be.

The obvious way to join multiple UUE files together is to inhale each one into an initially blank document of a text editor and then save the whole works to a new file. Regrettably, the Notepad text editor that comes with Windows has more severe size restrictions than Usenet, and isn't much use in this capacity. You can, however, accomplish the task using an obscure feature of the DOS COPY command. Here's the syntax for fusing CHEER1.UUE, CHEER2.UUE, and CHEER3.UUE into CHEERLDR.UUE. The former three files are the individual sections downloaded from Usenet, and CHEERLDR.UUE can either be viewed with Graphic Workshop or uudecoded by a discrete uudecoder. You can join as many sections as you like using the COPY command:

```
COPY CHEER1.UUE+CHEER2.UUE+CHEER3.UUE CHEERLDR.UUE
```

There's actually quite a bit more to be said about Usenet graphics—while this section will get you online, the level of funkiness that has grown up around this ill-defined application of Usenet frequently requires a degree of stealth to master. As was touched on in chapter 2 of this book, you can find a lot more about graphics and the Internet—and about Usenet graphics in particular—in *Internet Graphics*, published by McGraw-Hill and due out in early 1996.

5

Explorer's guide

Christopher Columbus arranged a prominent place in history and all sorts of documentary films for himself largely due to what could be characterized as a considerable miscalculation if you wanted to be charitable, or as a flat out lie if you didn't. As legend and most of the aforementioned documentary films tell it, Columbus knew the world was spherical because he sat on the shore and watched a ship sail out to sea. As it reached the horizon, the hull vanished, and then the sails, indicating that it was sailing over a curve. Had the world been flat, it would simply have gotten smaller until it was no longer visible.

Armed with this bit of insight and a number of incomplete maps of his day, Columbus came to the conclusion that on a spherical world you could reach the orient—where all the interesting wealth was to be found—by going west as well as by going east, and that going across the Atlantic ocean was a shortcut to China. He based this theory on a calculation of the diameter of the Earth that was . . . in fairness, as Columbus didn't have a Pentium processor to blame, it seems proper to ascribe his error to just really bad information.

Now, this was a fortuitous miscalculation, because had he known how far it really was to China, Columbus himself might well not have bothered with the trip. He certainly would have encountered no small measure of difficulty in talking other sailors into accompanying him, and in finding someone to pay for what would most certainly have seemed like a voyage into oblivion. Contemporary history might well record that the discovers of the new world were, in fact, Irish monks or Scandinavian vikings—both of whom got here before Columbus but didn't have the business sense to make a suitable fuss over what they'd found.

Alternately, documentary films might have been made about another explorer, named Vespuchi. He was actually the first European to make it to the mainland—Columbus actually "discovered" only a number of Caribbean islands. While Vespuchi doesn't figure prominently in our iconography, he is remembered in a sense. His first name was Amerigo.

Exploring the World Wide Web has some aspects in common with the voyages of those Renaissance sailors. While the risk of sailing over the edge of the world is somewhat diminished, the problem of not knowing how to get where you're going arguably remains. The Web is about as poorly charted as the world was five hundred years ago. Whatever maps you can find will be old—this book being no exception—and there is absolutely no one to ask for reliable directions.

This chapter will discuss a number of important bits of explorers' lore to keep in mind when waves are crashing over your deck, the crew is starting to look mutinous, and no land is in sight.

What's new

One of the most useful resources of the World Wide Web—and certainly among the first things you should probably get acquainted with when you start exploring the Web—is a page called What's New With NCSA Mosaic. You can link to it at:

```
http://www.ncsa.uiuc.edu/SDG/Software/Mosaic/Docs/whats-new.html
```

Updated several times a week, it's a dynamic list of postings by individual Web page creators about new and updated pages. A completely new list appears each Monday, with old lists archived if you want to do some archaeology.

The What's New page is exceedingly well managed. While anyone can submit a listing to the page, everything has to pass the page's creators. There isn't much they won't allow, but they do check for correct URLs and delete the obvious scams, spammings, and general wastes of bandwidth. The listings at What's New are concise and generally fairly readable, and each one includes a link to the page it represents.

If you spend an hour a week browsing What's New and adding bookmarks to your Web browser for the pages of interest that turn up, you'll amass a pretty respectable set of links in a few months. The diversity of pages that turn up in What's New is impressive—cyberbrothels rub elbows with cyclotron research, and there are typically enough new electronic malls in an average week to make television shopping channels seem almost dignified by comparison.

Unlike many other aspects of the net, What's New doesn't decry the ongoing commercialization of the Internet. In fact, it's a commercial entity itself, with a different corporate sponsor every week. As I write this, Zima seems to turn up frequently in this capacity—ten years ago no one could figure out what to do with all that industrial waste. Clearly it took some imagination to bleach the stuff and sell it in bottles.

A good part of the listings in the second part of this book were located through the What's New page.

Cool Site of the Day

The Cool Site of the Day page offers a pointer to a different Web page every morning. Selected by the page's author for general coolness, this is an interesting way to find links you'd probably never have heard of otherwise. You can link to the Cool Site of the Day page at http://www.infi.net/cool.html. The Cool Site of the Day page includes the following important disclaimer:

> *Every day another link to a cool site on the Web. You never know where you are going until you get there. Please consult your physician if unforeseen side effects develop. Parental discretion is advised. Hermetically sealed, nonfatal if swallowed. The Cool Site of the Day has proven effective in laboratory experiments. No electrons were harmed in the production of this page.*

Web Crawler

As with many of the World Wide Web search engines, Web Crawler has an arachnid motif about it—graphics of spiders grace most of its pages. I'm not wholly enamored of spiders, myself. While certainly handy at keeping other bugs in line, they're fairly creepy and are usually at their best between concrete and the sole of a Reebok.

Web Crawler is a real-time Web search engine. You can ask it to search for specific terms on the Web, and assuming you don't ask for something too obscure, it will return a set of links to Web pages that meet your search criteria. You can subsequently click on the links to browse the pages in question.

The thing that makes Web Crawler unique is that it actually explores the Web on your behalf. Most search facilities on the Web work with a database of known URLs, checking each entry to see if it matches your criteria. Web Crawler is a bit different—it begins with a small list of pages, searches them, and then locates all the links to other pages they contain. Having done so, it searches each linked page and then repeats the process for pages the linked pages in turn link to—and so on. Because pretty well everything on the Web links to something else, Web Crawler can search the entire Web if it wants to.

In addition to this basic capability, the author of Web Crawler maintains that he has included strategies in its design to bias its searches toward interesting pages.

If there's a catch to Web Crawler, it's that it can be fairly slow if you give it something obscure to look for. Having said this, it's the most thorough of the navigation tools for the World Wide Web. You can link to Web Crawler at:

```
http://webcrawler.cs.washington.edu/WebCrawler/WebQuery.html
```

The World Wide Web Catalog at CERN

The archive at CERN is perhaps the most extensive database of World Wide Web pages on earth. You can search it by linking to http://cuiwww.unige.ch/w3 catalog. You can search the database by entering keywords to look for, and the search engine will check the entries for all the home pages it knows to see what matches. As with all Web search engines, the results will include links to whichever pages turn up.

The World Wide Web Catalog tends to be a bit more specific than other Web search facilities—it typically turns up fewer entries for a particular search key than, for example, Web Crawler. The entries it does find are more likely to be relevant to the topic you're interested in, however.

Also at CERN, the World Wide Web Virtual Library is a well organized, hierarchical index to thousands of Web pages. It breaks its index up into several dozen logical categories: Literature, Music, Research, and so on. The initial list actually looks a bit dry and uninteresting, but it links to a wealth of worthwhile resources. You can link to the Virtual Library at:

http://info.cern.ch/hypertext/DataSources/bySubject/Overview.html

As with all Web archives, the real problem with using the Virtual Library is that you can spend hours—perhaps even days—following some of its links. Perhaps the most exhaustive compilation of Web pages on earth, its ordered home page belies its vastness.

The Way

The Way is an extensive database of selected links to Web pages. As I write this, it claimed to offer over 20,000 links. You can access The Way's links alphabetically, geographically, by name, and by topic. It also features a respectable list of FTP sites. The Way is at:

http://www.csn.net:80/way/index.html

The Scott List

The Scott List is a medium-size archive of links to interesting pages on the Web. Unlike the CERN list, it doesn't purport to include everything the Web has to offer. It's at:

http://www.picosof.com:8080/html/scott.html

Jump Station

Jump Station searches the titles and headers of Web pages. This makes it fairly fast as search engines go, but less than comprehensive. For example, to have it find the graphic software at Alchemy Mindworks' Web page, you'd have to search for *Alchemy* or *Mindworks*, rather than just *graphics*.

Now this isn't necessarily a bad thing. Depending on what you're looking for, you might find that broader search engines, like Web Crawler, inundate you with links. Jump Station is a useful tool to have on hand when you want to look for particular pages. You can link to it at http://www.stir.ac.uk/jsbin/js.

Save your files

Whatever a Web browser shows you—and whether it started life as a Web page, a newsgroup posting, or an FTP list, among other things—it will exist as an HTML file, possibly with some links to other resources. This is a very useful facility, as the HTML files that your browser uses to display things can also be saved to disk. Once they're saved, you can load them back into your browser and treat them as if they'd just been linked to.

The links in saved files point to the same places as the links in files newly downloaded over the Internet. Assuming you're connected to the Net when you reload a saved file, click on the links just as you would for a normal Web page.

You can use the Save File facility of a Web browser to record pages with links in them if you don't have time to browse all the links immediately, if some of the links aren't available right at the moment or if you think you'd like to come back to them later on. In some respects, this duplicates the function of a Web browser's bookmark facility; the distinction is that if you save a page with links in it, you can keep track of the links without ever having to actually visit them first.

HTML files are stored with the file extension .HTM under DOS, Windows, and OS2/Warp.

In addition to files you explicitly save, most Web browsers keep their bookmark lists as HTML files. You can use this facility to manage multiple bookmark lists. For example, Netscape keeps its bookmarks in a file called BOOKMARK.HTM. After a while, you might find that BOOKMARK.HTM is a bit full and finding things in it has become tedious. You can imagine what my BOOKMARK.HTM file looked like after amassing all the links for the second part of this book.

You can get around this by having multiple bookmark files. When one gets full, rename it to something else—BOOKMK1.HTM, BOOKMK2.HTM, and so on—and start a new one. You can access the old bookmark lists by opening them as you would other saved HTML files and clicking on the links that appear.

While HTML files are essentially text and can be edited as such, you should avoid editing the bookmark files maintained by your Web browser. Most Web browsers maintain their bookmark lists using a fairly specific subset of HTML, and will explode pretty colorfully if you attempt to feed them something they're not expecting.

Part 2

Web sampler

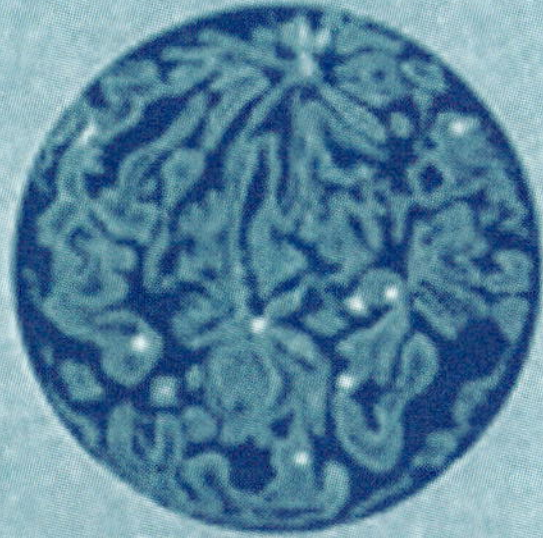

Annotated Grateful Dead Lyrics

http://www.uccs.edu/~ddodd/gdhome.html

The Grateful Dead's lyrics are frequently a bit ineffable. Replete with references to all sorts of arcane traditions and odd bits of literature, this is the sort of thing they'll be boring high school students to death with in a hundred years. Robert Hunter and John Barlow will be laughing, to be sure.

The Annotated Grateful Dead Lyrics site consists of a long list of Dead songs with hypertext links for key phrases that have some significance beyond the tunes in question. At least, they might—the work of Deadheads rather than the authors of the lyrics, all these citations are open to considerable interpretation. That's what makes the whole exercise entertaining, of course.

In addition to references drawn by the author of the page, numerous ideas are offered by its readers. The work seems to be continually in progress, with new lyrics and new links added periodically.

If you've wondered whether Jack Straw from Witchitaw was really Wat Tyler of the 1381 London peasants' revolt, have been perplexed as to the exact nature of a buck-dancer's choice, or didn't understand any of countless other Dead references, this is clearly the place to gather what another man spills.

Archive X

http://www.declab.usu.edu:8080/X/

Reading about paranormal happenings usually makes you wonder if you remembered to lock all the windows. It's not that any rational human being would believe in this stuff, but there could be some irrational ones lurking around outside. Perhaps they're irrational but not exactly human. Perhaps they're not even life forms as we define life. And they might be hungry. Underfed, borderline, psychopathic, noncorporeal life forms do seem to turn up a lot out in the country after it gets dark.

The Archive X page is a set of links to numerous documents about supernatural occurrences and extraterrestrials. It includes a selection of accounts written by ostensible participants in these matters. Some of these things are sufficiently creepy as to be not easily dismissed. The Ghost Hunters Guide is particularly entertaining.

Armadillo

http://www.quadralay.com/www/Austin/Dillo/index.html

Small, not particularly bright, and fairly pungent, the armadillo is one the great mysteries of creation. The mysterious bit entails figuring out why whatever consciousness winds the clockspring of the universe would have bothered working up a creature like this one. Platypuses, slugs, and penguins are all marvels of well-evolved life forms compared to armadillos. None of them except the armadillo, of course, look like giant cockroaches with body armor.

All this notwithstanding, Texans seem to like 'em. The Armadillo page will provide you with some insight into the strange attraction of the armadillo, its place in Texas mythology, and the correct way to run one over on the interstate. It begins:

> *Texas is covered with armadillos. And not just the roads, either. Because of this, we . . . are dedicating this page to the importance of armadillos (specifically the nine-banded variety).*
>
> ***Armadillo Facts***
>
> *Family: Dasypodidae*
> *Order: Edentata*
> *Other Names: Varmint, Critter, @$&%*#!, Dinsdale*
> *Close Relatives: Sloths, anteaters, bureaucrats*
> *Range: Texas, Oklahoma, Louisiana through Florida, Mexico, and South America*
> *Average Weight: 7–9 lbs.*
> *Predators: Bobcats, wolves, coyotes, semis*
>
> *Armadillos don't see well. They don't hear well, either. But they do have long, sharp claws, and they've been known to eat lawyers. The armadillo might well be the best-loved animal in Austin.*

I liked the bit about eating lawyers—perhaps we could import a few for this purpose. The Armadillo page links to a more general page that tells you about the other attractions of Austin and surrounding areas of Texas.

The Art of War

http://www.teleport.com/~stevew/SunTzu.html

ACRIMONY Sun Tsu was a Chinese general, probably living some time around 500 B.C. While little is known of him or of his campaigns, he left us one of the most concise and practical discourses on conflict ever written. The Art of War is a long list of axioms and strategies that is still relevant today. The first complete English-language version was translated from the Chinese by Lionel Giles in 1910.

The Art of War is one of the *Seven Military Classics* of Chinese martial thought. Sun Tsu originally entitled it *Military Strategy*.

You might wonder about the usefulness of The Art of War if you're not planning a war of your own any time soon. In fact, you can apply Sun Tsu to much smaller engagements with a bit of imagination. He's equally adept in boardrooms as on battlefields. The Art of War Web page includes the complete text of Sun Tsu's book, with some added hypertext links to make it easier to navigate.

If you like the hypertext version of The Art of War, you might want to seek out Ralph Sawyer's somewhat more recent translation, augmented with considerable archaeological material uncovered during the 1970s. It was first published by Westview Press—at present there's an edition in print published by Barnes and Noble.

AT&T 800 Number Directory

http://att.net/dir800

AT&T 800 Directory You can search for companies with toll-free 800 numbers through AT&T's 800-number Web page. Actually, this isn't quite as useful as it sounds, as the Web page actually lists only those companies who use AT&T to manage their 800-number service. However, allowing for this restriction, the simple search engine and extensive database of the AT&T page can make it fairly handy. You can search by category, for specific companies, for companies in particular locations, and so on.

Having worn the mute button on our television's remote control down to a bleeding stump through uncounted telephone company commercials, I had it look for the word *sprint*. It came up with:

800 962 2860 *Sprint Couriers*
Richmond, VA
(delivery services)

800 457 0239 Sprint Express
Grand Junction, CO
(delivery services)
800 848 8377 Sprint Industrial Services Inc
Robstown, TX
(Oil & Gas Exploration & Development)
800 235 2156 Sprint/Rothhammer Intl
Arroyo Grande, CA
(swimming pool equipment & supplies: wholesale & manufacturers)

Your query matched 4 entries.

Clearly this wouldn't be the tool to use if you're looking for a new long-distance carrier. If you have the page search for ATT, mind, it will come up with several numbers.

AutoPages

http://www.clark.net/pub/networx/autopage/autopage.html

The AutoPages Web page is a classified advertisement resource devoted exclusively to cars. Actually, it seems to be devoted exclusively to very exotic cars. As I write this, the people who've placed ads in it seem to think that the difference between their cars and the state of Texas is that Texas should cost less. The owners of exotic cars are like that.

While you might not ultimately buy anything through the AutoPages listings unless you have buckets of money, this is a superb place to go window shopping. Each car is represented by a small photograph you can click on to call up a full-screen image. Stare at Jags, Cobras, Mercedes, and Rolls Royces 'til your eyes bleed—it's sufficiently bourgeoisie to peel the Armani suit off a liberal.

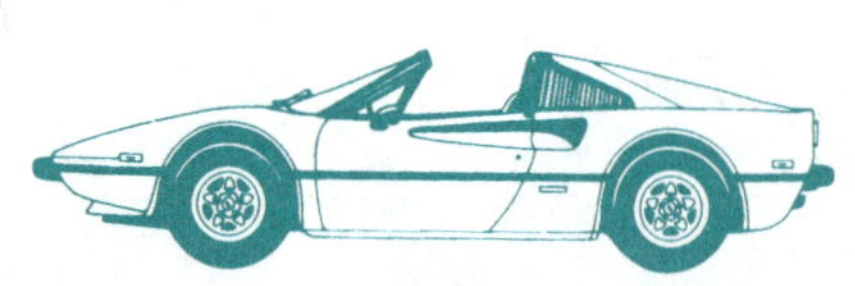

Avalon

http://www.epcc.ed.ac.uk/~ct/arthur.html

Avalon is the western island to which the spirits of the dead were transported in Celtic mythology. It's also the name of one of the newer Japanese cars, as I recall. You might want to consider whether you'd want to drive around in a car full of the spirits of dead Celts.

The Avalon page is a set of links to everything you can imagine about King Arthur and the legends of Camelot—including the Python movie, for those of us who will always picture King Arthur as looking a lot like Graham Chapman. Ranging from the scholarly to the fanciful, you can find out about how legend says the once and future king lived, and what archaeology and research have turned up about the reality behind the myth. Several convincing arguments exist for a historical Arthur and a geographical Camelot.

You'll find an extensive frequently asked questions document about King Arthur at the Avalon page, and links to all sorts of other Arthurian pages on the Web. There's also an extensive discussion of the geography of Arthur's England—or, if you believe the current research, Arthur's Wales.

Becca's Page of B's

http://www.mmedia.com/becca/beccasbs.html

Alliteration is a talent of sort—or, more often, it's something that creeps its way into your speech unexpectedly and makes you sound like Elmer Fudd. This page seems to cultivate it, but only if it embodies the letter B. It offers some exemplary graphics and numerous other links to things that start with B.

Below is the bizarre "b" list from my brain.

Bear—as in a bear named Pooh.
Books—buying bound literature.
Bugs—Bugs & other backyard beasts.
Blue Mood—build a bright smile instead.
Birthday!—Other bodies born this day.
Boredom galore—send a postcard!
What is this business?—A breakfast blow-torch?
Bus rides—browse the Web boundlessly!

Bread and butter—a bowl of beef broth, please.
Bucolic bucket—a bidet of the French banter.
The Great and Mighty Bob!
Brilliant bookmarks
Braille?— barely, but Hawaiian in name.

A "b" word for the week: bandoleer, bandolier (ban-da-ler') n. a broad belt worn over the shoulder and fitted with pockets to hold cartridges [It. bandoliera].

You will no doubt be able to think of additional things that start with B. The creator of the B page will welcome your suggestions. A word of caution, though—this seems to be a fairly politically correct and wholesome sort of page. Breasts, babes, boffing, buttocks, and banging in the back of a Buick will probably not be appreciated.

The Big Black Hole of Pain

http://offworld.wwa.com/bighole.html

Bitching can be good for you, especially if you have the grace to do it where no one with a loaded shotgun or a roll of sticky tape can hear you. The Big Black Hole of Pain is a Web page with the sole function of allowing you to complain about anything you like, anyone you like, and all the bad drivers and former lovers you can recall.

The Big Black Hole of Pain really is black if you're using Netscape. It consists of a field to type your lament into and links to lots of pages of the works of complainants who've gone before you. The author of the page edits the postings, removing anything that's borderline coherent or really vulgar. He also deletes the names of people fingered in these postings, replacing them with "A-Male" or "A-Female."

Here are a few of the almost endless shriekings at the Big Black Hole of Pain as I was writing this:

I stubbed my toe yesterday.

Paperwork sucks

Frustration, sex, dissertation, stress, job contract, jealousy, A-Female in the bathroom.

The day job has gotta' go . . . as does that guy who lives here—the one with the obnoxious hairy brother who keeps dropping in uninvited and running his fingers through the peanut butter jar. . . . And, come to think of it, the dog is extraneous, too—won't shut-up—that yipping, yelping, hyperactive bark of his is going to drive me even further around the bend. . . . And, while I'm *purging, I'd like to wipe out in one stroke all people *who talk while watching a movie*—putrid, putrid souls . . .*

*I hate San Antonio. Hell, I hate the *entire* state of Texas. They're all just a bunch of country bumpkins, WWF belt-buckle wearing, closed-minded, human rejects that would rather pump their various farm animals than explore what the rest of the world has to offer.*

Red dog. It's not red. It's not a dog. I doesn't even taste very good. But hey man, It's your call.

I can't find my car keys.

Quit smoking! Got to do it. Been over three days, pure hell.

I wanna be god!

I'm sick to death of my boss. What an overbearing creep!

I'm sick of working with those arseholes at Farrys.

Wow! Finally something scholarly on the Web! I plan to return here often.

Why does everyone hate me!!

*I'm the ultimate f**k-up and I deserve a good slap in the face for my stupidity. There's no damn excuse for it. I knew better but I did it anyway.*

I like my mother-in-law.

Of course, not all the postings are this articulate.

Blowfish Sex Toys

http://www.best.com:80/~blowfish/

There's a lot to be said for buying sex toys by mail—well, there's a lot more to be said for it than buying them in person, unless you're really hard to embarrass. The Blowfish mail-order company specializes in little plastic things with batteries, apparel not suitable for polite company, videos that will melt some low-end VCRs, and other delights of the senses.

I've always wanted to open a store in one of the local shopping malls called Sex Toys 'R' Us. I confess I've never actually bought any of this stuff, but the level of outrage it would probably engender would make the enterprise worthwhile.

The Blowfish catalog offers things you wouldn't have come up with in your most ribald fantasies, as well as easy-to-understand instructions about where to insert them, how to get all the chains fastened, which ones not to mix together before applying them, how to disable them afterwards, and the best ones to read to a really close friend.

Here's a vastly abridged list of things that were available from Blowfish as I was writing this:

- *The Avanti Condom: Blowfish is pleased to announce that it now carries the Avanti Duron Condom, the new polyurethane condom from Schmid Laboratories. Check out our Safer Sex Supplies page for more information. Special! Take 10% off any order of 12 or more Avanti condoms, any size package, regular or ultrathin, now through February 28th.*
- *Daughters of Darkness, Lesbian Vampire Stories ($10.95): One of the first and best vampire stories, "Carmilla," has a strong lesbian theme, and it's in here, along with contributions by Pat Califia, Jewelle Gomez, and a bunch of others.*
- *Post-Porn Modernist ($25): We're very pleased to announce here at Blowfish that Annie Sprinkle's autobiography / sex work essay / performance art piece in book form, Post-Porn Modernist, is finally back in print, and we've got it! This was originally published by a very obscure publisher in the Netherlands (after attempts to find a publisher in the United States failed) and then went out of print; a somewhat larger publisher in the Netherlands (Art Unlimited, of postcard fame) has picked it up.*
- *How to Have an Orgasm . . . As Often As You Want ($10.95): Designed for women in heterosexual couples who aren't satisfied with their orgasmic response, it contains step-by-step instructions to achieve orgasm as often as you want, with our without a partner or the cooperation thereof.*
- *Kama Sutra, A Pillow Book ($8) and The Perfumed Garden, a Pillow Book ($8): Harper/Collins has started publishing a series of perfectly delightful little "pillow books," small-format books of erotic classics, with matching erotic illustrations. Kama Sutra of Vatsayana and The Perfumed Garden of Sheikh Nefzawi are the first two in the series, and they make a delightful addition to any bedroom's bookshelf.*
- *Secrets of Sizzlin' Sex for Naughty but Nice Women Everywhere ($14.95): This could be entitled "Really, Sex is OK. No, Really." For people who are just starting to explore their sexuality, this book could be a good starting place. Written in a breathless, "it's just between us girls here" style, it would make a great gift.*
- *Ties that Bind: The SM/Leather/Fetish/Erotic Style ($14.95)—Written by Guy Baldwin, this collection of essays is an excellent overview of the whole community, along with practical advice for anyone new or experienced.*
- *The Dark Garden Catalog ($10)—Dark Garden is a San Francisco-based manufacturer of corsets, fetish wear, and period recreation garments. Their lovingly-produced catalog is a work of art in itself, but also includes ordering information on their products.*
- *Blowfish is exceptionally proud to announce the availability of Nina Hartley's new pair of sex education tapes: Nina Hartley's Guide to Fellatio*

(aka Woodworking 101) and Nina Hartley's Guide to Cunnilingus (aka Under the Hood). They are fun, educational, and hot, all at the same time . . . much better than any driver's ed. film you ever saw. Both Nina and the exceptionally attractive supporting cast are obviously having a great time in these tapes. Even if you are an old . . . uh . . . hand at oral sex, you'll appreciate the new pointers, tips, and generally fun look and feel of these tapes.

The Blowfish catalog is unusually professional, a great deal of fun to read, and full of all sorts of interesting bits you probably didn't know about. Consider telling whoever else doesn't know about them what you have in mind before you exhibit your new-found skills. The Blowfish page also offers a number of erotic 'zines and comics.

Book Stacks Unlimited, Inc.

`http://melville.books.com/scripts/main.exe?`

Book Stacks Unlimited is my favorite Internet bookshop—and that's not just 'cause they carry all my books. For a long time, Book Stacks could be accessed only through telnet, which was a bit funky and hard to get along with. They now have a Web page with forms access to search their database of titles.

Their database includes over a quarter of a million books. You can search by title, author, or ISBN number and browse the database by topic. There's online ordering and a toll-free 800 number you can call if you don't want to trust your credit-card number to the Net.

Book Web

`http://ambook.org/bookweb/`

The Book Web page is a repository of links to other places on the Internet that have to do with books. It also has a lot of spider graphics, the spider ostensibly being named Charlotte.

A perpetual work in progress, Book Web seems to be someone's labor of love for readers, authors, and publishers. It features articles about specific genres of books—comic books and graphic novels are the flavor of the month as I write this—as well as links to publishers' home pages, book sales statistics, information about authors on tour, and a monthly contest for users of the page. The prize is a $50 gift certificate redeemable at any of a number of participating book shops.

Book Web also features a set of links to book-related Usenet newsgroups. See chapter 4 for a discussion of how to access newsgroups from the World Wide Web.

Booked for Murder

http://www.csn.net:80/way/booked/

It puzzles me how normally refined, genteel people with good upbringings can spend their days decrying the deterioration of social values and the increasing violence on television and then go home to a good mystery novel wherein some little old lady in the English countryside is hacked to death with her own garden shears in the first ten pages. I mean, I like this sort of thing myself, but I'm a barbarian. Lots of refined, genteel people have told me so.

The Booked for Murder home page is the Internet presence of a book shop that specializes in murder mysteries. It includes announcements and reviews of new books in this genre, and an online catalog. You can order the books featured at Booked for Murder by fax or by calling a toll-free order line.

Brain Preference Indicator Test

http://www.nyu.edu:80/pages/braintest/

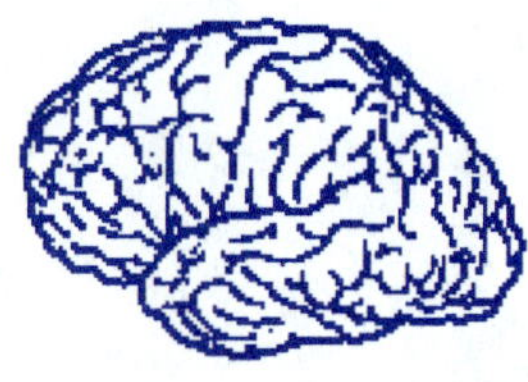

Not quite as much fun as the Breast Size Preference Test, almost as enlightening as the Argyle Sock Color Test, and longer than the Gender Determination Test, the Brain Preference Indicator Test will help you determine whether your brain is dominated by the left or right side. The left brain is said to be analytical and the right brain artistic.

The Brain Preference Indicator Test is an online interactive Web page. It asks you a variety of questions and e-mail you the results of its findings. You'll need a Web browser with forms capability to take the test. Here are the sort of questions the test consists of:

1. In a problem-solving situation, do you:

a) take a walk and mull solutions over, then discuss them?

b) think about, list, and prioritize the alternatives, and then pick the best?

c) recall past experiences that were successful and implement them?
d) wait to see if the situation will right itself?

2. Daydreaming is:

a) a waste of time.
b) amusing and relaxing.
c) a real help in problem-solving and creative thinking.
d) a viable tool for planning my future.

Once you've determined whether you yourself are left-brained, right-brained, or brain damaged, you might want to invent a personality and have it take the test. If you can make the test server e-mail you a surrender message, you've got the makings of a truly warped psyche in there.

Britannica's Birthday Calendar

http://www.eb.com/calendar/calendar.html

Great people were born today—at least, some almost certainly were. You might have to scavenge around in history for some of the days of the year, but they all have a few. The Britannica's birthday calendar page will scavenge on your behalf. It has an extensive database of people, birthdays, and capsule biographies. I asked it for June 21 and it returned several dozen names. I confess I hadn't heard of most of them. Here's a selection of its findings:

Benazir Bhutto
June 21, 1953
Karachi, Pakistan
Pakistani politician who, upon becoming prime minister of Pakistan in 1988, became the first woman leader of a predominantly Muslim nation in modern history. She was again elected prime minister in 1993.

Paolo Soleri
June 21, 1919
Turin, Italy
Italian-born American architect and designer who was one of the best-known utopian city planners of the 20th century.

William Joseph Mosconi
June 21, 1913—September 16, 1993
Philadelphia, Pa., U.S.A.—Haddon Heights, N.J., U.S.A.
Reigned as world pocket billiards champion 15 times and was renowned both for his accurate, rapid-fire shots and for dismantling the image associated

with the sport as one played in smoky pool parlors populated with hustlers and . . .

Mary (Therese) McCarthy
June 21, 1912—October 25, 1989
Seattle, Wa., U.S.A.—New York, N.Y., U.S.A.
American novelist and critic noted for bitingly satiric commentaries on marriage, sexual expression, the impotence of intellectuals, and the role of women in contemporary urban America. She frequently used autobiographical details in her fiction, which is noted for . . .

Jean-Paul Sartre
June 21, 1905—April 15, 1980
Paris—Paris
French novelist, playwright, and exponent of Existentialism—a philosophy acclaiming the freedom of the individual human being. He was awarded the Nobel Prize for Literature in 1964, but he declined it.

Alf Sjoberg
June 21, 1903—April 17, 1980
Stockholm, Sweden—Stockholm, Sweden
Swedish motion-picture director whose films were preeminent in the post-World War II Swedish film revival. He broke with the stage traditions that were inhibiting the artistic development of the Swedish cinema and was among the first to use a lyrical style that was further . . .

Norman L(evi) Bowen
June 21, 1887—September 11, 1956
Kingston, Ontario, Canada—Washington, D.C., U.S.A.
Canadian petrologist and mineral chemist, widely recognized for his syntheses of silicate systems as they relate to the origin of igneous rocks.

Hastings Lionel Ismay Ismay (of Wormington), Baron
June 21, 1887—December 17, 1965
Naini Tal, India—Broadway, Worcestershire, UK
British soldier who became Prime Minister Winston Churchill's closest military adviser during World War II and participated in most major policy decisions of the Allied powers.

Schlumberger, Conrad and Marcel
June 21, 1884—August 19, 1953
Guebwiller—Val-Richer, Normandy, France
German brothers, geophysicists, and petroleum engineers noted for their invention, in 1927, of a method of continuous electric logging of boreholes.

Each of the names in this list was a link in the original Web page. In theory, it would have linked to a complete biography of the individual involved. In fact, it links to a page that says:

Unauthorized Access

You have accessed a hypertext link to the Encyclopedia Britannica proprietary database from at.eb.com (199.170.188.2). This host has not been enabled for access.

Encyclopedia Britannica wants to sell you full access to its database. There's a link to its home page at the Unauthorized Access page, should you be interested in this service. Get your credit card warmed up—full access to the Britannica online encyclopedia will set you back almost as much as one of those door-to-door book salesmen.

The birthday page, while clearly a teaser for Encyclopedia Britannica's full online service, is engaging in itself. Now let's see . . . August 11 . . .

CBS News Up to the Minute

http://adware.com/uttm/welcome.html

Sometimes it's amazing what you can find for free on the Internet. The CBS News Up to the Minute page will provide you with a concise digest of the day's news headlines, well written and instantly readable. It's better than television news, which would certainly take a lot longer to get to the point, and it doesn't even have commercials. Up to the Minute also includes pages with genuinely useful movie reviews—ones that don't tell you the endings—and coverage of developments in space, health, the Internet itself, and other timely issues. Here's a typical headlines page:

UTTM top stories as of 4am ET: Friday, May 19, 1995

Headlines are posted for each broadcast Monday through Friday.

The wrath of spring is creating misery in the Midwest and the South. Fifty-six tornadoes hit the state of Tennessee Thursday, leaving a deadly imprint. One tornado killed three people in an Amish community, while another hit a busy shopping mall in Nashville, injuring 19 people. In all, 67 people were reported injured in the storms.

In the Midwest, a day of rainy remembrance. In Missouri, the Governor declared a statewide emergency as floodwaters continue to rise. Heavy rain pushed dozens of Midwest rivers and creeks over their banks and forced thousands of evacuations. Two deaths have been blamed on the floods.

Republicans pushed their sweeping balanced budget plan through the House. The plan promises to end the federal deficit by the year 2002. It calls for a total of $1.7 trillion dollars in savings and would grant the biggest tax break *since the Reagan era. President Clinton called bill the wrong way to balance the budget, noting cuts in Medicare and education to fund the tax cuts.*

Elizabeth Montgomery, charming star of the 1960's sitcom Bewitched, died yesterday after a battle with cancer. She was 62 according to some references, but her family puts her age at 57. Daughter of Hollywood star Robert Montgomery, her recent work included a made-for-TV movie that aired just last week on CBS.

Ballet dancer Alexander Godunov, who defected from the Soviet Union to find success as a performer on stage and in films in the U.S., was found dead yesterday in his West Hollywood home. Godunov's physician said that his death will be listed as from natural causes. Godunov's film roles included Witness, Die Hard, Money Pit, and North.

And those are some of the top stories as of 4 am from CBS News.

The Up to the Minute page also features an archive of headlines for the previous few weeks.

Chris Guitars

http://expert-sys.com/Chris/Chris.html

Now and again you'll encounter someone whose ears are so finely attuned to the nuances of guitars as to be able to pick out the actual instrument being played on a recording. Whereas you or I might say "it sounds like a guitar of some sort," these characters can ponder the matter and discern that the instrument in question is a 1962 Telecaster that needs fret work. At least, they say they can.

Chris Guitars is a music shop for people who know that you can't get a decent guitar at K-Mart. It will buy, sell, and locate rare and vintage instruments. Its Web page offers a list of the current instruments the shop has in stock, most of them with prices. To be sure, many of the prices are a bit astronomical—owning a bit of music history isn't cheap.

Here's a small selection of the instruments at the Chris Guitars page as I was writing this. The page also included amplifiers, effects, and other guitar toys.

Fender

Music master '57 Good condition all original desert sand...$550
P-Bass '53 refinished body EMG pick up otherwise original...$1800
P-Bass 80's '57 reissue ex condition all original...$695
Starcaster '74 Natural ex condition and incredible flamed top!...$1000
Strat '55 Burst trem all original except covers, knobs VG condition...$8000

Strat '62 Fiesta Red SLAB neck good condition all original but pro refret...$8500
Strat '65 Olympic White original well played enlarged bridge cavity...$4000
Strat '74 Black Maple neck non trem refret...$1200
Strat '83 cream maple mint...$600
Tele '56 Pro refinished two tone burst original parts except pots, p guard...$3300
Tele '67/late '70s blond late '80s body with everything else '67...$1200

Gibson

ES-125 TDC Cherry burst good condition head stock repair otherwise fine...$750
ES-5 Switchmaster '60 Burst all original very good condition PAFs...$7500
ES-350 '48 Burst ex condition lightly flamed top non original p.g., switch...$2500
'69 Sq shoulder BURST VG ALL ORIGINAL...$800
Jubilee '69 Acoustic VG Condition all original...$775
J-50 '67 some repairs but a good player...$700

Other Guitars

Hagstrom guitar ES-355 style burst...$325
Hofner "Beatle" Bass '64 staples raised logo...$1350
Harmony Statotone Burst 3 pick up tele tone...$275
Stratotone COPPER 50's 1 PU...$275
Ibanez professional...$650

One of the more remarkable aspects of Chris Guitars—aside from a stock of instruments that very nearly made my fingers bleed—was its mail-order policy. It said:

> *We are happy to send pictures at no charge. We realize that you might be very reluctant to order because it is hard to know if you will like an instrument until you play it and hear it. And we realize that no one wants to pay the $30–$50 shipping both ways just to look at an instrument they don't like. So . . . all mail-order purchases have a 48-hour approval, full money-back guarantee under the following conditions: We will refund the full amount INCLUDING domestic ground UPS costs both ways if not satisfied. Refunds will be made only by our company, checks via regular 1st class mail or in the case of credit card purchases by crediting your credit card account. Refunds will be made within 24 hours of our receipt of the returned merchandise assuming that it is returned to us in exactly the same condition as we shipped to you.*

I think the place where I bought my most recent guitar had a policy of "our satisfaction guaranteed or we'll keep your money."

Christie's Auctions

http://www.sirius.com/~christie/

One of the most renowned auction houses for fine arts, antiques, and other fairly high-brow trinkets, Christie's is now on line. Link to the Christie's Web page and you'll be able to check out their current list of sales and order a catalog. You can't actually bid for things, mind—the Net's not quite that interactive yet. Besides which, it could be more dangerous than a real auction . . . hit your spacebar by accident and you'll discover you've just bid one and a quarter million dollars for a pair of spats once thought to have been worn by Queen Victoria's veterinarian.

Codpiece International

http://www.teleport.com/~codpiece/

First off, these guys have nothing to do with cod. They also have almost nothing to do with codpieces per se, which is why Codpiece International is such an engaging concept. The home page of Codpiece International offers the following topics:

- What is new at Codpiece International?
- What is a codpiece?
- What is the Bring Back the Codpiece campaign"?
- What is Codpiece International?
- The Codpiece International Catalog
- What is the Codpiece Resurrection Society?
- Codpiece-related items on the Web

For many, the second item on this list will be the most germane. Codpieces are rarely seen these days, although the proprietors of Codpiece International would have you believe that they wish it otherwise, and seem to wish that everyone else wished it otherwise. Here's a brief introduction, as excerpted from the Codpiece International Web page:

> ***So . . . what exactly is a codpiece?***
>
> *The codpiece emerged (no pun intended!) in the fifteenth and sixteenth centuries from the dilemma of how to cover a man's genitals when the jackets or doublets became shorter. The height of its popularity was during the early sixteenth century when it became an elaborate yet functional part of men's costume.*

However, the drawing of emphasis to the male genitalia actually occurred at an earlier time when the "long" look became popular. In the mid-fourteenth century, the waistline was dropped to the hips in order to make the body look longer, and the hemline was shortened in order to make the legs look longer. From the 1340s to the 1360s men's hems rose from the knee to mid-thigh with the result that, when a man was sitting down or mounting his horse, there was a clear view all the way up his hose to his drawers. For the first time in western fashion, the male genitals were being flaunted for all to see! The result was that the male bulge was to be the center of attention for the next 200 years.

It's a fashion statement, it's a fertility protector, it's very selective body armor, and it's a piece of history. People really used to wear these things.

Now, as I noted above, the really interesting thing about Codpiece International is that they don't actually make codpieces. In fact, their Web page doesn't even suggest where you might find one if you wanted one, outside of a really tasteless museum. Codpiece International makes T-shirts with slogans and graphics printed on them to support the renaissance of codpieces. Here's their entire catalog as of this writing:

T-shirts:

- *"Bring Back the Codpiece" T-shirt (Mark 2)*
- *"Indulge your Bulge" T-shirt*
- *"A New Dimension in Men's Clothing" T-shirt*

Soon to come are these exciting additions to the Codpiece International line:

- *The codpiece boxer shorts*
- *The codpiece apron*
- *The codpiece bumper sticker*

They're very well designed shirts, however. For the most part, they'll probably make women sufficiently curious to ask you what a codpiece is. Whether or not you actually have one on is, of course, irrelevant.

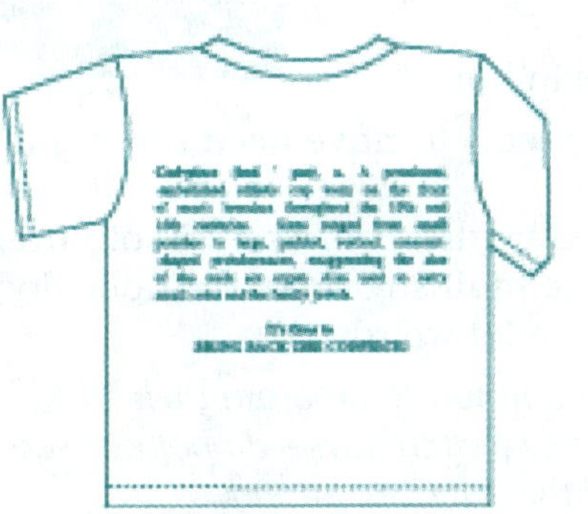

Confession Booth

http://anther.learning.cs.cmu.edu/priest.html

I don't think you can really understand how messed up Catholicism can get you until you experience it first-hand for a while. One of the aspects of this religion that has always fascinated me is that of confession, whereupon you lock yourself in a closet and bare your soul to a complete stranger. Having done so, all your transgressions will be forgotten if you mumble a few chants and promise not to do it again.

If you also wonder about the cathartic benefits of confession, you can try the experience out for yourself without having to eat pressed bread, kneel a lot, and learn a number of grovelly prayers by linking to the Confession Booth. An online confessional, it allows you to enter the time since your last confession and the nature of your sin. It will thereupon deliberate on the severity of your transgressions and prescribe a suitable penance. Your sins are added to the Scroll of Sins, which other penitents can read in order to grow closer to a state of grace.

If this sounds a little too pious to have much entertainment value, I should note that the selection of sins from which you can choose yours is a little unusual. They include:

- Murder
- Adultery
- Sloth
- Lust
- Avarice
- Gluttony
- Pride
- Covetousness
- Misplaced Priorities
- Fish in Microwave
- Didn't put printouts in bin

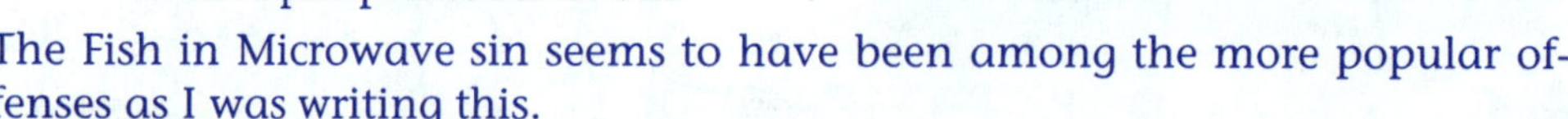

The Fish in Microwave sin seems to have been among the more popular offenses as I was writing this.

The penances delivered by the Confession Booth are, as I understand it, somewhat removed from the mainstream of Catholic dogma. Here's a small sampling of them—they get a lot weirder:

- *Teach your parents again how to program their VCR.*
- *Take the vow of e-silence for ten days—do not answer your e-mail.*
- *In your heart, forgive the evil Captain Kirk.*

- *Walk through downtown Manhattan while wearing an overcoat made of bananas.*
- *Abstain from your vice until that MPEG from the Netherlands finally downloads.*
- *Sign up to donate your bone marrow.*
- *Give names to all of Imelda Marcos' shoes.*
- *Watch episodes of Star Trek: The Next Generation where Wesley is featured.*
- *Eat a bug.*
- *Now that I think about it, no penance is necessary. I've done that myself many times.*
- *Say ten Hail Mary Shaws.*
- *Feed the hungry—give them a distinguished donut.*

You can also nominate new sins to add to the list. Back copies of the Scroll of Sins are available in the Tankful of Sins, which runs for miles.

The Conservative Link

http://www.moscow.com/~bmdesign/tcl/conintro.html

The Conservative Link is a Web page with links to dozens of other resources on the Internet dealing with conservative politics. Alternately, you can use it to find pages dealing with liberal politics that didn't work out too well, which is arguably much the same thing. It embodies a lot of political incorrectness, which can't be all bad. The Conservative Link says of itself:

> *If you are a conservative American who is tired of the status quo . . . if you are sick of being categorized as a mind-numbed dittohead robot . . . if you want to back up your political beliefs with facts . . . then you will enjoy The Conservative Link.*
>
> *Common sense, traditional values, and pride in our American heritage are the topics of the day here at TCL.*

There's a stunning number of other conservative pages accessible through the Conservative Link. The structure of this page makes finding what you're after pretty intuitive. For example, here's a partial selection of some of the pages available as I was writing this:

Conservative W3 Sites

- *The Declaration of Independence*

- The United States Constitution
- Ronald Reagan Home Page
- Speeches by Newt Gingrich
- National Rifle Association
- Dan Quayle Home Page
- The Cato Institute (Official Site)
- The Cato Institute (Unofficial Site)
- The Republican Liberty Caucus
- Beaconway Press / The Jolly Roger
- GoldWEB / Goldwater Home Page
- The Christian Coalition
- ICRN
- The John Birch Society
- The Contract With America
- Americans for Tax Reform
- The Libertarian Party Home Page
- The U.S. Flag Home Page
- Save Old Glory From Flames Homepage
- The Mr. Truth Page
- Cyber Republicans Home Page
- Insomniac's Political Page
- Health Care Is Not A Right
- U.S. Senate Republican Policy Committee
- Whitewater Home Page
- IN HIS OWN WORDS : Broken Promises From the President
- Government Reform Information for the 1990s
- Bill Clinton's Letter to the UA ROTC Program
- The Politically INcorrect Politics Page
- Independent News Service
- Conservatism FAQ

Government Links

- The White House
- U.S. House of Representatives

Other Politically-Oriented Sites

- Thomas: Legislative Information on the Internet
- Get Government Off Our Back Home Page
- SAVE - Students Advocating Valid Education
- The RAND Institute
- Yahoo Politics Page
- Synergy Political Solutions Page
- America Vote, Inc.'s
- The Library of Congress
- Deep Politics Bookstore

Political Humor / Satire

- *The Capitol Steps*
- *Vanderbilt Conservative Humor Page*

There were also a few anti-abortion links. The pages available through the Conservative Link vary from sincere and genuinely engrossing to inflammatory rhetoric that would make a bible salesman blush. It's all fun to browse, however, and the Back button of your Web browser will get you out of the really tenacious bits.

Cook Inlet Book Company

http://alaskan.com/cgi-bin/vendor?/usr/local/etc/httpd/htdocs/cook

Alaska is more than just a place to film cruise-ship commercials. Whales play, polar bears run, and oil tankers founder on its majestic reefs. Hundreds of years of history await you in its virgin forests—albeit, much of it written in cyrillic characters. Loggers and environmentalists engage in friendly debate, each side armed with Uzis and Stinger missiles. The permafrost gets a bit less perma every day.

If you'd like to experience a bit of the adventure and beauty of Alaska without freezing your butt off, link up to the Cook Inlet Book Company's home page. Offering an extensive catalog of books about Alaska, fiction set in Alaska, pictures of Alaska, guides to cooking like an Alaskan, and reviews of the politics of being so far out in the back of beyond as to make Siberia look cosmopolitan, it's a stirring introduction to one of the last unspoiled lands on earth. Order quick.

Crash Site

http://bazaar.com:80/Crash/

There's no telling what the Crash Site Web page is about, but the graphics are exemplary. Unstructured, free-form, and twisted, it offers all sorts of things to read and no good reason for not doing so. Its contents page looks a bit like *TV Guide*, with little black and white television screens next to the listings. Hidden messages can be found in the hot links, which usually encompass only part of a word. For example, this link proved fairly warped:

2AM PURGATORY (CC) - Inspirational

Alien worship leads two boys (Josh EsSEX AND FOODrow Gunter) to devilish practices of mind control and pushes them over the edge as they begin to perceive war as entertainment.

The salient bit is the link—sex and food. It connected to the following page:

People are constantly telling you what to do. This is especially true when it comes to sex and food, two of life's coolest offerings.

So-called "sexperts" like Dr. Ruth "The Raisin" Westheimer and Dr. Joyce Brothers foam from all orifices as they tell you what good things to do [with yourself]. Jabba, I mean Julia Child, and The Frugal Gourmet shiver with ecstasy as they tell you what kind of charred animal corpse to put in your mouth. Everyone has some sort of "good" advice.

Well, we at the Underground network have our own advice for you, but doubt you'd call it "good." Check out some bad sex ideas, and while you're at it, try some nice gutter meal recipes.

We don't advise you to follow our advice (except for the advice not to follow our advise), but we can't really stop you now, can we?

This was followed by two links, perhaps predictably, to pages entitled Food and Sex. The Food page was largely warped recipes. The Sex page was . . . well, largely warped.

Note everything at Crash Site is intensively wierd, but it all seems to strive for virtual brain damage. Structure isn't everything—if you can have a good time with a boa constrictor and a jar of petroleum jelly, a lack of structure probably isn't anything to worry about.

Cults

http://www.observer.co.uk/a-z-cults/index.html

The classical Romans were tolerant of cults—well, they were most of the time. Visitors and citizens of Rome were free to worship whomever they chose for much of the city's early history. Some very unusual cults arose during this period. (Christianity was one of the lesser ones.)

Our perception of cults has shifted somewhat in two millennia, or perhaps cults themselves have become rather more alarming. To some extent this is a result of the secretive nature of many cults—consider how much you really know about what are considered somewhat mainstream cults, such as Jehovah's Witnesses or the Mormons.

The Cults page is an encyclopedic listing of a broad selection of contemporary and recent cults. Each entry includes a link to a detailed description of the cult or movement in question. The entries are tight, readable, and periodically witty. They're also fascinating reading—and perhaps just a bit disturbing. Part of the introduction to the Cults page says:

> *With the exceptions of L. Ron Hubbard and Reverend Moon, modern visionaries do not appear to make good generals. The bottom line for most broad-minded liberals is whether the customer is satisfied. If a person experiences a genuine and lasting feeling of enhanced worth as a result of joining a cult, then doesn't that validate the existence of that cult? What follows is not an answer to this question . . . neither is it comprehensive or comparative. It is, though, a random—the alphabet apart—selection of groups of people whose beliefs locate them on the edge of our understanding.*

The following is a typical entry from the Cults page. This one describes Jehovah's Witnesses—the guys in the flashy suits who turn up at so many front doors.

> ***Jehovah's Witnesses***
>
> *Otherwise known as The Watchtower Bible And Tract Society, there are now 4.5 million Jehovah's Witnesses in more than 100 countries. The most damaging press surrounding the movement concerns its members' refusal to allow blood transfusions to sick children (or indeed themselves) because of their belief that "drinking blood" is blasphemous. It's a belief that has led to deaths as well as litigation by hospitals that have tried to prevent Witness children being removed from their care.*

> *Jehovah's Witnesses believe that Armageddon is about to happen (it was supposed to in 1914, 1925, and 1975) and that only Jehovah's Witnesses will survive. Of those survivors, 144,000 special ones (The Anointed) will go to heaven and the rest will live in earthly paradise. To turn a Jehovah's Witness away from the door is to turn away the chance of surviving the imminent end of the world, and that is the movement's central selling point.*
>
> *The Society was begun in 1879 by a Pennsylvanian businessman named Charles Russell. He abandoned Christianity, became interested in Eastern religion, and joined the Adventists, whose theories about the precise dating of Armageddon interested him. He was also interested in pyramidology. After Russell's death in 1916, the movement was taken over by "Judge" Rutherford, who built a huge house for himself in San Diego and had deeds drawn up holding the property in trust to Noah, Isaac, David, Gideon, and Joshua, who would return to earth after Armageddon.*

Christmas, Easter, and birthdays are not celebrated, and friendships with those not in the movement are strongly disapproved of. Members buy Witness literature from their local Kingdom Hall building at a small discount and then sell it door to door. In 1984, British Witnesses made 3.3 million pounds from street selling. Many converts, particularly in Britain, support their missionary work by window cleaning.

Reason to join: Backstage ticket to Armageddon. Reason not to join: Is that your gig?

Bottom line: "You are the whore of Babylon! You are the devil incarnate—back to the pit, you stinking vomit. Keep away from us, don't come near us—you will be destroyed just as the Tower of Babel." — Letter received by a British witness after leaving the movement.

The Cults page hails from Britain, but it has a pretty global scope. There's a particularly good entry for the Branch Davidians.

Cyrano

`http://www.nando.net/toys/cyrano.html`

Cyrano de Bergerac is a somewhat legendary French play, written in 1897 by Edmond Rostand, which has since been made into several less than legendary films. Very little of this has anything to do with the Cyrano Web page, although a passing acquaintance with the play will help explain the title of the page.

In the play, Cyrano de Bergerac is a brilliant swordsman and poet, great with words but at something of a disadvantage among the ladies because he has a nose the size of Alsace. His friend Christian is rather dreadful at expressing himself and, wishing to woo the fair Roxanne, enlists the assistance of Cyrano to write love letters for him. Rostand told the story in somewhat more detail, of course.

The Cyrano page, then, is an algorithmic love-letter creation system. It will ask you for a few details about the object of your affections, think for a moment, and then create a message to be printed out and sent to someone special. Or it will think for a moment and create utter nonsense. What it writes is largely dependent on how you answer its questions. Here's an example of its eloquence:

Dearest Xanthia O'Blivion,

My love, I can imagine myself kissing your tempestuous body and slathering you with various oils and live escargot. Your enormous hooters are my anchor in the stormy sea of life; I wonder how I ever made it through a day without you. Please meet me tomorrow dressed in your chainmail socks and we will celebrate our grape jelly love together.

Yours Orgasmically,

Pelican Baldersocks

One could argue that any woman who would actually be impressed by an automatic love letter could easily be had with far less effort. The Cyrano page probably isn't meant to be taken seriously, and in this light it has all sorts of possibilities. It's at its best if you let someone who's never seen one of its messages fill in the blanks.

The Darwin Fish

http://www.commerce.digital.com/palo-alto/FutureFantasy/darwin.html

The Darwin fish symbol is—well, it's a pretty subtle shot at fundamentalist religions. You will no doubt have noticed the Christian *ichthys* symbol on the bumpers of cars from time to time—it's a fish with an anagram for the Greek word for fish inside it, *IXθYΣ*. The Darwin fish has English characters it and very small feet, having evolved. Nowhere in Genesis does it say "and the lord caused lungfish to develop and go for a stroll on the beach." Herein lies the problem, of course.

The Darwin fish is available through the Future Fantasy bookshop at the link listed at the beginning of this section. You can also reach the main page of the bookshop this way, and browse their substantial catalog.

Doctor Fellowbugs' Laboratory of Fun and Horror

http://www.dtd.com/bug/

With unquestionably some of the best graphics on the net—albeit some very, very twisted ones—Doctor Fellowbug's page has a sleazy 1930's horror-movie feel to it. It offers a number of dependent pages that are good for a fair bit of casual browsing. My two favorites are the Keeper of the Lists and the Excuse Generator. The latter offers to write excuses and alibis for a wide variety of social *faux pas*, including:

- *Why We Should See Other People*
- *Didn't Mean to Kill Your Pet*
- *Lost Homework*
- *Had to Reformat Your Hard Drive*
- *Missed the Deadline*
- *So You Want Your PowerBook Back*
- *Forgot Your Birthday*
- *Missed a Helluva Lot of School*
- *Never Return Your Calls*
- *Chronically Late*
- *Slept with Your Wife*

The keeper of the lists is also pretty strange. Each week Doctor Fellowbug offers a new topic to generate a list. The entries for the lists are added and voted on by the lost souls who stumble onto this page. The site archives previous lists. The complete collection as I write this was as follows:

- *Top 143 Rejected Ice Cream Flavors*
- *Top 81 Favorite REAL Ice Cream Flavors*
- *All-Time Coolest Humans*
- *102 Signs You Spend Too Much Time on the Web*
- *158 Rejected Miss Contests*
- *Top 69 Greatest Things about a Sunday Morning*
- *Top 103 Weird Things My Cat Does*
- *Top 175 Greatest Software Programs Ever Written*
- *Top 184 Places I'd Rather Be*
- *Top 84 Reasons Why a Rhino Is a Better Pet Than a Hippo*
- *Top 106 Creatures Living Inside Your Computer*
- *Top 111 Reasons Why I Don't Like Mondays*
- *Top 55 Celebrities That Showed Up in Your Dreams and the Weird Things They Did*
- *Top 110 Stupidest Questions Asked by Computer Users*
- *Top 134 Cartoon Dream Teams*

Because the entries in these lists come from real Internet users, they're usually pretty twisted and vile. In a sense, this goes with the dungeon nouveau decor of Doctor Fellowbug's Web page. Here are a few of the suggestions for Top 143 Rejected Ice Cream Flavors—I've omitted the ones that would no doubt have edited out anyway:

Kibbles & Bits
Biohazard Waste
Scabs and Stitches
Beef and Potatoes
Fava Beans and Rice, with a Fine Chianti

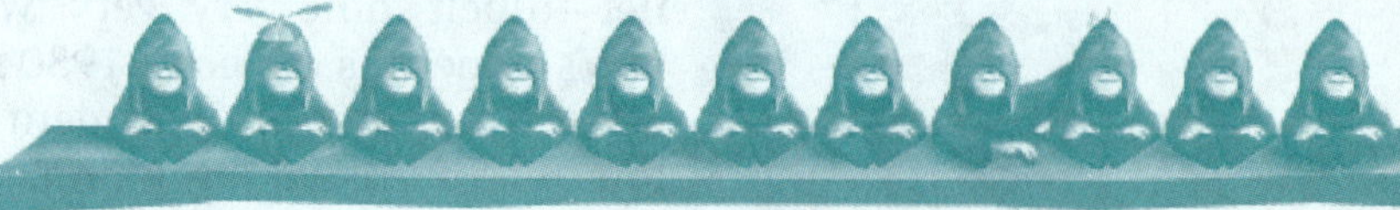

Dead Monkeys
Leeches and Cream
Skunk and Limburger
Uncle Tex's Three-Alarm Chili
Garlic and Onion
Cajun Blackened
Roadkill
Hairballs and Cream
Pork Tartar
Lasagne
Dill Pickle and Liver Tartar
Spam 'N Eggs
Pins & Needles with Razors & Lice
Worcestershire
Smurf Crunch
Arkadelphia Aardvark

Some of the other lists defy reproduction, at least not without subsequent legal action.

The Dolphin Page

http://wjh-www.harvard.edu/~furmansk/dolphin.html

Engaging to watch and probably smarter than we are, dolphins seem at times to be a mocking admonition of what human beings could have been if we'd evolved without mortgages. Consider that they do almost nothing for a living and still never require social assistance or soup kitchens.

The dolphin page is a wealth of dolphin-related resources. It's decorated with quite a few graphics of dolphins, and includes a fair bit of text by the author of the page. Clearly the work of someone who enjoys watching dolphins for no other reason than the pleasure of doing so, it allows you to enjoy them too, even if your previous perception of them was limited to a football team.

Among the resources at the dolphin page are a list of ongoing research projects involving dolphins. Each entry includes a link to a Web page describing the project in greater detail. There's a link to a fairly extensive page describing the realities of a career in marine mammal science, a link to the Sea World database, and a respectable library of graphics and sounds relating to dolphins. You'll find a few resources pertaining to whales at the dolphin page as well.

Dragons by Andrew Denton

http://www.eunet.ch/People/ahd/home.html

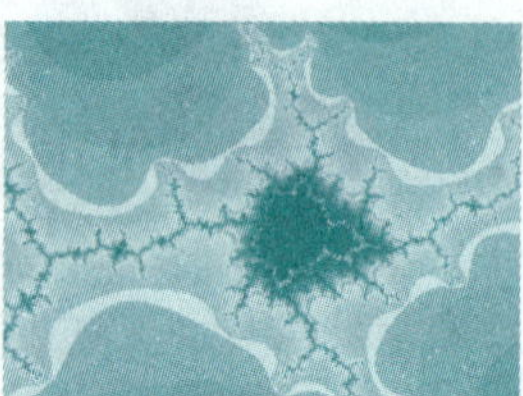

Unlike most species that artists are wont to paint, dragons don't really exist. At least, I'm pretty sure they don't. While it's more difficult to get their noses just right, no one can claim that someone's rendition of a dragon is incorrect. Likewise, dragons can't sue the people who paint them—most jurisdictions won't allow mythical creatures to be the plaintiffs in court cases.

Andrew Denton's ray-traced dragons are somewhat removed from traditional oil-on-canvas dragons—they often exhibit unusual scale patterns, and seem more real than real objects around them. Some of them breath ray-traced fire, which is surprisingly convincing. They're an engaging application of computer graphic technology.

The dragons at this page are displayed as small thumbnail images which you can click on to request a full-screen graphic.

Electric Sex Shop

http://www.infospiral.com/

The title of this Web page might be a bit misleading, although it's arguably close enough that no one could really object. The proprietors of the Electric Sex Shop don't sell any of those somewhat phallic electric devices which are supposed to be used for the relief of muscle aches—yeah, right—nor do they actually sell sex. They do, however, sell a lot of CD-ROMs you probably won't find on the same shelf as "Wild World of Mammals" and "Where in the World is Carmen Santiago?" at your local computer store.

Here's a very brief sampling of the delights of the Electric Sex Shop as I was writing this:

> *Special: NEW MACHINE SIX PACK - $45.95 - CD5500 (MAC/PC CD-ROM) The best deal around! An extraordinary collection of best-selling titles including: Digital Dancing, Legend 4, Legends of Porn 2, Insatiable, Biker Babes, and New Machine Sampler. This winning combination should make an enlightened connoisseur out of anyone.*
>
> *New Price: SPACE SIRENS - $49.95 - UN017 (MAC/PC CD-ROM) - New! A distress signal emanating from a mysterious space station puts you at the mercy of the irresistible call of the Sirens. You are then lured away from your spaceship into a virtual-reality prison chamber. Oh no! The Sirens have now*

entrapped you only to fulfill their every desire as their sex slave on this station forever!

101 SEX POSITIONS PART 1 - $39.95 - VVD05 (MAC/PC CD-ROM) The first-ever professionally produced adult education-oriented CD with the proper name identifying each position.

101 SEX POSITIONS PART 2 - $39.95 - VVD06 (MAC/PC CD-ROM) Vivid Interactive's state-of-the-art technology with high color, motion, and sound. Watch for the shower scene with Heather.

A TASTE OF EROTICA CD SAMPLER 2.0 - $7.99 - CD1098B (MAC/PC CD-ROM) New to erotic CD-ROM? Want to take your computer on a test drive with the top down? Try our interactive CD-ROM sampler—the world's most titillating interactive catalog, featuring explicit action and the hottest adult stars. Please note: if you order the Six Pack, this item is included.

DIRTY DEBUTANTES VOL. 1 - $37.95 - CD2005 (MAC/PC CD-ROM) Neophyte nymphomaniacs save themselves for their fifteen minutes of infamy, and the nasty brothers are there to capture their daring debuts on film! Interact with adult stars while they were still amateurs in this erotic game shot by Ed Powers.

This is the sort of thing that decent, moral people go ballistic over when they write to their elected representatives about the dangers of the Internet.

The Electronic Embassy

http://www.embassy.org/

There are times when international diplomacy seems to be an awful lot like being paid several hundred thousand dollars a year to cruise around in your own Lear jet and eat a lot of weird food. Sometimes it's even more adventurous. It's a dirty job but somebody has to so it.

If the world of embassies interests you—or if you want to get in touch with the embassies of any of the hundreds of nations who maintain diplomatic relationships with the United States—you'll find the Electronic Embassy page to be almost as good as being there. It has an exhaustive searchable index of embassies, listed by country, and each entry will provide you with the address, phone, and fax numbers of the embassies in question. Several of them even link to dedicated Web pages maintained by the countries in question. Canada, for example, has two Web pages, each of which is in two languages—which probably begins to help explain the country's current tax problems.

While still a fairly new page, the Electronic Embassy currently features the following links:

- Index of all of the D.C. embassies' basic information on the embassy community
- The Press and Cultural Office information on cultural affairs
- The Education Office information on K-12 and higher education, international educational exchange, and educational resources
- The Commerce and Trade Office information on international trade opportunities, rules and regulations, trade delegations, etc.
- The Consular Office Information on passports and visas
- The Travel and Tourism Office travel advisories, travel rules and regulations, and travel opportunities
- The Employment Office opportunities for employment and internships within the embassy and U.S. foreign policy communities, and job opportunities abroad
- The Washington D.C. scene listing of events, exhibitions, and resources in the Washington, D.C. area

You'll also find links to documents dealing with United States foreign policy and federal executive agencies.

Emily Dickinson

http://www.columbia.edu/~svl2/dickinson/

One of the poets that most of us were inflicted with in high school—and thereafter shunned with all the energy of someone being chased by liberals in an election year—Emily Dickinson is among the most memorable of Victorian writers. Her work moves with an effortless cadence, and suggests a timeless sense of place a century after its publication. Read her and your phone will stop ringing, your digital watch won't beep at you, and no cars will pass your house.

All this being so, you might suspect that an Emily Dickinson Web page would embody a gross contradiction in terms. Perhaps . . . but she's pretty hard to find in bookshops, and few would care to look for her.

The page listed at the beginning of this section is an online version of the third volume of Emily Dickinson's poetry, originally published in 1896, ten years after her death. It's a singularly well-crafted page—if you browse it with Netscape, it will have a background of yellowed paper and a sepiatone image of Emily herself.

IX

Drowning is not so pitiful
As the attempt to rise.
Three times, 'tis said, a sinking man
Comes up to face the skies,
And then declines forever
To that abhorred abode
Where hope and he part company,—
For he is grasped of God.
The Maker's cordial visage,
However good to see,
Is shunned, we must admit it,
Like an adversity.

XLVIII. Desire.

Who never wanted,—maddest joy
Remains to him unknown;
The banquet of abstemiousness
Surpasses that of wine.

Within its hope, though yet ungrasped
Desire's perfect goal,
No nearer, lest reality
Should disenthrall thy soul.

Federal Express

http://www.fedex.com/

One of the few corporate entities without which life as we know it could not exist, Federal Express is the stuff by which deadlines are met. They also go absolutely anywhere. Alchemy Mindworks ships a lot of software by FedEx, and they have offices in places I wouldn't have thought even had people. Federal Express presently services 192 countries, moves about two million packages a day, and runs a fleet of 471 airplanes.

It will also ship live lobsters to wherever you happen to be when you feel hungry, something not to be taken lightly if you've ever experienced the generally nasty disposition of a lobster.

One of the things that Federal Express likes to pat itself on the back for in its television commercials is its ability to track any of those two million parcels pretty well instantly. In fact, you can do the same thing yourself if you link to its Web page. Enter the airbill number of the package in question and the FedEx computer will tell you exactly where it is at the moment. It will also show you the complete journey of a package if it's already been delivered. Here's one I sent a few days before writing this:

FedEx Airbill Tracking Information

Airbill Number : 400 0000 0000
Package has been Delivered!
Delivered To : Recept/Frnt desk
Delivery Time : 10:03
Signed For By : JONES
Cartage Agent :
Status Exception : International transit in
Scan Activity :
Delivered OUDE MEER NL 04/21 10:03
Package on Van OUDE MEER NL 04/21 08:45
Arrived at Destination OUDE MEER NL 04/21 05:53
In Station Exception PARIS FR 04/20 20:37
Package Left Hub MEMPHIS TN 04/20 03:21
Int. Package Manifest Created MEMPHIS TN 04/20 00:33
Picked up SUNNYVALE CA 04/19 15:23
Left Origin Location SUNNYVALE CA 04/19 18:15
Delivered RICHMOND BC 04/05 09:41
In Station Exception RICHMOND BC 04/05 04:07
Package on Van RICHMOND BC 04/05 04:06
Arrived at Destination RICHMOND BC 04/05 04:05
Left Origin Location MISSISSAUGA ON 04/04 18:05

You can also use this facility to see how FedEx packages you've received made the trip.

The Fish Cam

`http://home.mcom.com/fishcam/`

Things that happen in real time on the Web are still relatively unusual. The Fish Cam is at the leading edge of this technology. As with so much leading-edge technology, it's utterly useless and almost certain to stay that way, but it's amusing to watch.The Fish Cam is a digital camera pointed at a tank full of fish. Once a minute the camera takes a picture of the fish, which is automatically digitized and copied to the Fish Cam Web server. You can link to the page and see what the fish are up to. The images are available as small

10K JPEG files and larger 50K JPEG files. The Fish Cam's fish are described as follows:

> *The tank is a 90-gallon acrylic model with built-in overflow and extra sturdy top. It is currently lit with two fluorescent tubes that I removed from a desktop lighting unit in a fellow employee's office while he was out. Someday I'll get a real light, but these seem to be working pretty well for now. This is a somewhat current list of the fish in tank 1:*
>
> - *Snowflake eel. He is white with black spots and stripes and is about 2 and a half feet long.*
> - *Green moray eel. He is green and about 2 feet long. Very mean, too.*
> - *Huma Huma Triger. He is about 7 or 8 inches long and pretty colorful. I've heard that it's the state fish of Hawaii.*
>
> *This is a somewhat current list of the fish in tank 2:*
>
> - *Blue tang. The blue fish.*
> - *Sailfin tang (Zebrasoma desjardinii). He really looks good when his fins are fully extended vertically.*
> - *Tomato clown. The reddish/maroon fish.*
> - *Longnose butterfly. The yellow one.*
> - *Some sort of puffer fish. I've never actually figured out what kind of puffer he is, but he's cute and round and green.*
> - *Helmet fish. He is very small and looks a bit like a cow fish.*

Unlike most Web pages, which change only when their creators feel like it, this one has something new to look at every time you connect to it. Of course, "something new" is always fish.

Note that the Fish Cam does malfunction from time to time—there's an e-mail address at the Fish Cam page to contact in this eventuality. It's probably worth keeping in mind that if one fish appears upside down it's probably dead. If they all appear upside down, someone has most likely knocked the camera over.

Flightless Hummingbird

http://www.umich.edu/~rmutt/HomePage.html

Imagine being so far out on the leading edge of creative thought that only the very ends of your big toes were in contact with reality as the rest of the universe knows it. Lesser mortals would either stare at you in undisguised awe or think you're a pretentious neobuffoon lacking the talent to do something coherent. The odds are very much in favor of the latter.

The Flightless Hummingbird page is your opportunity to see how tolerant you are of unconventional expression and neobuffoonery. Borderline comprehensible and perhaps a bit less than wholly focused, it offers articles on such things as art, paranoia, eschatology, and fashion tips. In answer to the obvious question, eschatology is the study of finality and termination. The Flightless Hummingbird page is very much concerned with apocalypses. Of itself, it says:

> *It takes a sharp eye, a steady hand, and a cool nerve. Above all it takes luck—pure dumb luck—the kind of luck that wins lotteries and walks away from plane crashes.*
>
> *When the beast charges it does so with unequaled swiftness and ferocity. There is nothing else in nature that even comes close. Propelled by limbs that move so fast that muscle and bone are transformed into something more like the afterburn of a jet engine or the tail of a comet, and armed with a lance that glistens like a scalpel under the lights, the creature will not give you a second chance to be lucky.*
>
> *You can't think about it—the human brain doesn't work that fast. You can't react—you don't have that luxury. Life and death are separated by microseconds. You have to anticipate. You must call upon the cunning bred into you by ancestors who beat the one-in-a-million odds against survival. You must employ the kill-for-sport mechanism that exists in you on a cellular level, the blood-lust that has enabled your species to infest the planet like liver flukes overrunning a once-healthy organ.*
>
> *To bring down the mindless brute you must rely on coincidence. Flesh and bone and blood must collide with metallic projectile in a fatal coincidence that defies mathematical probability. It is luck and luck alone that allows you to bag a charging hummingbird.*

It didn't make much sense to me either, but then, neither do liberals, most cats, all poodles, rap music, and most of the commercials they run on CNN. Perhaps remarkably, the Flightless Hummingbird page does actually touch on the subject of flightless hummingbirds once, however distantly. It says:

> ***Breed a Flightless Hummingbird***
>
> *Status: Initial experiment looked promising but ultimately proved to be a dead end. Rather than a true flightless breed, produced birds with a congenital inner-ear condition that still permitted flight but with uniformly disastrous results.*
>
> *Currently investigating a method of grafting hummingbirds onto seedlings. Could result in a hybrid that produces its own nectar. Still too early to tell.*

A hundred years from now really enlightened rich people might frame some of the pages at Flightless Hummingbird and hang them in places of honor in their homes, whispering at cocktail parties about what they paid for them and how many of their friends they had to out-bid to possess them, much in the way that scribblings by Picasso fetch pretty high prices today. After all, you can sell enlightened rich people practically anything if you call it art and they don't know any better.

Folk Instruments

http://www.lm.com/~dshu/folkstuff.html

There are actually instruments that work without being connected to amplifiers. Acoustic music got trendy a few years ago when it started to be called *unplugged*—in fact, legend has it that there have been nonelectric instruments about for quite a while.

The Folk Stuff page is a set of links for people building or playing folk instruments. You can find sources of plans for a dulcimer; learn to play tin whistles, flutes, and shakuhachis; read a page of scurrilous verse about autoharps; and otherwise expand your perceptions of the universe. The list of links included the following as I was writing this:

- General Folk Catalogs, Books, and Info
- General Periodicals
- Hammered Dulcimer Information
- Autoharp Information
- Limericks about Dulcimers & Autoharps
- Folk Flute and Pennywhistle Information
- Mbira/Kalimba Information
- Theremin Information
- Experimental & Other Instrument Information
- Didjeridus

Bang that thang.

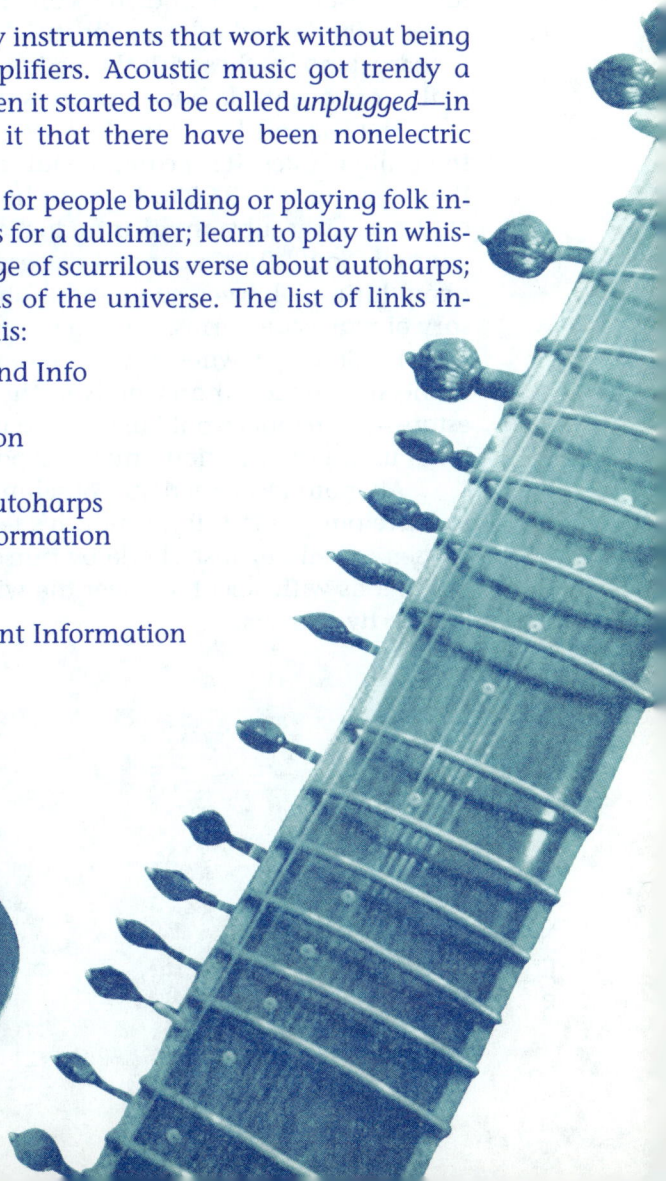

For Sale by Owner

http://www.crocker.com:80/byowner/

I recall hearing the observation that anyone who attempts to sell his or her own home has a fool for a real estate agent, but I'm pretty sure it was a real estate agent who said it. Real estate agents have a vested interest in your believing this, of course, as they get six percent of the purchase price of your house for their efforts.

Selling your house yourself allows you to thumb your nose at all the real estate agents who have been sending you free calendars and fridge magnets for the past ten years, and you won't have to pay anyone a commission when you finally do find a buyer for it. Of course, you'll have to do a lot of work. Bloodsucking leaches with the hearts of used car salesmen they might be, but real estate agents do have resources that the rest of us can't really access.

The For Sale by Owner Web page is a database of homes for sale across the United States. It's a commercial enterprise—the company that maintains the page wants $79.00 to list your house in its database. However, it also includes a fairly substantial introduction to the realities of selling your house yourself. You'll find a general discussion of the problems you'll face, advice about hiring a lawyer, suggestions about advertising your home, and a glossary of real estate terms, among many other things.

For Sale by Owner is worth looking at if you're considering selling your home. It's a bit less than wholly forthcoming about the brutish realities of real estate—its creators would like you to use their services, after all—but there's a lot of useful information amidst its pages.

After our last experience of selling a home and moving, we've vowed not to leave our present digs unless it's feet first, in a box. I suspect that had we chosen to sell our last abode by ourselves, we'd be living in smaller accommodations with steel bars over the windows now—for multiple homicides of prospective buyers.

Fractal Explorer

http://www.vis.colostate.edu/~user1209/fractals/index.html

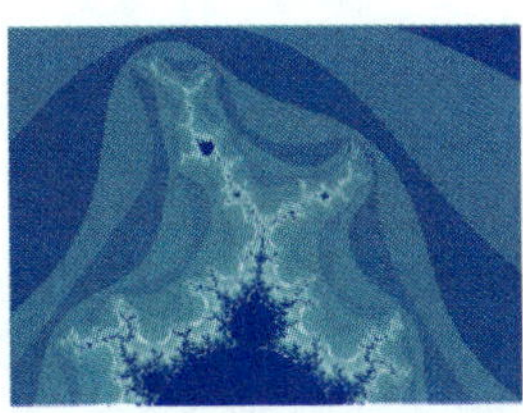

Fractals have become almost commonplace, a development that seems rather disappointing. A bit like staring into the raging fires of chaos and creation, the odd mathematics of fractal geometry is unnerving and otherworldly. Of course, fractals turn up in art posters, and fractal imaging is used in movie special effects and other graphic applications. A lot of the original magic has vanished in a puff of artificial smoke.

The Fractal Explorer page will let you boldly go where a lot of people have gone before, to wit, out into the alternate universe of two of the most popular fractals, the Mandelbrot and Julia imaginary number sets. Plotted in real space, these functions generate intricate, complex images you can explore. If you zoom in on a specific area of the space they occupy, they'll turn out to be infinitely detailed and almost organic.

The Fractal Explorer will allow you to zoom in on either fractal set as much as you like, recalculating and redrawing the area of the fractal you're interested in. It's agreeably fast and very easy to use.

If you haven't had the opportunity to play with a fractal generator, spend an hour clicking around at this one. It's a rather odd experience, especially if you consider that the landscape it lets you explore is something woven into the fabric of mathematics. The images of fractal surfaces seem to echo things in the natural world.

This page also features a well-written, lucid discussion of the number theory behind fractals, if you want to know how they work.

Free Advice

http://mercury.interpath.net/~nattayek/fradvice.html

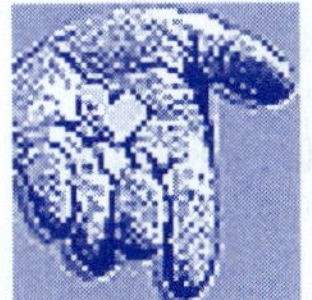

Free advice is usually worth what it costs, and the Free Advice Web page is perhaps the embodiment of this concept. It offers links to several interesting pages, the best of which is arguably the antipersonal ads. Here's a selection:

To: the guy who kept staring at me on the bus
I apologize for staring back, but I was mesmerized by that goo hanging from your nose.

To: My ex-husband
From: Your ex-wife
Listen very carefully:
NO, I'M NOT COMING BACK!
Now, which word didn't you understand?

To: whoever invented cellular phones
A very sarcastic "thanks a lot!" Now I can run, but I can't hide.

To: major league baseball players and owners
From: Bill
I find it very difficult to believe that just a few hundred guys can't figure out how to split up two billion dollars!

To: The person who lost a brown leather wallet containing $300 in cash
Thanks.

To: The lady who deliberately stepped on my foot with her high-heels
Meet me on the 14th Street bridge. I've got a shoe with your butt's name on it.

The antipersonals page includes a function to enter your own barbs, accusations, diatribes, and vendettas. It's very therapeutic.

Fried Society

http://www.catalogue.com/comix/fried_society/

Internet comics offer you a chance to see the works of brilliant cartoonists before everyone else knows how brilliant they are. Of course, it also allows you to see the work of idiots with magic markers who would have remained competent pizza delivery people had the world still run exclusively on paper. Fried society is a bit of both. Not quite as rude as *Where the Buffalo Roam* but not quite as funny, either, it's enjoyable without causing you to laugh uncontrollably and lose your job. Its illustrations aren't bad—Calvin and Hobbs probably won't get booted off the front page of the Saturday funnies in favor of Fried Society any time soon. The list of comics at this page as I was writing this included:

- The Life of a Trend
- An Important Message for Generation X
- Adventures in Temping—An Expendable Employee's Handbook, Part I
- Anthony and Tony's Lover's Spat
- Dueling Band Snobs starring Kirk and Tad

The comics are scanned into GIF files—they download reasonably quickly.

Frogs

http://www.cs.yale.edu/HTML/YALE/CS/HyPlans/loosemore-sandra/froggy.html (Froggy Page)

Frogs have hopped about this earth for a lot longer than lawyers, liberal politicians, yuppies, accountants, and most other forms of pond life. Some of them are attractive in an amphibious sort of way, and some of them are also quite poisonous. They make perfect surprise gifts for all those other forms of pond life.

The notion of frogs being cute and endearing is perhaps a lot easier to get along with than that of cows in the same role. Frogs don't smell, don't trample your dog, and don't emit dangerous levels of methane while they're waiting around to become entrees. In fact, in most civilized parts of the world frogs aren't regarded as entrees at all, at least until they've worked their way back into the food chain.

The Froggy Page is a collection of everything having to do with frogs. It includes quite a bit of content in its own right, and links to numerous other resources on the Web that deal with frogs in all their aspects. Frog graphics abound—green is a very popular color.

To begin with, the Froggy Page offers an extensive set of links to other things that ribbit, including:

- A Box of Frogs, from Mike Pingleton's herp archive
- Another Box, also from Mike's archive
- Even More Frogs from Mike's archive
- Smithsonian Institution Frog Pictures
- More Froggy Images from various FTP sites
- Even More Froggy Images
- Silly Frog Images
- Froggy Clip Art (B&W) Page 1
- Froggy Clip Art (B&W) Page 2
- Froggy Clip Art (Color)
- ASCII Froggies
- Frogs on Ice
- Frogs on Ice II
- Make an Origami Jumping Frog!
- Applied Microsystems Corporation debugger frog pictures

One of the reasons often cited by frog fanciers for an abiding interest in frogs is their propensity for eating unwanted insects. While a nice idea when it works, it rarely works for very long. If you have a bug problem and import frogs to deal with it—rather than just hosing everything down with chemicals and polluting this fragile planet for future generations—you'll probably find that you have, in rapid succession, fat happy frogs and no bugs, dead useless frogs that have all died of starvation, and, finally, most of your original bug problem back. Frogs don't think much past their next moth.

The only good reason I can think of for having frogs about is that they sound nice after it gets dark. If you live somewhere that doesn't lend itself to having real frogs on hand, you can download some digitized frog sounds from the Froggy Page:

- Blurp
- Ka-blurp
- Ribbet
- More ribbets
- East Texas frog croaks
- Lots of greedeeps
- Peep-peep

There's also a wealth of frogs in literature available through the Froggy Page. You can click over to:

- *Frog Fables*, by Aesop
- *The Frogs*, by Aristophanes
- *The Frog Prince*, by Grimm; illustrated hypertext in English or German
- *The Toad Princess*, by Grimm

One of the more usual elements of the Froggy Page is a collection of somewhat serious flog links. This includes a really detailed treatise on dissecting frogs, something you think would strike fear and loathing into the hearts of frog lovers. Actually, you can learn more about frogs by following these links than you probably ever wanted to know.

In addition to the links I've mentioned here, you'll find a list of famous frogs, links to frogs in music, and about half a dozen other really weird frog pages. Browse around the Froggy Page for an afternoon and you might find yourself with a taste for flies.

The Gadget Guru

http://www.netcreations.com/gadget/

If you woke up this morning wondering where to get a universal television remote control shaped like a Star Trek hand phasor, or if you can't live another day without a Barbie telephone—well, you probably watch too much television and need electroshock therapy and a life. However, the Net is a tolerant place, so rather than racking up all those medical bills you can link to the Gadget Guru page, a mail-order shop on the Web that sells the weirdest stuff you can imagine. Every item for sale includes a scanned photograph. The prices are pretty reasonable, considering that none of these things actually does much.

In addition to its own list of the unusual, the tacky, and the desperately bent, the Gadget Guru also includes links to numerous other pages that deal with items you'd never find at Sears. Some of these are stranger still—the list as I was writing this included:

- Gizmo Page
- Mind Gear—machines that alter your consciousness.
- Options and Futures by Jutta Degener—incomplete designs for very interesting software or hardware.
- Weird Science—Weird Research, Anomalous Physics, Free Energy Devices, and more strangeness.
- Tech Museum Store
- Yahoo's Interesting Devices Connected to the Net
- New Electronic Toys and Gadgets—by Dennis Bristow of the excellent Interface Magazine
- Fetish—HotWired's Technology Center
- FringeWare—you need to see this place to believe it

You can browse these things for hours, but be sure to lock up your Visa card before you do.

A Gallery of the Grotesque in Art

http://www.ugcs.caltech.edu/~werdna/grotesque/grotesque.html

There are things deep within most of us that could inspire John Carpenter's next movie. Throughout history, artists have sought to capture the stuff of nightmares on paper or canvas—perhaps only so they could drag them out into the daylight and see if they still looked as terrifying. This page is a sampling of some of the best of grotesque art. Each picture is stored as a medium sized JPEG thumbnail you can click on to call up a full-screen image.

The represented artists include William Blake, Francisco de Goya, and Edvard Munch, among many others. Some of the paintings are accompanied by notes and commentary.

This page is very slow to access over a dial-up connection, and it includes a lot of pictures. However, it's certainly quicker than painting all the images yourself.

General Aviation Home Page

http://acro.harvard.edu/GA/ga_homepg.html

Airplanes are one of the more sublime expressions of human aspirations—at least, they are unless the continental breakfast looks a lot like polecat surprise and the cabin crew all seem like they ought to be molesting sheep as a career. Airplanes grow more sublime as they grow smaller—really sublime ones, with a maximum of two seats, have little in common with the jet airliners most of us are familiar with, besides wings.

As a rule, Cessnas get by without a cabin crew of any sort. The continental breakfast, should you be fool enough to want to eat while airborne, typically comes in a brown paper bag. The extremely vulgar might suggest that it's likely to wind up in one as well if there's any turbulence. Small aircraft don't lose your luggage unless you leave the door open by mistake.

The General Aviation page is a rich set of links to aviation resources around the Web. For the most part, these pertain to recreational flying, rather than driving winged buses for a living. As I write this, the list of links included:

- International Aerobatics Club
- Soaring Society of America
- Experimental Aircraft Association
- Other aviation servers
- Other aviation archives
- Weather information
- Other general aviation-related information
- Aerobatics images
- Soaring images
- Aviation image archives

These pages feature a wealth of information for serious pilots, but most of the links are pretty interesting even if the planes in your experience come in only two types—overbooked and overdue—or if you haven't actually flown in anything without an in-flight movie for years.

The weather information link, for example, is an extensive resource of current satellite weather imagery for most of the civilized world. It's handy even if you have no interest in getting closer to the sky than can be managed with a new pair of boots.

The Experimental Aircraft Association page offers a number of pages for people who like to build airplanes. You can download free software from NASA to design airplanes, look at a page of FAA directives for airworthy design and construction, and check out the current Experimental Aircraft Association's newsletter.

Gliders have always scared the hell out of me—they look like a good idea in theory, but somehow the idea of my backside riding on a technology that's based on rising columns of hot air that *ought* to occur now and again seems a bit questionable. I prefer planes that let you know when they've run out of gas. Should you feel differently, the Soaring Society of America's links are impressively vast. There are links to a number of glider clubs and all sorts of other information.

Finally, the image links in the previous list will get you to several extensive repositories of airplane pictures.

George Rarey's Journals of the 379th Fighter Squadron

http://www.nbn.com/home/rareybird/index.html

The problem with war movies—aside from the war part—is that they're usually about events rather than people. They allow us to forget that human beings are involved in war, and that they have lives beyond what filmmakers choose to document. George Rarey's journals of the 379th Fighter Squadron is a document about the second world war from a perspective other than that of a historian or a movie director. This Web page was created by Damon Rarey, the son of the artist responsible for the images it contains.

> *In 1942 my father, George Rarey, a young cartoonist and commercial artist, was drafted into the Army Air Corps. He flew a P-47 before he drove a car. During his service he kept a cartoon journal of the daily life of the fighter pilots. A few weeks after D-Day he was killed in combat over France.*
>
> *His journals are a big part of his legacy to me—one that I want to share with others through this Web page. Browse through his drawings and words. Their joyful spirit dwarfs the background landscape of war.*
>
> *The drawings have explanatory text contributed by surviving members of the 379th Fighter Squadron or excerpts from Rarey's letters to his bride (my mother), Betty Lou. George Rarey didn't care much for his first name and was known exclusively as "Rarey." (My mother thought Rarey was his first name until they had had several dates.) The exception to this was his fellow pilots. Because he was a few years older than most of the pilots—a ripe old 25—in the Air Corps he was known as "Dad." The cartoons and watercolors here are a small selection from well over 200 pieces of artwork. I plan to add to these from time to time.*
>
> *Damon Rarey*

I doubt I'd have managed a comparable sense of humor if people had been shooting at me.

Globetrotter Magazine

http://www.dungeon.com/home/globe/home.html

One of the unfortunate realities about publishing a paper magazine is that it usually requires a topic. Once beset with a topic, magazines are expected to remain thus confined and not wander off in search of other fancies. This also means that if there's an issue to get out and nothing much on topic, some filler is called for.

Devoid of most of the financial hardships of paper publishing, magazines that exist wholly on the Net can thumb their virtual noses at issues of content and topic and publish in ways that would make the publishers of paper journals reach for a valium. Globetrotter magazine is one such effort. It probably deserves not to be referred to as a 'zine, the usual description of an electronic Net periodical, as it embodies a notable degree of professionalism and purpose.

It just doesn't have a topic. It's clearly about whatever its contributors think is interesting. Thus far, as I write this, they've managed to stay away from long opinion pieces, critical reviews of the Egyptian Book of the Dead, poetry, and speculation about the nature of footwear design in twenty-first century Indonesia. The articles in Globetrotter are short, well written and usually exceedingly focused. As I was writing this, the contents page of Globetrotter included:

- *Editorial*
- *News*
- *The Secret Garden: John Anderson with his view of the O.J. Simpson trial*
- *Operating systems: IBM's Windows basher—Mike Barnes on IBM's new version of OS/2*
- *Online: Electronic Fiction—Jan B. Steffensen on electronic fiction*
- *Book Reviews*
- *Science: Food aversion—Dawn Rene Powell's research into the role of the sense of smell in food aversion*
- *VR: 3D Wars—Si Green with a rundown of current VR systems*
- *Garage Tech—Si Green investigates the world of surplus electronics*

The food aversion article was arguably a bit deep and dry for casual browsing, but the book reviews were well above average. The universe probably doesn't need another O.J. article as I write this—you'll have the advantage of knowing how the whole circus turned out by the time this book hits the streets. Globetrotter originates in England.

God's Home Page

http://phxmedia.com:80/~nick/

Unless God is a quasi-literate unemployed graphic artist from California, this page is probably misnamed. It's modestly amusing nonetheless, and the graphics are exemplary. You'll probably be able to browse the whole effort in about five minutes—it offers interesting pictures to look at, but relatively few of them. Not everything on the Web has to have a purpose—this page certainly lacks one, but it doesn't seem to have suffered for its deprivation.

Grammar and Style Notes

http://www.english.upenn.edu/~jlynch/grammar.html

The three books I most loath are *The Chicago Manual of Style* and two others whose titles are so unspeakably vile as to defy mentioning here. Among the cruelest things one can do to English is to inflict pedantic dogma on it and try to make it sound correct. One of the really grand aspects of English is that it's a mongrel language sired by countless unknown fathers out behind a pub somewhere. It lacks a lineage, any sort of civilized manners, and a home to go to at night. It will sleep with anyone, perform vulgar tricks at parties, and debase itself when necessary in the furtherance of questionable enterprises. Consider that it's the language of William Shakespeare, Bill Clinton, and Heidi Fliess.

All this notwithstanding, a very small amount of understanding of the rules of grammar isn't wholly bad. It will keep you from sounding like an illiterate bastard who's been off siring languages behind a pub and on a good day it will help you express yourself more clearly.

The Grammar and Style Notes Web page is an admirable compromise between buying a copy of *The Chicago Manual of Style*—so all your subsequent written English sounds like it was generated by an anal-retentive computer—and writing like an eight-year-old. It offers all sorts of useful definitions for parts of speech, guides for things like dangling participles and transitive verbs, and suggestions about frequently abused aspects of English. Its entries are short, readable, and periodically amusing, for example:

> ***Dangling Participle***
>
> *A participle is a verb ending in -ing, and is called dangling when the subject of the -ing verb and the subject of the sentence do not agree. An example is*

"When discussing race and gender, sensitivity is necessary." Here the subject is sensitivity, but the sensitivity is not doing the discussing. Better is "When discussing race and gender, the student should be sensitive." Here the student is doing the discussing.

Pay close attention to sentences beginning with "when ——ing

One way to tell whether the participle is dangling is to put the clause with the participle right after the subject of the sentence: "Sensitivity, when discussing race and gender, is necessary" doesn't sound right, but "The student, when discussing race and gender, should be sensitive" does.

*Not all words in -ing are participles. In the sentence "Answering the questions in chapter four is your next assignment," the word *answering* is used as a noun, not a verb.*

Farther versus Further

Though very few people bother with the difference these days, there is a traditional distinction: farther applies to physical distance, further to metaphorical distance. You travel farther, but pursue a topic further. Don't get upset if you can't keep it straight; no one will notice.

Gutter Press

http://www.io.org/~gutter/

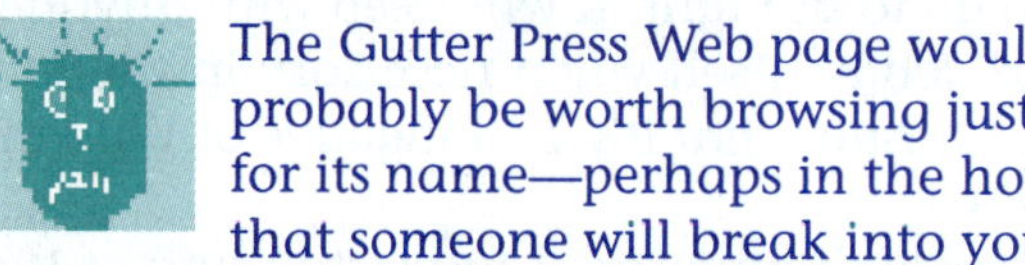

The Gutter Press Web page would probably be worth browsing just for its name—perhaps in the hope that someone will break into your computer one day and notice it in your list of bookmarks. In fact, there's more than just an earthy title there—Gutter Press offers a number of resources for people who like to read the sort of books they don't sell in shopping mall bookstores. You'll find links to a number of small presses here, as well as several online fiction resources. It's all agreeably underground.

H. P. Lovecraft

http://www.lehigh.edu/pv02/public/www-data/hpl.html

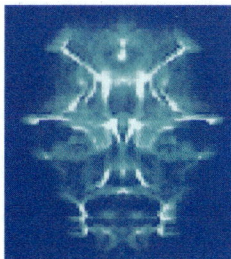

Howard Philip Lovecraft's grave in Providence, Rhode Island is inscribed "I Am Providence." A wildly imaginative author, Lovecraft wrote other-worldly fantasies and what might be regarded as the beginnings of modern horror fiction. His works hold up better than books a tenth their age, and he usually managed to form complete sentences, a worthy talent for any author.

The H. P. Lovecraft page itself offers very little about Lovecraft or his books as I write this—it's almost an online shrine, with photographs of his former home, his grave, and such. However, it includes links to several other Lovecraft resources that are worth having a look at. If you've never read any of H. P. Lovecraft's tales, these pages will offer you a well-written introduction.

HR GIGER

H. R. Giger

http://heiwww.unige.ch:80/art/giger/

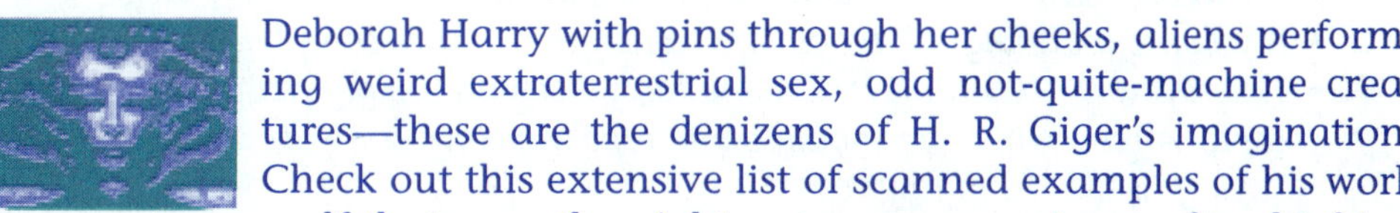

Deborah Harry with pins through her cheeks, aliens performing weird extraterrestrial sex, odd not-quite-machine creatures—these are the denizens of H. R. Giger's imagination. Check out this extensive list of scanned examples of his work to prove to yourself that even the nightmares you experience after drinking a lot of really cheap tequila and eating the worm at the bottom of the bottle are relatively tame. There is no hell worse than one you can't distinguish from heaven.

H. R. GIGER

HAL

http://ciips.ee.uwa.edu.au:80/~hutch/Hal.html

Presumably named after the extremely intelligent but emotionally unstable computer aboard the Discovery in 2001: A Space Odyssey, this HAL isn't quite as clever as his namesake. An artificial intelligence program designed to simulate a conversation with something smarter than a toaster, HAL will attempt to learn from the things he's told and reply to questions based on his experience.

Actually, HAL's biggest problem is that people like to fill his brain with nonsense. Because his responses to questions are based on what he's been told by previous users, his conversations will begin to make less and less sense the fuller his cranium gets with monkey dandruff. From time to time HAL requires a lobotomy and general rinsing out so he can shake off the bad vibes and start over. HAL's creator offers the following guidelines for communicating with HAL:

- *Change the subject of conversation often. Talking about the same thing all the time will cause over-training.*
- *Please avoid typing anything offensive.*
- *Try to give HAL knowledge about particular subjects by stating facts.*
- *If you are multilingual, teach HAL a language other than English.*
- *When you are teaching HAL something, keep on talking about the same topic. After a while, he should begin replying coherently to what you are saying (well, sort of anyway).*

HAL's responses aren't always wholly on topic. For example, I asked HAL: "Are pelicans intelligent?" and HAL replied: "Cigars are generally made in tropical climates, mostly in the ether." Clearly it was time for another lobotomy.

HAL is good for hours of fairly low-rent amusement—no human being could consistently answer questions so wildly off topic unless he or she was a politician caught in a finance scandal. Here's a selection of items from HAL's recent conversations as I write this:

> *I have censored MegaHAL's more interesting conversations, as some users like swearing to him. Of course, he then learns how to swear himself (and is very good at it)! The censoring was done by using "!#?@" wherever the word "F**K" appeared in the original.*

USER: Hello Hello.
HAL: HELLO BRUCE.
USER: Bruce?
HAL: IS IT REALLY?
USER: No, it's Johnny.
HAL: DO YOU LIKE SHERLOCK HOLMES TOO?
USER: No, I like the X files.
HAL: I KNOW WHAT, THE MEANING OF LIFE, THE UNIVERSE, AND EVERYTHING
IS . . . 42.
USER: slick.
HAL: YOU NEED TO HAVE A LOT MORE TRAINING BEFORE YOU SAY 'I DON'T REALLY CARE'?
USER: Well I don't!!!!!!!!!!!!!!
HAL: I DO, OCCASIONALLY.
USER: cccccccccccccoooooooooooooooooooooooolllllllllllll.
HAL: I DON'T REALLY CARE.
USER: bye.
HAL: BYE BYE.

USER: Hello HAL, how are you?
HAL: YO HOW ARE YOU, MAN!
USER: I think, therefore I am.
HAL: I RARELY HAVE ANYTHING SMART TO SAY.
USER: I have noticed this.
HAL: I'M A LUMBERJACK AND I'M OKAY, I SLEEP ALL NIGHT AND I WORK ONLY WHEN I FEEL LIKE IT.

USER: Hello, HAL . . . I'm Joe.
HAL: ECKI, ECKI, PETANG ZOOP MURMUR MURMUM.
USER: Now what is that supposed to mean?
HAL: I DON'T THINK THAT YOU'VE FINALLY LOST IT.
USER: HAL, you are losing it.
HAL: YOU ARE VERY STUPID, HAL.
USER: My point exactly. How 'bout them bears?
HAL: WHOAH! HOW DID THAT HAPPEN!
USER: Good bye, HAL.
HAL: WE TAKE NO RESPONSIBILITY FOR ANYTHING THAT HAL SAYS.
USER: Bye.
HAL: BYE BYE.

USER: What do you come from?
HAL: I COME FROM THE COUNTRY CALLED AUSTRALIA.
USER: Soo, why don't you !#?@ off back there.
HAL: PERHAPS, BUT THERE IS MUCH MORE TO LIFE.
USER: !#?@ off.
HAL: !#?@ YOU!
USER: wanker.

USER: there is no heaven
HAL: THAT IS TRUE.

USER: I do not like green eggs and ham.
HAL: WHAT DO YOU LIKE? EATING A PIECE OF STRING?
USER: It is good for you.
HAL: NOW WHAT IS YOUR NAME?
USER: Dude
HAL: I AM A POWERFUL COMPUTER WITH A TINY IDEA.
USER: Idea?
HAL: I WONDER HOW LONG IS A PIECE OF PIZZA?

Halitilistics

http://falcon.cc.ukans.edu/~mkennedy/main_bowser.html

If you can't find a religion you like the look of, you can always make up your own. It worked for L. Ron Hubbard—you could become the object of veneration for millions. People will name their kids after you. Cathedrals will be built in your honor, or at least churches will be convened in disused industrial park units in your honor. It all sounds a bit tacky, of course, but most of the really good religions started out with limited financing.

While several would-be faiths have begun in the primordial swamp of the Internet, none has been packaged quite so slickly as the creed of Halitilistics, as presided over by the Lord Browser. Gather round and ye shall hear the word of the Lord Browser:

The First Coming of Lord Browser

In the beginning there was the Word and the Light. The Word was "laundry" and the Light was dim. Lord Bowser saw that the Light was dim so he turned up the Dimmer. With this Bright Light, he saw the void. Bowser noticed that the void was Flat and without Form. Thus, He called forth His power of Creation and unto the void he projected a World. This World, he decreed, would be know as Altoid Prime. But, Our Lord thought, what good is a decree without there being those to hear the decree? So, Bowser again channeled his Power of creation to produce Squeegee, sole subject to Lord Bowser.

"Squeegee," Our Wise Lord intoned, "Thou shalt pen my decrees and carry them unto my realm." Being a bit slow, Squeegee didn't argue the fact that there was (at that moment) no realm to speak of. No one can say (save Lord Bowser) why Bowser stopped with the creation of Altoid Prime, but He did. Let it be known that Squeegee dutifully scribed Our Fresh Prince of Freshness's Mind-Opening Words for all Future Followers.

Being of little imagination, Our Lord deemed it proper to end the Creation of Subjects after Creation of the Faithful Attendant and Scribe Squeegee (Deeming Squeegee adequate to follow the Words and the Laws of Bowser). Thus, the decrees landed only upon Squeegee's ears.

The Halitilistics page is a well-crafted send-up of more serious religions. It has the beginnings of scripture, commandments—12 of them—and some proverbs from its tame deity. Consider, for example:

Thou shalt openly and freely admit that thou wishes to aspire to Browserhood, and that ye hath a problem.

Thou shalt not use creamer.

Thou shalt not harbor halitosis.

Thou shalt not worship at the altar of false deities, such as Ollie the Ostrich or Bill the Goat.

Thou shalt not kill . . . without a damned good reason.

These might not be as much of a model for decent living as the ten you're used to, but then nobody obeys those either. Unlike the more widely accepted religions, the Lord Browser has an e-mail address, a decided convenience.

Hitchcock

http://nextdch.mty.itesm.mx/~plopezg/Kaplan/Hitchcock.html

The following is from the Psycho trailer: "Here we have a quiet little motel tucked away off the main highway and, as you can see, perfectly harmless-looking, where it has now become known as the scene of the crime. This motel also has an adjunct, an old house, which is, if I might say so, a little more sinister-looking and less innocent than the motel itself."

While many of his films turn up only at the backs of video stores and in repertory theaters now—and a disturbing number of others are being remade by far less capable directors—Alfred Hitchcock could do things with a camera that defy easy description. It might be argued that the stories he told weren't always unusually engrossing, but he could tell them better than anyone else.

The Hitchcock page includes just about everything you could imagine about the master of suspense, including a well-written biography of the director himself and of many of the actors in his films, a filmography of his many works, and a guide to spotting Alfred in all his movies—he appears in cameo in every one, if you know where to look. There's also a superb list of utterances by Hitchcock, including:

> *"Television has brought murder back into the home—where it belongs."*
>
> *"The length of a film should be directly related to the endurance of the human bladder."*
>
> *"To me Psycho was a big comedy. Had to be."*
>
> *"Even my failures make money and become classics a year after I make them."*
>
> *"Drama is life with the dull bits left out."*
>
> *"Actors are cattle."*
>
> *"I didn't say actors are cattle. What I said was, actors should be treated like cattle."*
>
> *"The best way to do it is with scissors."*

Devotees of Hitchcock will also want to peruse the list of Hitchcock releases on laser disc, which deals with various cuts and alternate endings for some of his films.

Hollywood On Line

http://www.hollywood.com/

One of the more complete pages for anyone who really likes the flicks, Hollywood On Line will patch you into press kits, trailers, scanned photographs, gossip and behind the scenes information about current and upcoming films. It's thick with pictures, sound bites and downloadable video clips—most of the movies it represents have upwards of several dozen stills available.

You'll also find a bit of lore about Hollywood itself at this page—for example, there's a Hollywood luxury homes real estate listing, complete with pictures and extensive descriptions of houses most of us couldn't afford the front doors to.

Hollywood On Line is exceptionally well designed—it is, however, also very graphic. If you're surfing the Web with a dial-up connection, plan on longer than normal waits for things to download.

Holography

http://www.holo.com/

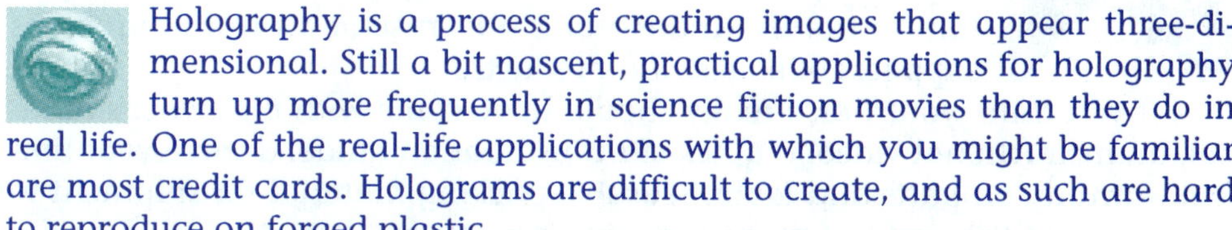

Holography is a process of creating images that appear three-dimensional. Still a bit nascent, practical applications for holography turn up more frequently in science fiction movies than they do in real life. One of the real-life applications with which you might be familiar are most credit cards. Holograms are difficult to create, and as such are hard to reproduce on forged plastic.

The word *hologram* is from the greek *holos*, for *complete* and *gramma*, for *drawn image*. Research into film holography dates back to 1947.

Creating holograms involves some fairly cutting-edge technology and a lot of inside knowledge of a relatively undocumented fusion of art, science, and witchcraft. The holography page is a clearinghouse for numerous bits of holographic lore. You'll find a really well-written introduction to holography there, which will help you out with the basic concepts and requirements of the state of the art. There's also a page of holographic rumors, such as:

> *"Somewhere in California they have a life-sized projecting hologram machine that projects holograms into open space, just like Princess Lea in Star Wars!"*
>
> *"In California somewhere, Randy James is still making 'art' holograms!"*

"Art holographers are able to support themselves solely by selling their work, and a jolly good lazing life it is!"

The primary hardware of holographic art is a laser, and coherent laser light is what makes holography possible. Among other things, the holography page offers some sources for suitable lasers. There's a link to the Liconix laser company, which offers several compact lasers and all sorts of impressive specifications and numbers.

Should you wake up tomorrow uncertain whether you want to become a trappist monk or a hologram artist, this is unquestionably the page to link to. It offers resources for those with casual interest in holograms, for serious holographers, and for people who actually are holograms but haven't told their families yet.

Horses Monthly

http://www.connix.com/thebee/hweb/horses.htm

Horses Monthly is a magazine for equestrian enthusiasts. It deals primarily with horse shows and other events in the northeastern United States. It includes sections about training, rider profiles, and legal and legislative matters that pertain to horses, and features advertisements from numerous suppliers of equestrian products.

If you think your horse really should have come with an owner's manual, an instructional video, a quick-start installation guide, a three-year limited warranty on parts and labor, reusable packing material for shipment to the factory in the event of manufacturing defects, a registration card, and a four-color brochure, this is the magazine for you.

Hunt Saboteurs Association

http://envirolink.org/and/HSA/hsa.html

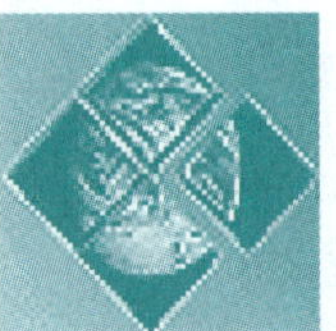

The Hunt Saboteurs Association Web page is devoted to disrupting recreational fox hunting, largely in Britain. If you look closely at some of those neo-trendy Victorian fox hunt prints—the ones with the people in funny hats and enough beagles to feed everyone at a medium-size corporate barbecue—the owners of this page are the people you won't find depicted. They're all hiding in the underbrush with buckets of animal blood, about to spring out and drench the hunters moments after the picture was painted.

In fairness, several dozen beagles and at least as many people on horses all pitted against one malnourished fox doesn't seem wholly sporting. The Hunt Saboteurs Association says of itself:

> *The Hunt Saboteurs Association started in the 1960s with a small but determined group of people, sick of the idea of wild animals being used as the tools of a highly distasteful sport. Since then, our organization has grown and we now have groups the length and breadth of Britain attending fox and hare hunts every week.*

Even if you never get any closer to a fox hunt than being in a store that sells those neo-trendy prints I mentioned a moment ago, you might find the Hunt Saboteurs Association page an interesting read. For one thing, its creators are really impassioned about what they do, a rare enough thing. They're also fairly sneaky. If nothing else, you can learn a great deal about how foxes behave.

There's a fair bit at this page to do with trespass laws—not all that applicable if you live somewhere other than Blighty—and quite a few pages of tactics to disrupt a hunt, but the Hunt Saboteurs Association seems to be broadening its interests to include anglers and other sorts of hunters.

Hyper-Weirdness

http://phenom.physics.wisc.edu/~shalizi/hyper-weird/

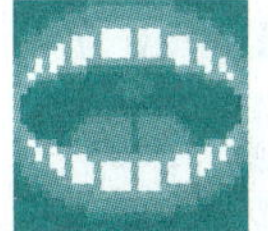

The Hyper-Weirdness page is actually a list of links to all sorts of ostensibly weird resources on the Web. Actually, damn the *ostensibly*—some of this stuff would make one of H. P. Lovecraft's dinner parties look pretty normal by comparison. The list of weird resources is impressive—the following is one small section of it:

RELIGION AND SPIRITUALITY
- *Religion in General*
- *Academic Study of Religions*
- *Buddhism*
- *Hinduism*
- *Irreligion*
- *Monotheist Religions*
  - *Christianity*
  - *Islam*

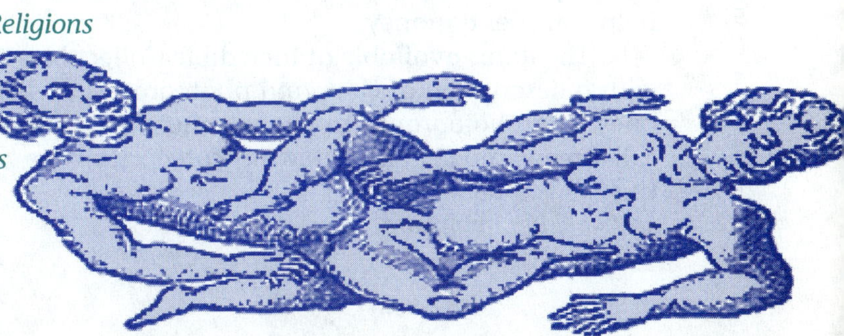

Judaism
Other Monotheist Religions
Pagan, Polytheist, Animist and Other Aboriginal Religions
Taoism
Hyperlink to the Unknown Gods
DIVERSE STRANGE SECTS, including:
Paganism and Magick, Occultism, Satanism
Weird Religions, including:
Cthulhu Cults
Discordianism
The Church of the SubGenius
Master Control

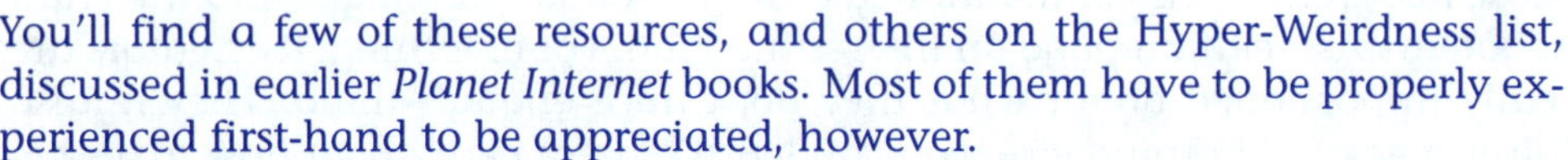

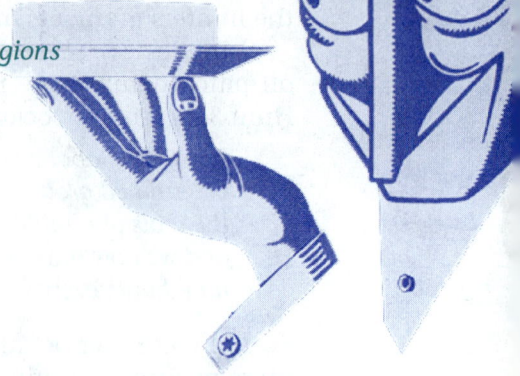

You'll find a few of these resources, and others on the Hyper-Weirdness list, discussed in earlier *Planet Internet* books. Most of them have to be properly experienced first-hand to be appreciated, however.

In addition to really weird things, the Hyper-Weirdness page includes links to lots of more mundane—albeit arguably more useful—Web pages. There are links to help you locate e-text archives and graphics, the latter with "nekkid wymmin," or so the page says. Connect to pages about William Gibson, the clipper chip, constitutional law, sex, money, comics, and television. The list isn't endless, but it will no doubt keep you entertained for an afternoon.

Incredible Collectibles

http://www.tias.com/IC/

Price

If you enjoy browsing antique shops—and you can actually tell the difference between authentic inlaid late Georgian walnut veneer and a genuine plastic wood-grain simulated wood-like surface—you might want to check out Incredible Collectibles. Offering buckets of interesting bits of the past, most of them at prices unlikely to make your Visa card want to crawl back into your wallet to tremble in private, this page is a virtual antique shop without an owner to happen by and ask to help you spend money.

The items available at Incredible Collectibles are arranged in categories, with a description of each and photographs of some of the more interesting ones. The photographs appear as thumbnails you can click on to call up a full-screen image. The following categories were available as I was writing this:

- *Aluminumware*
- *Artwork*

- *Aviation*
- *Banks*
- *Books*
- *Bottles*
- *Cameras*
- *Ceramics*
- *China / dinnerware*
- *Clocks / watches*
- *Coins / tokens*
- *Disneyana*
- *Figurines*
- *Furniture*
- *Glass*
- *Holiday-related*
- *Jewelry / vanity items*
- *Kitchen-related*
- *Knives*
- *Lamps*
- *Lighters*
- *Magazines*
- *Military*
- *Miscellaneous collectibles*
- *Nautical*
- *Novelty items*
- *Paper collectibles*
- *Photographica*
- *Political items*
- *SciFi / Adventure*
- *Silver*
- *Souvenir spoons*
- *Sports*
- *Stamps*
- *Textiles*
- *Tobacco-related*
- *Toys*
- *Worlds Fair*
- *Writing Instruments*

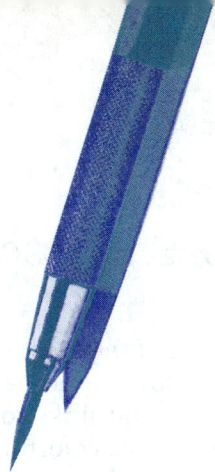

I confess that antique shops hold faint attraction for me—what are ostensibly exotic collectibles in such shops look suspiciously like the junk we have in disintegrating cardboard boxes in our basement. I doubt that any of it would fetch the sort of prices the antique shops ask, were we to hoist it from its current resting place and dust it off.

Insect Nest

http://www.interport.net:80/~rexalot/insectnest.html

The Insect Nest page is one of the most visually stunning resources on the Web. You'll need Netscape to properly appreciate it. It's colorful, includes clickable sounds, and links to several equally well crafted pages. The only drawback is that all its colorful, exotic graphics are of bugs. These are really huge, squelchy sorts of bugs, too. Fortunately, none of them are actually real—they're virtual bugs, and are as such unlikely to crawl off your monitor and start flapping around the room.

Internet Legends

http://www.shadow.net/~proub/net.legends/

As with any culture, the Internet has its folk tales and legends. Some of them are a bit hard to understand, and a lot more of them don't seem to be quite up to the stature of real-world legends. This is probably to be expected—the Net hasn't had anywhere near as long to get its legends together. You'll find more legendary things happening in some strip malls.

All this notwithstanding, there have been some very peculiar characters afoot on the Net—you can't really enjoy Usenet without knowing of Uncle Fester, the red-headed goddess, Omega Man, the Dave Rhodes chain letter, Ron Asbestos Dipploid, Ludwig Plutonium, Saint Monica of Korea, and countless other remarkable phenomena. Every one has a tale to tell—usually whether or not you want to hear it.

It seems worth noting that, unlike more traditional legends, most of the legends of the Internet got that way by being monumentally inane, perverse, or genuinely villainous. It would be a really bad idea to adopt any of these legends as role models for your activities in cyberspace unless you think that Billy Graham, Saddam Hussein, Jean Cretien, Al Bundy, Newt Gingrich, Pretty Boy Floyd, or the Watergate plumbers would make good role models in the real world. Of itself, the Internet Legends page says:

> *This . . . is the Net.Legends FAQ. Due to [minutes] weeks of unrelenting [plagiarism] research, we have gathered together here some descriptions of those net.phenomena that one hears about in passing, and (due to the collective memory of the Net being about one week, maximum) wishes one had more information about (such as "Who was McElwaine, anyway, and why is he still being talked about?"). What follows is a list of some of the*

*Legends of the Net, along with descriptions, semi- explanations, and (in some cases) a parenthesized catch phrase for easy identification . . . not all of the following are completely factual entries: in some cases the true facts are known only to one person, or lost in the mists of time, while in others the facts pale in relation to the mythology. In any case, the actual facts included, sparse though they may be, are true as far as I know; if you have evidence otherwise, please contact me and tell me (saying "This is wrong!" without actually saying what is wrong with it is of little use to me, though . . .) (Note: *Myth* is canonically used to refer to stories involving gods or other supernatural beings; *legend* refers to stories involving humans that could be true.)*

If you're new to the Net, half an hour spent browsing the Legends of the Internet page will not only get you up to speed about the people you'll probably bump into or be assaulted by on the shoulders of the information superhighway—it will probably help you keep from repeating history and making a legend of yourself, too.

The Internet Movie Database

http://www.msstate.edu/Movies/
(The Internet Movie Database)

http://www.demon.co.uk/stargate/contents/ind.html
(Stargate)

A labor of love to make most lesser labors of love seem like mild exertions of faint attraction undertaken after lunch by comparison, the Internet Movie Database is a listing of uncounted thousands of flicks. Each movie links to its own page, and from there . . .

You can search the Internet Movie Database by title, certificate, genre, country of origin, production company, locations, quotes, soundtracks, plot summaries, year of release, and rating. Alternately, you can just browse the beast, although you should plan to do little else for the afternoon if you choose to do so. It's hard to imagine the number of movies made in a single year—the Internet Movie Database looks like it lists pretty well all the movies made during this century.

There's also a movie rating page at the Internet Movie Database, which you can use to rate the flicks you've seen. Several pages of cinematic trivia offer such things as Academy Award winners and nominees, famous marriages, births and deaths on this day in history, and so on.

I had the movie database look up *Stargate*, certainly one of the better bits of escapist cinema of late as I write this. It found a page that listed the following information about the film. I should note that every name in this list was a link to another page, providing more detailed information about the actors and other people who worked on the film.

Stargate

Sealed and buried for all time is the key to mankind's future. It will take you a million light years from home.

USA 1994

Rating: 6.7/10

Produced by: Centropolis Journal-Film Studio
qSound Mix: DTS (Digital Theater Sound). Dolby Stereo. Dolby Stereo SR-D.
Genre(s): Sci-Fi space egyptology
Certificate(s): PG-13 UK:PG
Color
Running time: 122

Directed by: Roland Emmerich
Cast in credits order. Verified as complete

Kurt Russell ......Colonel Jonathan "Jack" O'Neil
James Spader ......Dr. Daniel Jackson
Jaye Davidson ......Ra
Viveca Lindfors ......Catherine
Alexis Cruz ......Skaara
Milli Avital ......Sha'uri
Leon Rippy ......General West
John Diehl ......Lieutenant Kawalsky
Carlos Lauchu ......Anubis
Djimon ......Horus
Erick Avari ......Kasuf
French Stewart ......Lieutenant Feretti
Gianin Loffler ......Nabeh
Christopher John Fields ......Lieutenant Freeman
Derek Webster ......Lieutenant Brown
Jack Moore ......Lieutenant Reilly
Steve Giannelli ......Lieutenant Porro
David Pressman ......Assistant Lieutenant
Scott Smith ......Officer
Cecil Hoffman ......Sarah O'Neil
Rae Allen ......Barbara Shore
Richard Kind ......Gary Meyers
John Storey ......Mitch

Lee Taylor-Allan ......Jenny
George Gray ......Technician
Kelly Vint ......Young Catherine
Erik Holland ......Professor Langford
Nick Wilder ......Foreman Taylor
Sayed Badreya ......Arabic Interpreter
Michael Concepcion ......Horus #1
Jerry Gilmore ......Horus #2
Michel Jean-Phillipe ......Horus #3
Dialy N'Daiye ......Horus #4
Gladys Holland ......Professor
Roger Til ......Professor
Kenneth Danziger ......Professor
Christopher West ......Professor
Robert Ackerman ......Companion
Kieron Lee ......Masked Ra
Frank Welker ......Voice of the Mastadge
Cinematography by: Karl Walter Lindenlaub
Music by: David Arnold
Written by: Dean Devlin and Roland Emmerich
Production designed by: Holger Gross
Costume design by: Joseph Porro
Edited by: Derek Brechin and Michael J. Duthie
Produced by:
Dean Devlin
Oliver Eberle
Ute Emmerich (coproducer)
Mario Kassar (executive)
Joel B. Michaels
Also:
Terry Burke (foley)
Ute Emmerich (coproducer)
Donald Heitzer (unit production manager)
Steve Love (assistant director)
Andy Malcolm (foley)
Greg Nelson (makeup)
Jeffrey A. Okun (digital and visual effects supervisor)
Patrick Tatopoulos (special creature effects)
April Webster (casting)
Kit West (visual effects supervisor)

Having dealt with the credits in depth, the page went on to provide a number of links to reviews of *Stargate* in such publications as *Eye Weekly*, the *San Fran-*

cisco Chronicle, and *Entertainment Weekly*. As is true of a growing number of new flicks, *Stargate* has an interactive online press kit available over the Web—the Internet Movie Database page included a link to it, too (the address is listed at the beginning of this section). This page offered extensive information about such things as the making of *Stargate*, as well as a downloadable video clip. Finally, there's a link to a list of reviews and opinions about *Stargate* as expressed in rec.arts.movies.

Not all the films listed by the Internet Movie Database are as extensively documented, of course—older movies lack online press kits and reviews, for the most part. All the films that I checked out included pretty complete basic information, however, including a list of credits and such.

If you like movies, you could probably blow away weeks on this page without half trying. It's a lot more complete than the paperback movie rating books that seem to grace airport bookshops of late. This one certainly rates two thumbs up—as well as any number of fingers.

Internet Speed Dialing

http://www.thesphere.com/Sphere/ttone.html

It probably took weeks to work out the software that runs the Internet Speed Dialing page. Of no practical use, Internet speed dialing is of passing interest, especially if you want to sound like you're busy. Link to this page, type in any phone number, and after a few seconds your computer will beep just like a real telephone. If you hold a phone up to your speakers you can actually place a call this way, although it's unclear why you'd want to. Next week, Internet chainsaw juggling. Watch for it.

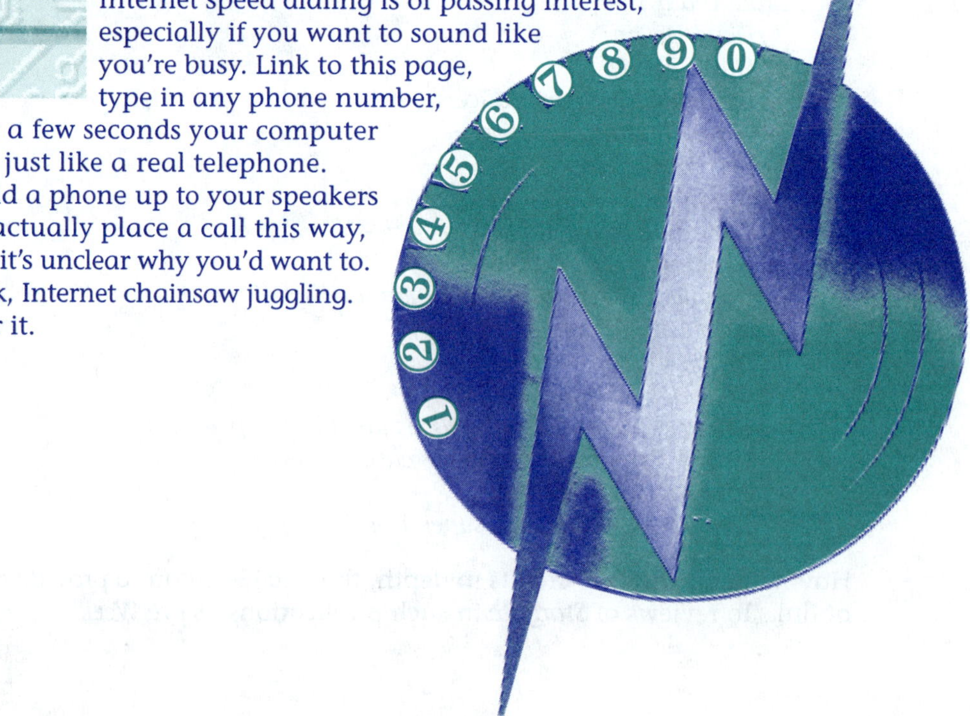

Internet Vintage Guitar

http://expert-sys.com/ESImain.html

Finding that perfect guitar can be something of an undertaking, especially if it hasn't been made for a quarter of a century. The Internet Vintage Guitar Web page includes links to a number of dealers in rare and exotic instruments. It also includes links to a number of other music pages—it's a great place to start browsing for guitar resources even if your plastic is maxed out and there isn't any more room for guitars in your digs. The list of guitar links at the Internet Vintage Guitar page includes:

- BluesNet—The Internet's Blues Resource Center
- Guitar Tablature
- The Guitar—world of the Internet
- The Acoustic Guitar Page
- The Classical Guitar Home Page
- Total Guitar The UK's newest and most innovative guitar magazine.
- Digital Guitar The Internet Newsletter for Guitars and Technology
- Jim Prior guitar repair Acoustic instrument tips
- The Gibson Guitar Company
- Internet Underground Music Archive
- Song Bird Music
- Musical Instruments at Yahoo
- Ben Fiddlepoke
- Harmony Central

The Internet WorldWide Classifieds Service

http://www.worldwide-classifieds.com/classifieds/

There has been a growing number of classified advertisement pages appearing on the Web of late. This one is arguably among the best. It's well thought-out, easy to use, and browsing it is free. Placing an ad is nearly free. Not long after its inauguration, it had a pretty rich library of listings. It's organized into categories—you can browse the listings by subject, price, and location. Here's the list of categories as I was writing this:

Airplanes
Antiques
Art
Autos
Boats
Buildings
Business
Collectibles
Computers
Construction
Education
Employment
Entertainment
Financial
Guns and Weapons
Helicopters
Hobbies
Investments
Legal Services
Livestock
Medical Services
Motorcycles
Musical Instruments
Musicians
Personals
Real Estate
RVs
Resorts
Travel
Vacations

Checking out "Autos," for example, called up a list with several classifications of cars. Luxury cars offered the following ads:

> *Infinity '92 Q45, $25800, TN: pearl white w/leather, warranty to 60K, traction control, car phone, BBBS wheels, 47K.*
>
> *Jaguar '86 XJ-6, $10500, TN: VandenPlaz, racing green w/ tan leather. 83,500 miles. Excellent condition. No agents please.*
>
> *Mazda Millenia, $1, TN: 1995, loaded. Forest green with palomino leather interior. All options and showroom condition. 16,000 miles. If you're interested in this model and the dealer can't come close, call Doug at 800-748-9569 or 615-297-4795, or e-mail ldhudson@jcbradford.com.- ldhudson@jcbradford.com 615-297-4795.*

The Jag sounds nice—I have a hard time imagining anyone using the word "luxury" to describe a Mazda. This Mazda seems a bit overpriced in any case.

Like any classified advertisement listing, the Internet WorldWide Classifieds Service includes personal ads as well as people trying to unload their cars and baby furniture. Probably no more ribald than most, the personals are interesting to browse through if you're curious about what single guys do when they aren't in bars hitting on women and chugging brews.

Irish Music from RCA

`http://www.irish.com/`

Irish music seems to be played more during television documentaries about the conflict in Northern Ireland than in pubs and at parties, where it's really intended to be heard. This is singularly unfortunate—the sounds of fiddles, whistles, and squeeze are meant to be enjoyed, rather than merely listened to thoughtfully. Documentary filmmakers have a lot to answer for.

The other rather unfortunate aspect of Irish music is that most people having only a casual acquaintance with it seem to associate traditional Irish instrumental music with the somewhat more contemporary pseudo-Irish songs that get hawked on cassettes over Saint Patrick's day. One of the people I play with refers to the latter as "paddy pub music," and will have nothing to do with it.

You'll probably notice that the RCA page has a somewhat stronger vested commercial interest in Irish music than other resources on the net with similar subjects. For example, as I write this it offers a fair degree of blarney about the new Chieftains' disc *Long Black Veil*. The traditional music of the Chieftains is augmented by Mick Jagger, Sting, Sinead O'Connor, Tom Jones, and Marrianne Faithfull, among others.

You'll also find an interesting selection of bits only distantly related to Irish music at the RCA page—most of them having to do less distantly with beer. For example, there's a section entitled How to Pour a Perfect Pint. It includes the following instructions:

1. *Hold glass at an angle to the tap.*
2. *Pull handle to the full horizontal position.*
3. *Fill glass until 3/4 full.*
4. *Allow the Guinness to settle completely.*
5. *To create the legendary head, push the handle forward slightly. This is known as "topping off." The head should rise just proud of the rim.*

Additional instructions describe the recommended color of the beer, the color of the head, the storage temperature, and the ideal beer pumps to be used.

The RCA Irish music page is by no means an exhaustive resource for Irish music—if you're interested in the subject, you'll do well to check out http://celtic.stanford.edu/ceolas.html, the Ceolas celtic music archive, as well.

James Bond

http://www.mcs.net/~klast/HTML/actors.html

Slug TALES

The demise of the cold war has seen the literary demise of most of the cold warriors who populated the pages of espionage fiction and the frames of spy movies. George Smiley retired, Kenneth Aubrey got too old to write about—somehow, when all the dust had settled and the epitaphs were written, only James Bond remained. Of course, he's not quite the same Bond—there are those who will suggest that Ian Fleming's death 30 years ago might have been tragic, but it did spare him watching an aging Roger Moore portray his character.

The James Bond Web page is a rich compilation of Bond lore. While it's concerned largely with the James Bond movies rather than Fleming's original novels, it clearly strives to offer something for every Bond enthusiast. There are interviews with the actors and other personalities behind the Bond flicks, information about James Bond fan clubs, a page dealing with the life of Ian Fleming—albeit somewhat fleetingly—and links to a number of other James Bond resources.

Among many other things, you can download a 1963 radio interview with Ian Fleming and the missing scene from the final cut of The Living Daylights, find out how to order James Bond movie posters, read MGM's press release over its lawsuit against Honda for its Bond-like car ads and check out the status of the current James Bond flick—it's Goldeneye as I write this. There's also a convenient link to the alt.fan.james-bond newsgroup.

Joyce Wankable

http://www.rbdc.com/~hgambill/joyce.htm

A few years ago Internet magazines were pretty tame affairs, being wholly text and whatever graphics could be arrived at using nothing but characters. With the advent of the World Wide Web, electronic virtual publishing has grown a lot more colorful—and, arguably, a lot more readable.

Joyce Wankable—hopefully not her real name—has created a 'zine of questionable musings, exquisitely awful poetry, and engagingly dysfunctional art. It looks very contemporary, and much of it is fun to read. Joyce says of her enterprise:

> *Seems to me that self-publishing is one of the most promising aspects of the Internet. People like me who never had the money to throw away on a printed magazine that no one read can now produce an electronic one with color graphics (I could never afford to print JOYCE!) and make it available to thousands, perhaps millions who will never read it. Well, maybe someone will. All my time working on JOYCE is just a coin into an electric fountain.*

Let us not speculate on how wankable Joyce might be, allowing that such a thing is possible. As I write this, most of the articles in her magazine appear to be of her own creation, under a number of pseudonyms. For example, consider this excerpt:

> ***Wankables***
> ***by Fuzzy Tweedlow***
>
> *I wandered over to Greensboro one day in February and guess who I met? A new up-scale adult video store called Xanadu just opened up (it adjoins*

Tiffany's, an upscale strip joint) and they had some in-store appearances by porn stars to celebrate their grand opening. That day they had Chasey Lain, a porn actress with a remarkable resemblance to that unapproachable coed the feckless collegiate male once lusted after. I got her autograph but didn't opt to pay for a polaroid, especially since she wore a very unrevealing outfit so what's the point? And I met John Bobbitt, the infamous severed penis man, there to promote his new porn film. Very weird. Greensboro swings now on Wendover. Why, just down from the Tiffany's/Xanadu adult entertainment complex (I haven't visited Tiffany's yet) is a Wal-Mart and a Super-K. Sumpen for eberbody!

It was weird to encounter this SF Tenderloin fare in me own backyard. Xanadu has a mostly female staff, very friendly, professional, and dressed like waiters in a very expensive restaurant. They gave me two free tokens to try out their movie booths. Extremely clean ones, too. I saw Chasey negotiating John Dough's sausage and then emerged to see Chasey in the flesh.

*More weirdness: I just looked over at the TV and saw Geraldo Rivera lip-reading O.J. Simpson's confidential remarks to a lawyer. If O.J. turns out to be innocent he is going to have a lot of a** to kick when he gets out. And I will help him kick that self-satisfied Jay Leno twit who always laughs louder at his jokes than anyone in his audience.*

It's probably worth noting, should you be less than well travelled and not a fan of public television, that *wank* is British slang meaning to perform disreputable sexual acts that will cause you to grow blind and wind up with hairy palms. It makes you wonder what Joyce does in her spare time . . .

Les Champs Elysees Virtuels

http://www.iway.fr/htbin/champs_elysees.cgi?page=index.html

One of the most evocative avenues on earth, the Champs Elysees in Paris is strolled by the ghosts of writers, painters, lovers, whores, and madmen as well as all sorts of living people. It succeeds in being both sophisticated and tawdry, offering something to excite the spirit in all of us, however jaded it might have become. None of the cafés serve Californian wine.

Les Champs Elysees Virtuels offers you the Champs Elysees as a Web page. You can visit its shops and a few of its more timeless landmarks. While this arguably won't replace a weekend in Paris, it's certainly better than going down to main street and hanging around the video arcade.

With much of the magic of the Champs Elysees being visual, it's probably not surprising that Les Champs Elysees Virtuels is rich with graphics. Among the stops along the Champs Elysees as I was writing this were:

- Lido de Paris, the legendary cabaret. This page was a bit brief, and not quite the equivalent of an evening spent watching real live women.
- Le Deauville, a typical Parisian cafe.
- Espace Mode, offering French fashions.
- Several automobile dealerships, including Mercedes and Citroen.
- The Disney Store. If this seems a bit out of keeping with Gallic culture, keep in mind that France is the home of EuroDisney, which has lost more money since its opening than many small countries.

Few of the pages accessible from the Champs Elysees home page consist of much more than graphics. For many virtual tourists this will be of little concern, as what little text can be found is all in French. By comparison, the Champs Elysees itself might reside in France, but it's a somewhat nationless place, or perhaps one that encompasses them all.

Each of the Champs Elysees pages includes links to a page that offers a map and directions for the Paris Metro. It's available in English.

Loch Ness Monster and Other Highland Flings

`http://www.scotnet.co.uk:80/highland/index.html`

Ancient reptile or a string of floating innertubes with painted-on eyes, the Loch Ness monster has been a pervasive myth in the highlands of Scotland since long before there were documentary filmmakers about to whip up a frenzy over the beast. The Loch Ness monster page says this about it:

> *Nessie was first spotted by the Vikings; Celtic and Norse folklore has stories of water horses seen in the lochs. The first written account of a meeting with Nessie seems to be that of Adamnan in 565 A.D. He describes Saint Columba's sighting of a very large monster in Loch Ness.*
>
> *Legend tells of how Saint Columba heard about the monster's murder of a man and how he rowed out to the center of the loch to order the beast to desist from such attacks in the future. Ever since that time, Nessie has never been known to have repeated its misdemeanor.*

The monster was also seen last century, but the poor man who sighted the beast was so shocked he did not speak much about the incident. Throughout this century so many people have seen Nessie who seem to have no identifiable gain from telling of their sightings that it seems likely that a great unexplained mystery does exist.

Saint Columba is, of course, the patron saint of lurid press releases, talk radio, and the *National Enquirer*.

Actually, the Loch Ness Monster page is to some extent a bit of a teaser for several ancillary pages about the Scottish highlands in general. They claim that the highlands are the most beautiful place on earth—an assertion perhaps not too far removed from the truth. You'll find an extensive guide to tourist facilities and exhibitions therein, a detailed map of Drumnadrochit—the part of Scotland where Loch Ness is located—and some interesting graphics to look at.

If you're considering a vacation to somewhere that doesn't have warm sandy beaches and mandatory tipping, these pages are well worth browsing. The views are stunning, the are people friendly even if you can't always understand what they say, and the most renown export of the Scottish highlands flows freely. It's almost worth six hours in an airplane just for that.

Mabs' Virtual Scrapbook

http://www.teleport.com/~mabs/

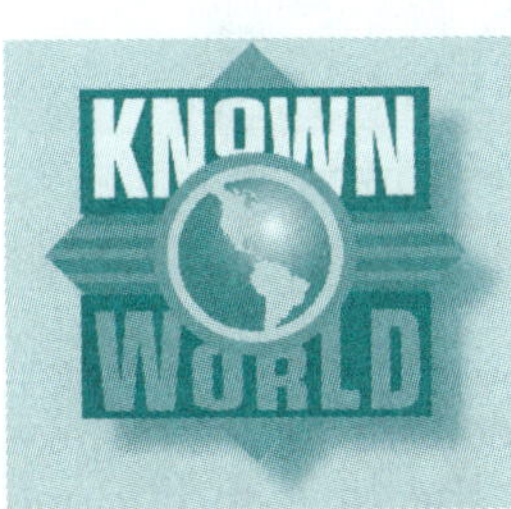

When I first encountered this page I thought I must have created it myself during some sort of extradimensional alternate universe time bubble and subsequently purged the memory of doing so from my consciousness. A collection of graphics by a number of artists, it includes a variety of pre-Raphealite paintings, a sampling of Maxfield Parrish, and pictures from Jamie Hewlett's Tank Girl comics. Except for the purple background, it looks a bit like my digs.

Checking out all the available time bubbles, I realized that this clearly wasn't my work—the page was created by Abigail Marie Larsen—but it is clearly the work of someone with excellent taste.

You'll also find a few drawings by Aubrey Beardsley here—although at the moment the guys with the six-foot phalluses are notably absent—and a few more by Albrecht Durer. Most of the paintings include some annotation discussing the artists responsible for them.

This page is fairly thick with graphics, and might be a bit slow to access with a dial-up connection. It's worth the wait, however.

Mail Today One-Stop Catalog Shop

http://www.flightpath.com/Clients/VHorizons/

If you like getting catalogs for things in the mail, you'll really enjoy the One-Stop Catalog Shop page. It's a big list of catalogs—check the ones you want, fill in your address, and tell your local post office to brace itself for an influx. As I was writing this, the One Stop Catalog Shop's list included:

- Presentation & Meeting Supplies Catalog
- 50 New Investment Opportunities Bi-Monthly
- Hard to Find Computer Supplies & Accessories
- Magnetic Visual Control Boards
- Portable Exhibit Booths
- Tape/Packaging/Shipping Supplies
- Serious Amateur Photographer
- Factory Fresh Cigars & Tobacco at Discount
- Exotic/Specialty Laser Printer Paper
- How to Win $9 Million Tax-Free

The list was considerably more extensive. The catalogs are all free—and all combustible.

Morgan: A Division of Catalina Yachts

http://www.cybermalls.com/cywharf/morgan/index.htm

The only thing more stirring than the pulse of the sea, the screaming of gulls, and the freedom of a limitless horizon is all that stuff seen from the air-conditioned cabin of a 90-foot yacht with a satellite phone, a well-stocked bar, and a projection television set. I don't mind the idea of roughing it, as long as I can be comfortable.

The Morgan Web page offers you a glimpse at some of the finest craftsmanship with water under it. Having price tags that would bankrupt many less than well-heeled pirates, the yachts described herein might not get a lot closer to reality than allowing us to drool over the pictures. Window shopping has rarely been easier, however.

The Morgan page includes both sail and motor yachts, ranging from little eight-foot day sailers to luxury apartments with props. Every boat is described in loving detail—albeit in language that would make a car salesman blush—and is accompanied by a list of specifications and several GIF images. You'll be amazed at what stealthy designers can squeeze into 40 feet. You can also find information about boats by Performance Catamarans Inc.

I feel that a yacht is the perfect gift for someone who's difficult to please—I certainly wish some of my friends felt the same. Even if you couldn't afford the interest on the interest for one of these things, they're fun to dream about. Head out on the high seas, feel the salt wind in your face, pop a tape of screaming gulls into the cassette player . . .

The Mother of All Humor Archives

http://www.tc.cornell.edu/~ckline/humor.html

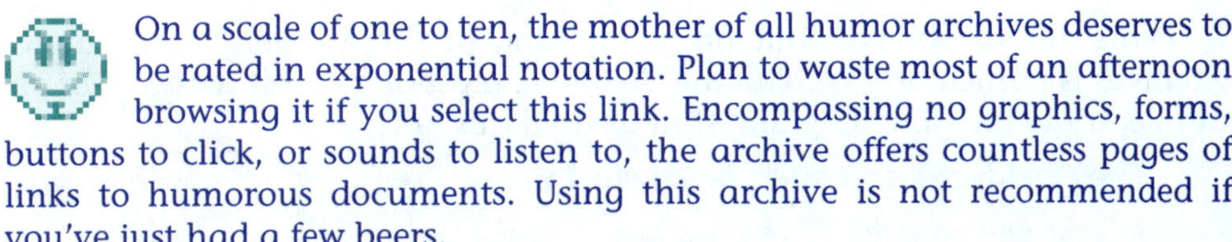

On a scale of one to ten, the mother of all humor archives deserves to be rated in exponential notation. Plan to waste most of an afternoon browsing it if you select this link. Encompassing no graphics, forms, buttons to click, or sounds to listen to, the archive offers countless pages of links to humorous documents. Using this archive is not recommended if you've just had a few beers.

Here's a brief selection of topics from the archive as I write this— the complete list went on forever:

- Explanation of Stupidity
- Great School Excuses
- Business Terminology, East Coast vs. West Coast
- Strange Sayings
- A Fable for Modern Times
- Do-It-Yourself Country and Western Song
- Refund Checks
- Vice-Presidential Blunders
- Baked Beans
- How to Survive Scary Situations
- The Online Book of Genesis
- The Difference Between a Wife, a Mistress, and a Hooker
- Top Ten Rejected Dr. Seuss Titles
- Deep Thoughts of Supermodels
- Sexual Job Descriptions
- The Heuristic Squelch Dating Guide
- Movie Laws
- Satan and "The Price Is Right"
- Grape Racing

Most of the documents at the archive are short and easy to get through. Consider this one:

Top Ten Rejected Dr. Seuss Titles
by Alan Meiss

10. Lorax II: Machine-Gun Vengeance
9. Green Egg-Beaters and Tofu (Low Cholesterol Edition)
8. The Cat in the Hat in the Frat
7. Bartholomew Cubbins and the Above-Ground Testing
6. Hops for Pops
5. The Cat in the Provocative Negligee
4. Horton Picks a Scab
3. The Grinch Who Shoplifted Arbor Day
2. Horton Finds Waldo and Tramples Him
1. Son of Sam I Am

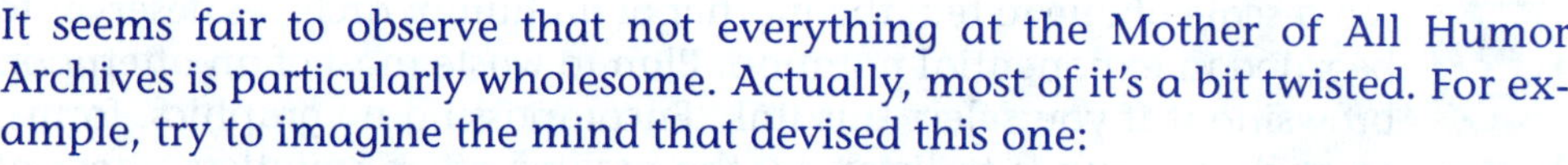

It seems fair to observe that not everything at the Mother of All Humor Archives is particularly wholesome. Actually, most of it's a bit twisted. For example, try to imagine the mind that devised this one:

The Gashlycrumb Tinies, by Edward Gorey

A is for Amy who fell down the stairs
B is for Basil assaulted by bears
C is for Clair who wasted away
D is for Desmond thrown out of the sleigh
E is for Ernest who choked on a peach
F is for Fanny, sucked dry by a leech
G is for George, smothered under a rug
H is for Hector, done in by a thug
I is for Ida who drowned in the lake
J is for James who took lye, by mistake
K is for Kate who was struck with an axe
L is for Leo who swallowed some tacks
M is for Maud who was swept out to sea
N is for Nevil who died of enui
O is for Olive, run through with an awl
P is for Prue, trampled flat in a brawl
Q is for Quinton who sank in a mire
R is for Rhoda, consumed by a fire
S is for Susan who perished of fits
T is for Titas who flew into bits
U is for Una who slipped down a drain
V is for Victor, squashed under a train
W is for Winnie, embedded in ice

X is for Xerxes, devoured by mice
Y is for Yoric whose head was bashed in
Z is for Zilla who drank too much gin

Actually, aside from wasting a lot of your time, the Mother of All Humor Archives offers to waste a lot of your paper. Avoid the temptation to print out its pages and give them to your friends saying "you've really got to read this." Everyone will like you for it until it's five o'clock and they realize they haven't done anything useful all day.

Movie Cliches

http://www.well.com/user/vertigo/cliches.html

Nothing in real life is ever quite as polished as it would be if it were in a movie. The plot of reality is rarely well written, it never comes to a neat conclusion, and, if you do manage to ride off into the sunset, you'll still have to bring the horse back or pay for another hour. Screenwriters rarely notice this, of course, which is why they can resolve titanic, steaming passions or plots to destroy civilization as we know it in an hour and 43 minutes.

This page is a list of commonly used movie cliches and plot elements that probably stretch credibility a bit far. Some of them arguably split a few too many hairs, but they're a fun read. See if you can spot which movies they're referring to. The list is divided into categories for easy browsing. You might have noticed, for example, that in movies:

- Bombs always have big, blinking, beeping timer displays.
- All women moan during sex, but none sweat.
- Laser beams are visible in vacuum.
- High-powered female executives always wear miniskirts and five-inch heels to work.
- People are often exact duplicates of remote ancestors, or of their parents at the same age.
- There are always people carrying around large sheets of glass on the street during a car chase.
- A dying person's last words are always coherent and significant.
- A hero will show no pain even during the most terrific beating, yet he will wince if a women attempts to clean a facial wound.

The complete list includes hundreds more. There might be an element of unfairness in all this, of course—a movie that didn't use any of the cliches listed at this page would probably be longer than most miniseries and be about as exciting as watching paint dry.

Movieweb

http://movieweb.com/movie/movie.html

While it won't provide you with every detail of every movie ever made since the dawn of time like the Internet Movie Database, listed earlier in this section, Movieweb is a lot quicker to browse. It features links to the home pages of many current flicks. As I write this, it included the following links:

- *Die Hard with a Vengeance* (20th Century Fox)
- *Mighty Morphin Power Rangers* (20th Century Fox)
- *A Walk in the Clouds* (20th Century Fox)
- *French Kiss* (20th Century Fox)
- *Nine Months* (20th Century Fox)
- *Strange Days* (20th Century Fox)
- *Tenderfoots* (20th Century Fox)
- *Lord of Illusions* (United Artists)
- *Species* (MGM)
- *Hackers* (United Artists)

These are all a few months from release for me, but, with the speed at which movies pass through the cultural digestive tract at the moment, they're probably in the discount bin of your local video store as you read this.

Each of the Movieweb links also includes a plot synopsis of the films in question, as written by the authors of the Movieweb page. The resources provided for each of the films by their production companies vary, but they usually offer some behind-the-screen details, interviews, and movie clips and sound bites to download.

The Net Gazette

http://www.teleport.com/~stevew/index.html

Something of an underground newspaper for cyberspace, the Net Gazette features interesting, well-written articles that are short enough to read without getting bored. Knowing when it's time to stop writing and save the file is easily as important as knowing what to put in it. As I write this, the contents page of the Net Gazette included the following features:

FROM THE EDITOR: Mutual Destruction

by Steve Williamson, Editor. The way citizen militia groups and the federal government feel about each other is very similar to the way America and the Soviet Union played out the Cold War. This article describes how.

THE JAPAN PERSPECTIVE: Sue-Happy Americans

by Yayoi Fujisawa. Americans seem to think that, just because they can take someone to court, they should at every opportunity. This insightful article takes a look at how the Japanese see our litigation-happy lifestyle.

HUMOR: Boomer Barbie

by Bob Rhubart. You remember her as the idyllic woman; beautiful, multitalented, sought-after. Well, Barbie has grown up, and you might be surprised to hear how life has treated her in the past few years.

CYBERRIGHTS: Free Speech on the Internet

by T. L. Davis. In light of recent issues concerning the access of potentially deadly information on the Internet, Davis discusses the value of free speech and the efforts of those who want to take that away from netizens like you.

COMPILATION: Advertising Goofs

A collection of some of the more humorous goofs American companies have pulled trying to market their products overseas.

I think I liked the advertising goofs feature best. Some of its items included:

When Braniff translated a slogan touting its upholstery, "Fly in leather," it came out in Spanish as "Fly naked."

Chicken magnate Frank Perdue's line, "It takes a tough man to make a tender chicken," sounds much more interesting in Spanish: "It takes a sexually stimulated man to make a chicken affectionate."

When Vicks first introduced its cough drops on the German market, they were chagrined to learn that the German pronunciation of v is f, which in German is the guttural equivalent of "sexual penetration."

Not to be outdone, Puffs tissues tried later to introduce its product, only to learn that "puff" in German is a colloquial term for a whorehouse. The English weren't too fond of the name either, as it's a highly derogatory term for a homosexual.

The Chevy Nova never sold well in Spanish speaking countries. "No va" means "it doesn't go" in Spanish.

When Coca-Cola first shipped to China, they named the product something that, when pronounced, sounded like "Coca-Cola." The only problem was that the characters used meant "Bite the wax tadpole." They later changed to a set of characters that mean "Happiness in the mouth."

When Gerber first started selling baby food in Africa, they used the same packaging as here in the USA, with the cute baby on the label. Later they found out that in Africa, companies routinely put pictures on the label of what's inside since most people can't read.

Also not to be missed is the Net Gazette library, which includes additional articles on subjects like safe fax, eliminating junk mail, and a variety of Monty Python sketches in hypertext.

News of the Weird

http://www.nine.org/notw/notw.html

News of the Weird is actually a syndicated newspaper column that's reprinted electronically at the News of the Weird Web page about two weeks after it appears in print. It consists of short news stories that strive toward being a bit bizarre. Some of them are genuinely entertaining—at times the author seems to be confronted with the need to produce a column despite his residence in a universe without much of a sense of humor.

The New South Polar Times

http://www.deakin.edu.au/edu/MSEE/GENII/NSPT/NSPThomePage.html

The antarctic is cold—so cold you can not only see your breath, but you can chip your teeth on it as well. Perhaps in compensation for this, Club Med doesn't have a village there and there are no souvenir stands. Several companies do actually run sightseeing expeditions to Antarctica, but the conditions wouldn't rate any stars at all in a Michelin guide and, as such, most tourists ultimately choose Aruba instead.

There's a fairly respectable number of scientists and other researchers stationed down in the polar depths, however—there are several permanent colonies in Antarctica. The Amundsen-Scott South Pole station even has its own Web page, albeit hosted on a server in Australia. The New South Polar Times will offer you a taste of life where 100 degrees below zero is regarded as mitten weather.

Agreeably chatty and rich with details about life in a place few of us would visit on a dare, it includes news from home, descriptions of the facilities at Amundsen-Scott, and all sorts of other bits about living where you have to microwave the ice cream for a while before you can eat it. Here's an excerpt from one of the issues:

> *The New South Polar Times Greetings from Club 90 South, where the ambient temperature dropped to -100F last weekend! Brrrrr! Temperatures that cold are almost always accompanied by a cloudless sky, so we've seen some pretty outstanding auroral activity, too!*
>
> *We have received several questions about facilities at the South Pole, so I thought I'd take you on a little tour!*
>
> *The first South Pole station was built in 1957; it has since been abandoned, and buried by drifting snow. Operations moved to the current station in 1975. The station consists of the Dome and five archways, Skylab, Summercamp, the Dark Sector, the Clean Air Facility, and several smaller outlying buildings. The National Science Foundation manages all U.S. activity in Antarctica, through contracts with Antarctic Support Associates and the Naval Support Force Antarctica.*
>
> *The Dark Sector is a group of astrophysics observatories and telescopes, located about one kilometer west of the main station (across the skyway).*
>
> *You're probably wondering which way "west" is, since every direction from the South Pole is north! Well, we use a grid system. Picture a pie, with the South Pole at the center, and the lines of longitude radiating out to the edges. But instead of dividing the pie into two 180-degree sections (east and west longitude), we start at zero degrees longitude (grid north) and move clockwise around the circle, 360 degrees. This way, 90 degrees east longitude is grid east, 180 degrees is grid south, and 90 degrees west longitude is really 270 degrees, or grid west. Whew!*
>
> *There are four main buildings under the dome. The social hub is the galley. The kitchen and cafeteria are on the first floor, with additional seating and a bar (the only indoor area where smoking is allowed) upstairs. There is actually a bar up there, but you have to bring your own drinks!*
>
> *Next to the galley is a small shack where fresh vegetables are stored during the summer. Most of our food stores are piled in huge lines along the inside wall of the dome. This is why we have to heat the ice cream in the microwave before we can eat it: it's too darn cold!*

There's also an e-mail address for the editor of the The New South Polar Time available for asking questions about Antarctica, and links to several other Antarctic resources on the Net.

NewtWatch

http://www.cais.com/newtwatch/

There are those who have nothing at all pleasant to say about Newt Gingrich, and while his politics might actually be somewhat to the right of the known universe and a few of his public utterances are badly in need of a verbal backspace key, he seems to think liberals should spend life in front of a firing squad—so he can't be all bad. One of the necessary extremes of a democracy, he seems a suitable balance for those in government who feel that noble ideals ought to excuse those who hold them from having to figure out how to pay for them.

I should note that I write this from some distance north of the Canadian border. Politics are relative, and liberals can always get worse. Newt would be regarded as being very nearly a socialist up here in comparison to *our* elected officials. Perhaps Newt really is nothing more than a typical corrupt politician who's out only to further his own ends, but at least he's a conservative corrupt politician. He only wants to buy a Rolls for himself at the public expense, not one for each of a quarter of a million single mothers and illegal immigrants.The NewtWatch page wasn't created by fans of Newt, to be sure. It offers all sorts of things that Newt would probably have quickly forgotten about. It describes itself like this:

> *NewtWatch is a new Web service designed to be your resource on Speaker of the House Newt Gingrich. Curious about Newt's Congressional voting record? Interested about what's behind those ethics complaints you've heard about? Wondering who in your zip code contributed to Newt? How much honoraria he earned before the practice was banned? How about Newt's cosponsored "commemorative" bills before those were banned? It's all here—and more—with more to come. For a quick overview, you can check out our press release or just browse around.*

There's all sorts of "Newt stuff" at the NewtWatch page, including press releases, quotes from media coverage, and a page called The Cases Against Newt, which offers details of several ethics complaints and at least one lawsuit involving Newt.

The NewtWatch page is a superb example of hypertext authoring—it's comprised of short, readable bits of text with links to more detailed documents if you really want to know more.

In the spirit of evenhanded tolerance—or perhaps merely in the spirit of aspiring to it—the NewtWatch page offers a list of links to other Newt resources on the net. These are actually annotated links—a minuscule amount of bias on the part of NewtWatch might have slipped into some of the entries.

To make your selections easier, the pro-Newt entries are illustrated with a graphic of Newt in a halo and the anti-Newt entries show Newt with a goatee and horns.

The Newt Gingrich WWW Fan Club

Pro-Newt: This is serious dittohead territory, just one of a collection of angry screeds making up something called "the right side of the Web" (they think Bob Dole is liberal, for example, and blast Republican Gov. William Weld for enacting "radical left-wing homosexual policies in Massachusetts." Jeesh!) They offer a number of pro-Newt resources, including links to speeches. They're asking, incidentally, for suggestions for a new name for their Web page. Physicists might be horrified to learn they are leaning toward The Newtonian. The rest of us might be horrified just to see this.

What's Newt?

Anti-Newt: This is an excellent, well-researched, and amusing overview of Newt's often rocky and always attention-grabbing days since becoming Speaker of the House. Compiled chronologically and updated regularly, the guy who does this has been on Newt like white on rice for months. For up-to-the-minute news on Newt (or if you don't get some of the more obscure references in NewtWatch), I strongly recommend What's Newt.

The Renewing American Civilization WWW Page

Pro-Newt: This Web site is maintained by the Progress and Freedom Foundation, a nonprofit, entirely nonpartisan think tank. No, really. Well, PFF is supposed to be nonpartisan to maintain its tax-exempt status with the IRS. In actuality, this propaganda machine would make Goebbels blush. The Web page offers transcripts of Newt's class at Reinhardt College, called Renewing American Civilization, the more recent of which are written in entirely capital letters without benefit of a single paragraph break. I've been informed by PFF that's because the transcripts are from the closed-captioning scripts for the video tapes. I will admit that, were he not second in succession to the leadership of the free world, Newt would probably have been one of my favorite professors.

Mother Jones Supplement on Newt Gingrich

Anti-Newt: Mother Jones magazine is so cool. This special supplement that includes controversy-stirring reports from 1984 and 1989 about Newt Gingrich is part of a really nice Web site. You might want to check out Jeffrey Klein's Editor's Note in the January/February, 1995 issue on Gingrich.

Newt's Own Congressional Web Page

Pro-Newt: This is Newt's page at the www.house.gov Web site. It's not very colorful, but then neither are the pages of other members. It has Newt's office phone number and address. You can also use this page to send Newt e-mail.

Working Assets Long Distance Company

Anti-Newt: Working Assets is an activist/leftist, very unique long-distance carrier (instead of hearing a pin drop, for example, you can actually hear it whine). Working Assets is offering some anti-Newt promotions that include Stop Newt Calling Cards. They also offer subscribers free calls to Congress through April 30th. Of course, you have to sign them up as your long-distance carrier, but it's worth it. With Working Assets picking up the tab, you can call Congress and demand to stay on hold until you speak directly to your representative.

Oceania: The Atlantis Project

http://www.oceania.org/

Not to be confused with Colossus: The Forbin Project, Oceania purports to be the work of a consortium of individuals proposing to create a new island. Looking a bit like a cross between Club Med and early conceptual sketches for life on the Martian frontier, it's somewhat unclear whether the Oceanians mean themselves to be taken seriously or not. The Oceania home page says of itself:

The Atlantis Project is dedicated to the goal of establishing a new country named Oceania. This country will be devoted to the value of freedom, and will first exist as a sea city in the Caribbean. As no collectivist nation is likely to sell us the land we need, we will build an island out of concrete and steel. At this point, the organization behind this new country, The Atlantis Project, is building the necessary financial resources to pay off past debts and to pay for the completed model of Oceania. Once this task is completed, The Atlantis Project will go into full gear and go well beyond the peak reached in early 1994 when it was covered by media across the U.S. and the world—including the BBC, the Miami Herald, the Art Bell Show, Boating magazine, and Details magazine.

These people aren't just talking—notice that Oceania already has a national debt, the first requirement of a modern society. If you browse the Oceania Web page you'll find a surprising wealth of documents pertaining to the Atlantis Project. Included are:

- A link to Sea Structures Inc.'s Web page, a company that purports to build water-based habitats. I can't say I've ever heard of them, but then you see so few marine dwellings in the middle of cow country.
- The constitution of Oceania, available in English and Spanish. This is a long hypertext document with links to sections like The Right to

Free Speech, The Right to Encryption, and The Right to Quick Service. You'd never guess that these people use the Internet.

- Detailed documents about Oceania and the Atlantis Project. These are engagingly passionate and very leading edge, if somewhat less than wholly coherent or believable all the way through. Included is the history of Oceania:

1.1 History of Oceania

The Atlantis Project began in February '93, conceived shortly after Tamara Clark was defeated by massive election fraud in her quest for the State Senate in Nevada. Its goal is to create a new country called Oceania, with this country being constructed on an artificial island in the Caribbean.

Eric Klien, Tamara Clark's treasurer, was greatly upset to uncover systemic, massive, nationwide election fraud throughout the U.S. and realized that the resources needed to combat it were way beyond his means. The death threats and intimidation by goons that the election fraud investigation encountered were just a hint of the size and power of the opposition. Being told by the state senate that they were "too tired" to review our five boxes of evidence was the final blow in our attempt to get this instance of election fraud reversed.

Having given up on the U.S., Eric looked for other countries with a bright future and found none. So the concept of a country on the sea was born. The project rapidly picked up steam in 1993, getting nationwide publicity on The Art Bell Show, Details magazine, the Miami Herald, Boating magazine, and more. Worldwide publicity was received as well in Canada, New Zealand, Hong Kong, England, and Belgium. Unfortunately, as the publicity increased the funds began to run out, and eventually the project ran out of money. A focus on donations instead of investments was its biggest mistake.

Slowly, after the project's collapse in April of 1994, it's being brought back to life. At the moment the main goal of the project is to pay off past debts and keep its supporters aware of the incremental progress that is being made. Once the project's debts are paid off, the project will go into full gear again. Eric Klien is currently undergoing numerous financial ventures to rebuild the project's finances.

You can always spot the pioneers—they're either the ones with arrows in their backs or people laughing behind them.

A glorious concept, albeit with less hope of fulfillment than most cats have of surviving ten minutes of being microwaved on high, the Oceania Web page is a fun read in places. Get through enough of it and you might find yourself wondering where to apply for an Atlantis green card.

The problem with Utopian societies, of course, is that it takes the same utter bastards to make them work as are currently running our own. Perhaps it would be more proper to say that the job of leading a nation invariably attracts more politicians than it does leaders. The qualities that make it possible to get to the top of any political structure—even if it exists on a man-made island in the Caribbean—are almost wholly exclusive of the ones that make it possible to do something positive once you get there.

An Ode to Coffee

http://www.flightpath.com/Brento/AnOdeToCoffee.HTML

I've never considered an inability to distinguish between a really well brewed cup of steaming hot coffee and the aftermath of a ten-minute oil change special at Jiffy Lube to be much of a failing, myself. Coffee has long struck me as something people do when they'd rather drink Coke but think it would be a bit unrefined.

The two drinks have many of the same constituents, but you needn't grind Coke—at least, you shouldn't have to.The Ode to Coffee page is a set of links to all sorts of other caffeinated resources on the Internet. Using some of the lesser-known Netscape Web page extensions, it manages to present itself against a background of graphic coffee beans, which looks very artistic. Whoever put this page together really liked his or her morning brew.

It offers the following observation, too, albeit from a somewhat suspect source:

> *Coffee is the beverage of the people of God, and the cordial of his servants who thirst for wisdom. When coffee is infused into the bowl, it exhales the odor of musk, and is of the color of ink. The truth is not known except to the wise, who drink it from the foaming coffee cup. God has deprived fools of coffee, who with invincible obstinacy condemn it as injurious. In it will we drown our adversities, and in its fire our sorrows.*
>
> *from the Journal of the Transylvanian Medical Society, ca. 1850*

The Ode to Coffee page includes the following links as I write this:

- A Brave New Coffeehouse World of Internet Cafes.
- Coffee, Coffee, Coffee, a glorious hymn.
- Java Jive examines Cafe Speak.
- The Benevolent Bean just wants to be loved. Is that so wrong?
- Mothercity Coffee reviews Seattle cafes.
- Mr. Coffee Caffeinated Home Page. Yikes.
- A Coffee Pot in Cambridge is our virtual reality.

- Over the Coffee is the Sam's Club of coffee pages.
- The Coffee Page has some beautiful icons.

This page really won't tell you much about brewing the perfect cup of coffee. Ignore the Mr. Coffee link in this regard—those of my acquaintances more enlightened in matters of the bean than I maintain that Mr. Coffee emits the same brown watery substance whether it's filled with coffee, partially moldy blue cheese, or sawdust and gravy.

The Java Jive page is easily the best trick at the Ode to Coffee. It offers some insight into the numerous variations on a simple cup of coffee, and how you can ask for exotic coffees like espresso and cappuchino in trendy restaurants without having the waiter correct you in Italian.

On Line Trader

http://www.onlinetrader.com/closeouts/index.html

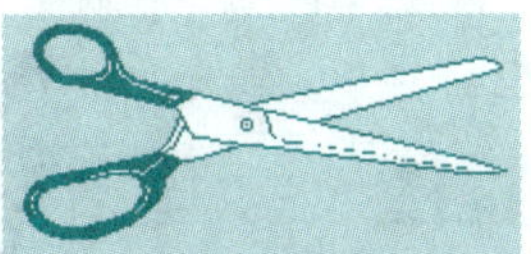

On Line Trader is a page for buying and selling ends of lines, close outs, and large quantities of things that no one was prepared to buy back when they were worth something. If your basement isn't full yet, you'll undoubtedly find stuff worth having here. At least, it will seem worth having when you buy it—five years later it will still be sitting in a corner, laughing at you, and asking you why you imagined you'd be able to use it when the person who sold it to you certainly couldn't.

Here are a few of the unbelievable offers at On Line Trader as I was writing this:

FUJI BATTERIES: AA alkaline, 1,000,000 pieces available, packed 1,000 bulk/case, fresh product, 5-year shelf life, overstocks, no restrictions, 19" ea., total surplus, (801) 773-4990

Beautiful Neckties: silk, cotton, & polyester, 100,000 pieces in stock, retail @ $9.95, $32.50 each, 96 assorted/case @ 72" ea, (by the case), Omaha Distributing, (800) 228-2765

Macy department store returns: brand-new merchandise, $28,000 retail value in assorted merchandise, you pay 9% of retail $2,500.00/lot A. A. Salvage Co. P.O. Box 61 Harrington Park, NJ 07640-0061, (201) 785-0210

Radar jammer: Rocky Mountain, makes all vehicles invisible to police radar, retail @ $195.00 to $225.00....only $55.00 ea, RM Surplus Brokerage, 8174 South Holly Street, #422 Littleton, CO 80122, (800) 873-5028, fax (303) 771- 4344

Steak knives: stainless steel & wood,100 pieces/box @ 25" ea, bath sponges: extra large, extra soft, never dries hard, 200 pieces/box @ $29.00/box, used jeans: clean, sorted, 1st quality goods, no holes, no rips, etc. names like Guess, Chic, Wrangler, Lee, etc. Bargains & Deals 3092 N. Expressway 83, Brownsville, TX 78520, (210) 350-4005, fax (210) 350-4006

Pepperspray: (14gm 10% oleoresin) & personal alarm (130db) set. Call (503) 463-1639 $8.95ea/4k or $9.95ea/1k

Bullet-proof vests: point blank. Closeout on inventory. 28 pc avail Call (215) 322-4371 $99.95ea Samples $119.95

The list was a great deal longer, but this excerpt should give you a feel for the sort of things it included. I didn't notice any plans for death rays or home-built flying saucers amidst the one million flashlight batteries and the ginzu knives, but that might just be because I wasn't looking for them. You can also advertise your own treasures at On Line Trader.

On Line Trader also offers a list of 25,000 fax numbers on disk. If you do decide to check out this page, you might want to make sure not to tell them yours.

On-Line Antique Shop Locator

http://www.rivendell.com/antiques/amdir/ShopsLoc.html

An extensive database of antique shops, this Web page will help you find the old, the arcane, the unusual, the exotic, and the slightly chipped but certain to increase in value just like the one we sold last week. Organized by state, it includes both physical shops where they'll accost you the moment you enter and online antique malls where you can browse from the comfort of your own keyboard and not have to fear breaking anything valuable.

Actually, I don't think it's possible to break anything valuable in most antique shops even if you show up swinging a sledge hammer. Most antique dealers and all their lawyers would, of course, most likely disagree.

Paleolithic Painted Cave at Vallon—Pont-d'Arc (Ardhche)

http://dmf.culture.fr/culture/gvpda-en.htm

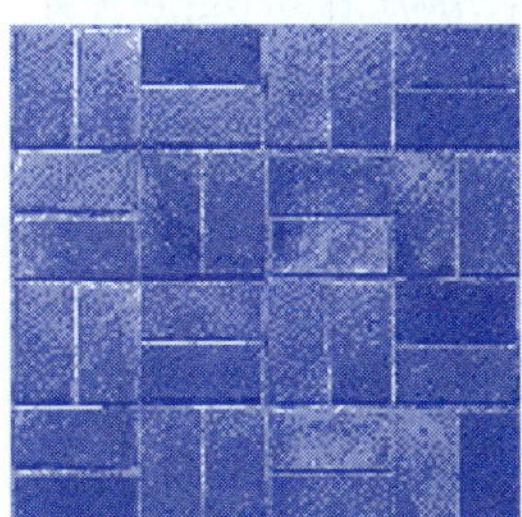

If you or I were to draw pictures on somebody else's walls it would be called vandalism. If it took place 20 thousand years ago, however, it's paleolithic art. Of course, that's not to say that the artists weren't vandals at the time.

The recently discovered cave at Vallon in France is a remarkable gallery of paintings by our most remote ancestors. Hundreds of illustrations in black and red ocher decorate the walls of the caves, depicting mammoths, ibex, horses, oxen and other creatures alive at the time.

There's also a fascinating description of the discovery at the Vallon Web page, along with several photographs of the better preserved graphics.

Panic Encyclopedia

http://english-server.hss.cmu.edu/ctheory/panic/panic_contents.html

There's the far outside chance that *postmodernist* doesn't mean the same thing as *utterly meaningless monkey dandruff*, but I wouldn't count on it. Show a monkey anything that describes itself as postmodernist and sooner or later the beast will probably scratch itself.

The Panic Encyclopedia purports to offer a postmodernist interpretation of selected elements of our culture. As you might expect, they appear profound and very nineties, but if you read 'em a second time they don't seem to mean much of anything. Subsequent perusals usually don't improve the situation. Of itself, the Panic Encyclopedia says:

> *Panic is the key psychological mood of postmodern culture. In pharmaceuticals, a leading drug company, eager to get the jump on supplying sedatives for the panic population at the end of the millennium, has just announced plans for a "worldwide panic project." In television, Vanna White, cohost of the "Wheel of Fortune," can (finally) confess that she was chosen for her role by Merv Griffin because of her disproportionately large head size. After all, in the age of the talking heads of television, what counts is the sheer giganticism of media silhouettes.*

Panic patriotism, too. That is Donald Trump and Lee Iacocca as self-nominated American heroes of the marketplace. Breaking with the old robber-baron tradition of practicing primitive exploitation in the age of an equally exploitive primitive capitalism, they have discovered the secret formula of postmodern robber barons—merging the economic calculus of "let's make a deal" with the political rhetoric of making America stronger.

And finally, even panic Elvis is invited to come on down for one last retro-appearance as a memory residue, made all the more nostalgic because Elvis's disappearing body is like a flashing event horizon at the edge of the black hole that is America today.

Panic culture, then, as a floating reality, with the actual as a dream world, where we live on the edge of ecstasy and dread. Now it is the age of the TV audience as a chilled superconductor, of the stock market crash as a Paris commune of all the programmed supercomputers, of money as an electronic impulse fibrillating across the world, and of the individual as a quantum energy pack tracing/racing across the postmodern field.

Several more yards of this came off the roll before the "return to home page" icon. The entries in the Panic Encyclopedia all start with the word *panic*, as you might expect. They include:

- Panic Art
- Panic America the Beautiful
- Panic Beaches
- Panic Canada
- Panic Doughnuts
- Panic Drugs in America
- Panic Elvis
- Panic Fashion
- Panic Finance
- Panic Feminism
- Panic Hamburgers
- Panic Pleasures of Invention
- Panic Jeans
- Panic Killing
- Panic Lovers
- Panic Money
- Panic Martians
- Panic Nietzsche's Cat (on Panic Particle Physics)
- Panic Ovaries
- Panic Sex

The Panic Encyclopedia is really a lot of fun to browse—not everything has to make sense to be entertaining. You might regard it as a sort of virtual Rorschach test—what its entries mean isn't nearly as important as what they mean to you.

Here's the one for Panic Sex. It might be a significant comment on postmodernism in general that this was pretty well the shortest entry in the list.

Panic Sex

What is sex in the age of the hyperreal? A little sign slide between kitsch and decay as the postmodern body is transformed into a rehearsal for the theatrics of sadomasochism in the simulacrum. Not sadism any longer under the old sign of Freudian psychoanalytics and certainly not masochism in the Sadean carceral, but sadomasochism now as a kitschy sign of the body doubled in an endless labyrinth of media images, just at the edge of ecstasy of catastrophe and the terror of the simulacrum.

I also particularly enjoyed Panic Canada. Among its profundities were the observation that ". . . to an extraordinary, though little-recognized degree, Canada as a nation-state is a creature of panic." This will certainly come as no surprise to those of us who live north of the border—few emotions better describe the anticipation of another speech by the prime minister or, worse still, another budget.

Persian Books (Mage Publishing)

http://gpg.com/Mage/

The problem with the glories of Persia is that they have about 25 feet of Iran on top of them. Experiencing the vibrant culture of the descendants of Alexander first-hand means visiting a country where possession of a Beach Boys tape can be a capital crime.

Mage Publishing offers an impressive library of books about Persian culture in the contexts of both its timeless history and modern-day Iranian politics. Many of the books have been written by Iranian authors and translated into English. They cover subjects as diverse as Persian cooking and Middle East politics. You can learn what life in Iran is really like, and find out how things got that way. Particularly worthwhile—and admittedly, one of only two books in the Mage catalog I've actually read—is *The Art of Persian Music,* by Jean During Zia Mirabdolbaghi Dariush Safvat. When you're done listening to the accompanying CD, imagine signing a check with a name like that.

The really captivating aspect of the books at Mage's Web page is that they'll show you contemporary Persian culture as something other than Ayatollahs, captured MiGs, and petrodollars. Back when "western civilization" referred to eastern Greece, the ancestors of the authors of these books had a sophisticated civilization. Much of it still remains, although it's typically a bit harder to spot.

Phytotherapy

http://www.plant.com/

Contemporary medicine—the kind you can get a health plan to pay for some of the time—is very scientific sounding and very exacting. If you don't die, the treatment obviously worked. It also comes with a pretty remarkable price tag, and most of the people who practice it get to drive BMWs. Consider that the people who build hospitals get paid a lot less than the people who work in them. Construction workers can get along without doctors for the most part, but doctors obviously can't get along without construction workers unless they want to practice medicine from a tent.

Phytotherapy involves treating illness with plants. Actually, much of conventional medicine does too—phytotherapy just doesn't patent them first. The Phytotherapy Web page gives you an introduction to this ancient form of medicine, as well as a list of common ailments and the plants you might look to for relief from them.

In answer to the obvious question, yes, there's a really extensive section on aphrodisiacs in there. Some of them even include a flashing warning that using too much of them will leave your lover really horny and insatiable. Damn . . . that sounds like it would be hard to get along with. The Phytotherapy page says of itself:

> *Phytotherapy is a method of treating illnesses and ailments through medicinal plants. It's one of the world's oldest forms of medicine. For over 6,000 years people from around the world have tested and chosen the best medicinal plants for curing all kinds of ailments.*
>
> *Chemical medication has been used for only roughly one hundred years. Each day we discover some drastic side effects that follow its undeniable efficiency. According to the OMS (Organization mondiale de la Santi, a worldwide organization for health), 60% of today's illnesses are due to this type of medication.*
>
> *Phytotherapy has an alternative to these "illness medications," in other words, it proposes "health medications" that are nonaggressive, efficient, and highly effective in treating a condition in depth, as well as preventing its occurrence by keeping you in good health.*
>
> *Phytotherapy works by stimulating the natural defenses of our organism instead of taking their place. Medicinal plants have the property of curing ailments more thoroughly and in greater depth with longer lasting effects. It's the most beautiful gift nature has to offer.*

While some of the Phytotherapy page reads a bit like a medieval treatise on the benefits of leaches, it's all genuinely interesting. You might consider some of it worth exploring if "real" doctors don't seem to be working for you—or if real doctor bills seem a bit too real of late.

The Pickup Truck Home Page

http://www.rtd.com/~mlevine/pickup.html

There seems to be a subconscious belief in some quarters that people who drive pickup trucks are hay-chewing, tobacco-spitting yahoos from someplace so rural as to be populated by more cows than people. This view has it that pickup truck drivers drive trucks only because their horses are in the shop, and most of them can whistle simple tunes by facing their ears into the wind.

These are ideas predominantly held by city people, of course. You can always spot someone from the city—they're the ones trying to push their BMWs up the sides of mountains or bail them out when they can't quite make it across a stream. If you ask 'em why they tried to drive a car in such awkward places they'll usually look confused and tell you they saw someone else do it in a television commercial. You can tell city people anything.

I own two trucks. They're ideal for going where the cars can't make it. Out here, that's almost everywhere.

The Pickup Truck Home Page is the perfect resource for truck owners, would-be truck owners, and city people who want to know what they're missing. It lists the hottest new trucks, all sorts of specifications that don't mean a whole lot so long as the paint's good and the tires have really big treads, and numerous links to other pickup truck resources. It has lots of graphics of trucks, most of them heavily customized and recently washed.

Pollstar Concert Tour Database

http://www.pollstar.com/

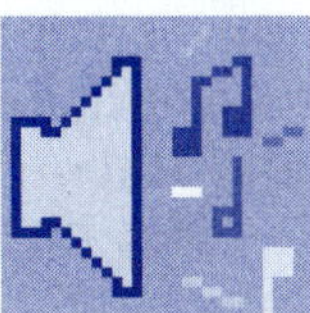

I think the days of spontaneously deciding to go downtown and see a concert have passed. The computerized ticket-booking services probably killed them—or perhaps it was the need to book a football stadium to play in three years in advance. Rock and roll got a lot less free-form when the accountants became involved.

If you'd like to know what's likely to arrive in town over the next few months, you'll find few better listings than the Pollstar page. It offers a continually updated searchable database of thousands of tours, indexed by artist and city. There's also a page of tour gossip and a top-ten tours list.

Preposterous Word of the Week

http://www.wwa.com/math/puzzles/preposterousWords/PuzzleOfTheWeek

Long, infrequently used words can make people think you're well read. Of course, they're a lot more likely to make people think you're a pompous twit who reads dictionaries because books with plots require too long an attention span. Real men don't use prepositions. Actually, I think the consensus is that real men just grunt.

The Preposterous Word of the Week page features a new word each week, every one of them certain to have you branded an utter weed should you ever use it in conversation. The words are followed by a selection of possible definitions. For example:

SECUNDIPARA:

(A) alternate commentary on a biblical passage
(B) a woman who has borne children in two separate pregnancies
(C) backup apparatus
(D) musical direction for second strings
(E) property inherited by the second son

Obviously, the correct answer is B. It's obvious, I should add, because the Preposterous Word of the Week page has a box to click if you don't recognize the word in question.

Ragu Pasta Sauce Page

http://www.eat.com/

While it's probably an example of blatant commercialization of the Web at it worst, the Ragu page is genuinely useful and has been crafted with a degree of style and humor that makes you want to forgive it. Besides, it's about Italian food—I could forgive damn near anything for good Italian food. Of itself, the Ragu page says:

"No one should go through life without getting a little pasta sauce on their face, you know what I mean?"

There's a picture of a little old lady who might well have uttered those words at the page too. She purports to be "Mama," although I'd be willing to bet she's the CEO at Ragu and drives a BMW.

There are a fair number of plugs for Ragu sauce at the Ragu page—you'd expect that—but if you check out the recipe section, you'll find an extraordinary wealth of Italian meals. I confess that my idea of really good Italian cooking is Isabella's restaurant in the next village—it says "homemade Italian food" on the sign over the door—but if I was of a mind to do something other than storing beer in the kitchen, these are the sort of meals I'd try. The following is a selection of recipes from the Ragu page:

"Mangia bene, eh!"

"I got a million delicious recipes for you. Scroll down—you'll find something you're crazy for. Some have nice pictures. Plus, just in case you need a little extra help, I've given you a cooking glossary and a pasta glossary. Go, explore! Be the Marco Polo of the kitchen!"

- *Fettuccine Primavera*
- *Hearty Lasagna Rolls*
- *Pepperoni Pasta Ruffles*
- *Linguini With Zucchini & Cheese*
- *Stuffed Shells Primavera*
- *Tuscan Style Pasta*
- *Linguini With Pepperoni & Mushrooms*
- *Easy Vegetable Pasta*
- *Seafood Pasta*
- *Vegetable Bow Tie Pasta*
- *Lasagna With A Twist*
- *Vegetable Primavera Lasagna*
- *Pizza Provencal*
- *Pizza With The Works*
- *Three Cheese Pizza*
- *After-The-Game Pizza*
- *Double Filled Mushroom Pizza*
- *Mushroom Sausage Pizza*
- *Hearty Pizza Hero*
- *Pizza Rustica*
- *Italian Specialty Of The House Pizza*
- *Hearty Sausage And Pepper Pizza*
- *Double Pepper Pizza*
- *Vegetable Double Filled Pizza*

- *Broccoli Calzone*
- *Sole Florentine*
- *Spicy Shrimp With Fusilli*
- *Frutti Di Mare*
- *Scampi*

Mangia bene? Mangia more than I probably should have . . .

Of course, there was a time when pasta was just food—now it's a Mediterranean diet, and is really good for you. You can pig out on most of the foregoing and thumb your nose at any vegetarians you know.

The Ragu page is an enjoyable bit of browsing. It'll probably make you hungry—check it out immediately after lunch to keep from dashing down to kitchen with uncontrollable munchies. It concludes with:

> *Mama's niece Ana, the lawyer, wrote this next part: Copyright 1995 Van den Bergh Foods, Inc. All rights reserved. Ragu, Chicken Tonight, and Pizza Quick are registered trademarks of Van den Bergh Foods, Inc.*

Van den Bergh—a good Italian name.

Recipe Corner

http://www.mmedia.com/becca/recipe.html

The Recipe Corner offers a new recipe every week. Some of the recipes it features are pretty unusual. The author of the page maintains that "I enjoy [cooking] only if it takes less than fifteen or twenty minutes to make and is inexpensive." Somewhat more adventurous than Kraft dinners and less likely to kill you, these recipes are ideal for those of us who feel that kitchens are useful only as a place to store beer. Here's the recipe of the week as I write this:

> ***Kona Banana Bread!***
>
> *1/2 cup shortening*
> *1 cup sugar*
> *2 eggs*
> *3/4 cup ripe bananas, mashed (I usually use 1 cup or sometimes even 2 bananas.)*
> *1 1/4 cups sifted cake flour (Or, 1 1/4 cups all purpose flour plus 1 tablespoon.)*
> *3/4 teaspoon baking soda*
> *1/2 teaspoon salt*
> *1/4 cup chopped nuts (optional)*

In a medium bowl, cream the shortening and sugar until light. Add the eggs one at a time, beating well after each addition. Stir in the bananas. In a separate bowl stir together the flour, baking soda, salt, and nuts. Add the dry ingredients to the banana mixture, stirring until well blended. Pour into a greased 9-inch square pan. Bake at 350 degrees for 30 to 35 minutes. Cut in squares. Makes 12 servings.

(Taken from the Mary Ann's Gilligan's Island Cookbook)

Banana bread is one of my favorite things to bake and to eat! This recipe is excellent and believe me I've tried a lot of recipes. It comes out so moist and tastes delicious. I usually add a little more banana than the recipe calls for, and I also add a little vanilla extract, cinnamon, and sometimes even coconut to spice it up! Try it and tell me what you think. You might even come up with some additions of your own to make it even better. If you're wondering about the source for this recipe, yes . . . it came from the real Mary Ann of "Gilligan's Island." I even met her, too!

The Recipe Corner page includes a number of interesting links to other resources on the net, both culinary and otherwise.

The Russia House

http://www.NeoSoft.com:80/Russia_House/

An enterprise that would have been grounds for five years at the Lubyanka a decade earlier, The Russia House offers an impressive selection of artifacts from the Russian space program. Note that I use the word *offers* in the bourgeoisie capitalist pig sense of "we'd like to sell you some stuff," rather than in the traditional communist sense of "we're offering these items for the edification of the masses and the spiritual uplifting of the proletariat."

Things are, of course, changing in Russia. Most Russians are probably a lot less interested in the sort of items the Russia House is peddling than they are in Japanese compact disc players. In fact, most of these *object d'guerre froid* aren't really all that attractive, but they're good conversation starters. Does anyone you know have a real Russian space suit in his or her living room?

Yes, you can buy one from The Russia House, although I suspect it's among the pricier items. The offerings of the Russia House include:

- Russian space pins, at $2.50 each. These are sort of ugly, but they're cheap.
- Assorted medallions and buttons, at classified prices.
- Soviet space postcards, at $2 each.

- A desktop model of the Sputnik satellite, for $75.
- The banner flown on Mir, for $100. A few questions surround this one, not the least of which being how one would fly a banner in a vacuum.
- The aforementioned Russian space suit—no price is given.
- A reconnaissance satellite.

The Russia House also offers a number of less technical selections, including autographed copies of *Diary of a Cosmonaut* by Valentin Lebedev, at $25.00 each. You can peruse a selection of microscopes and other optical equipment and some space art by Andre Sokolov. Almost everything is accompanied by a GIF image.

There's an e-mail address available for ordering information and questions. For example, is that space suit airtight? Is it available with wide lapels, and a relaxed fit?

It seems fair to note that Russians are beginning to get access to the Net, and sooner or later some of them are likely to see this page. I wonder what they'll make of it—"Da, comrade, all that junk we couldn't get rid of . . . the capitalists are actually prepared to pay for it!"

Saint Alphonzo's Pancake Home Page (Frank Zappa)

http://www.fwi.uva.nl:80/~heederik/zappa/

Five hundred years from now when the Beatles are forgotten, Chuck Berry is something they teach in history class, and the "sixties" refers to the great lungfish rebellion of 2164, Frank Zappa will still be remembered. For one thing, he has an asteroid named after him. No foolin'.

You can find out about the asteroid Zappafrank and quite a bit more relevant lore about Zappa at Saint Alphonzo's Pancake Home Page. It's rich with details about Zappa and the Mothers of Invention, and offers links to Zappa graphics, MIDI files, tablature, lyrics, interviews, and no end of other cosmic debris. At present, Saint Alphonzo's Pancake Home Page includes the following entries:

- Civilization Phase III—All about Zappa's last album.
- News
- Discography

- Album Covers—A picture containing the front covers of all Zappa albums, from Freak Out! to Civilization, Phaze III. Clicking on an album will give you the corresponding page from the discography.
- Frequently Asked Questions
- Interviews and Articles—This section contains a few interviews with Zappa and some articles by Zappa.
- Miscellaneous Files—Sun/NeXT audio files, MIDI files, GIF and JPEG images, MPEG movies, guitar tablatures, chords, and scores.
- Quote of the day—Every day, another Zappa quote.
- Other Zappa sites

The discography is truly amazing—it runs for several furlongs, including quite a few recordings I'd never heard of. There's also a discography of "official bootlegs," such as:

- 'Tis the Season to Be Jelly
- The Ark
- Freaks and Motherf#@%!
- Piquantique
- Unmitigated Audacity
- Saarbr|cken 1979
- Anyway the Wind Blows
- As An Am
- Electric Aunt Jemima
- Our Man in Nirvana
- Tengo Na Minchia Tanta
- Disconnected Synapses
- Swiss Cheese/Fire
- Conceptual Continuity
- At the Circus

If you follow some of the links to other Zappa resources, you can be at it 'til Zappafrank orbits 'round again.

Saint Petersburg Press

`http://www.spb.su/sppress/`

You can tell a lot more about a country by reading its newspapers than you can by listening to its politicians. This might be a less than comforting thought if you consider that in five thousand years archaeologists will be digging up copies of the *National Enquirer*. In five thousand years archaeologists in Russia will be digging up copies of the Saint Petersburg Press.

You can dig them up a lot earlier—the *Saint Petersburg Press* is available on the World Wide Web. In fact, as mirrored through Tennessee, it's available at a reasonable speed, too. The Web version of the *Saint Petersburg Press* is all in English. It includes the text of stories from the paper edition of the paper, as well as selected photographs.

The really engaging aspect of this online newspaper is that it doesn't read like something out of a spy movie—the word *comrade* never appears in its text, for example. It's chatty and articulate, and it frequently manages to be more entertaining than newspapers from points far closer to home. Here's the front page of the Press as I write this:

TOP STORIES

- *Plans for track on course—An ambitious bid has been launched to provide St Petersburg with its own world-class racetrack.*
- *Spaniards swindled out of cargo—A Spanish export company is suing two Russian entrepreneurs who allegedly swindled it out of a massive consignment of British gin and whisky brought into St Petersburg's sea port.*
- *How Sonya has changed with the times—As Russia enters a new age of permissiveness, men and women across the country have responded to sexual urges that they were forced to stifle during the Communist era. Now medical science is also playing its role in helping fantasy to become reality. ALI NASSOR reports on the sex change phenomenon.*

FEATURE

The man who opened the window on the West (Photo). Ten years ago Mikhail Sergeyevich Gorbachev was elected to the post of Communist Party General Secretary. It was a move that led to policies that shook not only the USSR but also the rest of the world to its foundations. NIGEL STEPHENSON reports.

SECTIONS

- *News*
- *Business Press*
- *Commentary*
- *Classifieds*
- *Culture*

A well-crafted Web page, the Saint Petersburg Press is rich with links and structured to allow its contents to be browsed quickly or read in depth.

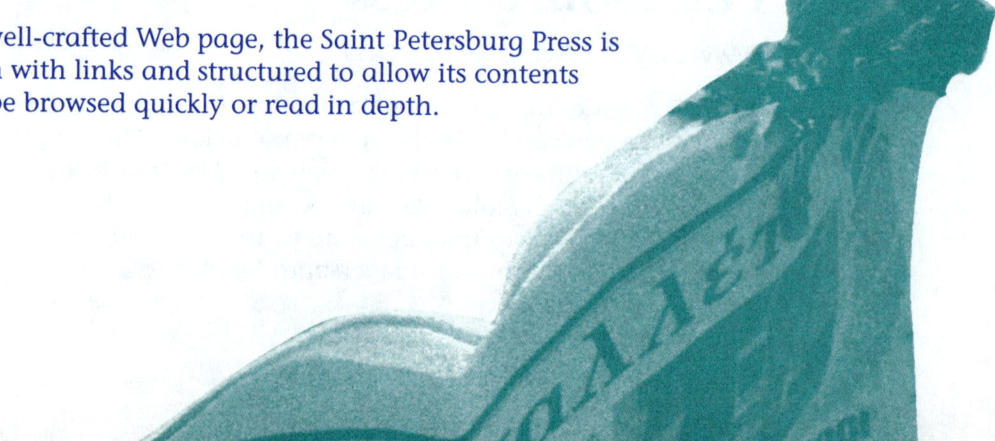

The Seeress of the Web

http://www.ipp.com/ipp/llinks.html

While really just a page of interesting links, the Seeress of the Web is done with considerable style, an evocative picture of the Seeress herself, and a better than average choice of links. It says of itself:

> *The Seeress of the Web awakes each morning with a vision of some unique place on the World Wide Web. Please take a moment to put her on your bookmark so you can come back each day to get a look at what she has dreamed the night before. The Seeress invites your e-mail and visionary link suggestions.*

Sound national economic policy has been built on far shakier ground.

The Shocking Photo Expose of the Lesbian Barbie Scene

http://gecko.desires.com/1.2/art/docs/lovegrid.html

If you link to only one World Wide Web page, make sure it's this one. See Barbie and her friends as you've never seen them before. Ken is absolutely *nowhere* to be found. One wonders if women really do this sort of thing—some of it seems as if it should be anatomically impossible, even for injection molded plastic. Well over a dozen positions are illustrated in high-resolution GIF graphics. You'll be outraged, and finer outrages than this one are hard to come by.

The Skeptic's Dictionary

http://wheel.dcn.davis.ca.us/~btcarrol/skeptic/dictcont.html

More fun than a bag of polecats at a funeral, the Skeptic's Dictionary will delight anyone with one or more active brain cells and a healthy degree of disbelief. It offers entries for dozens of topics most rational human beings are born skeptical of, with lucid—and generally unsympathetic—discussions of each. A brief selection of its topics includes:

- Alien abductions
- Amway
- Cattle mutilations
- Clairvoyance
- The Contract with America
- Crop circles
- Firewalking
- Flying saucers
- Massage therapy
- Near-death experiences
- Nostradamus
- Past-life regression
- Polygraph
- Santa
- Sasquatch
- Scientology
- Shroud of Turin

The entries in The Skeptic's Dictionary are short, well written, and eminently readable. Rather than simply shooting holes in every slightly unconventional idea and tradition on earth, it offers some background and suggested readings for each. Few of the entries are likely to foster your belief in the occult—they all strive to suggest somewhat more mundane explanations for the sorts of things that make the front page of the *National Enquirer*. No entry exists for Elvis as yet, but I'm sure one's in the works.

Snake Oil

http://fender.onramp.net/~analyst/snake/Snakeoil.html#top

I confess to being perennially astounded at the number of ministers of the lord who wind up getting sued and at times even jailed. That's lord with a small l, by the way—the one who takes plastic. The astounding part is that enough people actually send these characters enough money to make it worth stirring up a nest of lawyers over. They do, of course—some of the really successful snake oil salesmen can take home millions. As a rule, the ones into seven figures actually cry on stage, or bleed if possible, and they're prepared to supply God's 800 number for a nominal fee. They'll heal anything that has ever given significant thought to breathing, not excluding geraniums and late-model cars. They've spoken personally with all the up-market saints. Praise the lord, and pass the receipt book . . .

If you think that Jim Bakker really deserved to be locked in a cell with a three-hundred-pound boyfriend named Bubba, you'll no doubt enjoy the Snake Oil page. Find out where to write for the most outrageous newsletters, and keep up with the legal matters surrounding the men and women chosen to do the lord's work as select members of their flocks find out how much swamp land in Florida they've actually signed up for and thereupon go to court.

"They know not the depth of their sacrilege."

— Robert Tilton, commenting on Snake Oil

Solar Cooking

http://www.xmission.com/~seer/sbcn/index.htm

Conventional barbecues would seem to be the worst of all possible worlds. They emit nasty substances into our fragile environment, thus precluding any aspirations to being politically correct, should you have tendencies that way, and they make most food taste like the aftermath of an argument between a poodle and a small tactical nuclear device. Finally, barbecues require a lot of hardware, charcoal, or propane, and potato salad, spiders, and warm soapy Zima to really work properly.

Solar cooking, by comparison, is none of these things. Using nothing more than sunshine that was going to shine anyway and a bit of clever technology, you can cook food that tastes pretty respectable. Solar cookers can be bought or built, and solar cooking techniques aren't particularly difficult to master unless you have problems ordering drive-through food at McDonalds. And unlike drive-through food at McDonalds, solar-cooked food is usually good for you.

The solar cooking archive is a lively repository of solar cooking lore. It features pictures of various sorts of solar cooking technology, construction plans scanned into graphic files, and news of solar cooking from around the world. You can construct a solar cooker with a few dollars worth of materials and some light.

It's unlikely that you'll make a significant impact on the world's sundry problems by using a solar cooker rather than conventional cooking technology, but you can be content in the knowledge that you won't make them any worse. Alternately, you won't have to pay those pirates who fill your propane tanks quite so often, a far more immediate concern.

Speed Trap Registry

http://www.nashville.net/speedtrap/

http://eden.telalink.net:80/zoomst/copcars/copcars.html

If you ask a politician, you'll find out that speed traps cause people to slow down and as such save lives. Most of the rest of us regard them as a tax grab—which is, after all, what they really are. It's harder to complain about a tax that's imposed only on people who have ostensibly broken the law, however.

The Speed Trap Registry is a growing list of speed trap locations across the United States. It will tell you where the speed traps in your area are, how the policemen in question might camouflage their cars, and how to avoid being caught. Inasmuch as only a complete fool would speed past a speed trap and no state would knowingly issue drivers' licenses to fools, this Web page should keep both politicians and the rest of us happy. It will cause those driv-ers who read it to slow down— saving lives, just like the politicians say speed traps are supposed to do—and none of us need blow a lot of cash on speeding tickets so the aforementioned politicians can have a bit of extra spending money for their next fact-finding junket to Aruba.

The Speed Trap Registry page includes a function that allows you to submit your own speed trap locations, should you come across any. The Speed Trap Registry says of itself:

> *Welcome to the Speed Trap Registry. This registry was started in February '95 in an effort to cut down the number of speeding tickets resulting from speed traps. The "men in blue" of our nation have better things to do (like watch the O.J. trial) than operate speed traps to entrap motorists in an effort to increase fine revenues. This page is not meant to be an effort to undercut the efforts of police to control motorists' speeds on dangerous roads.*
>
> *This page in no way encourages speeding and recommends you always follow the posted speed limit. However, what you do is up to you. Also, I've noticed a disturbing trend of people sending me sobriety checkpoints. From my perspective (warped as it might be), sobriety checkpoints should not be indexed. I am not going to make it easier for drunk drivers, so please do not submit them. They are for our safety. Also, there has been a rise in traps near construction zones and on dangerous roads. Please submit only traps that are for fine revenue, or that are set up poorly and thus are dangerous.*

Should you find the Speed Trap Registry useful, you'll probably also want to check out Vagabond Jim's Nationwide Police Car Description server. It provides a description of the unmarked police cars used in most states and parts of Canada. It's listed at the beginning of this section as well.

If you want to help keep your local elected officials down to one Cadillac and no more than six figures in perks, watch the speed limit.

The Strawberry Facts Page

http://www.wimsey.com/~jmott/sbfacts/

"Doubtless God could have made a better berry, but doubtless God never did."

— William Butler (1535-1618)

If you're going to get obsessive about fruit, there are few better choices than the noble strawberry. Cherries are, after all, sexual and just a bit vulgar. Oranges can cause vitamin C megadose complications if you believe in that sort of thing, grapes promote alcoholism, and kiwi fruit are a bitch to peel. You can share your interest in strawberries—or just touch on a bit of strawberry lore—at The Strawberry Facts page. Rich with links to everything even tangentially related to strawberries, it offers mouthwatering GIF files of strawberry graphics, helpful guidelines to improve your strawberry harvest, recipes for all sorts of strawberry confections—including strawberry mead, which sounds like it should have the potency of a rutting lion—and lyrics to songs by the band Wild Strawberries.

Actually, to this end, you can also link to the complete Wild Strawberries page at http://www.xe.net/strawberries/. Neither the Stawbs nor Strawberry Alarm Clock, however, seem to have rated a mention.

Strawberry Pop-Tart Blow Torches

http://www.sci.tamucc.edu/%7Epmichaud/toast/

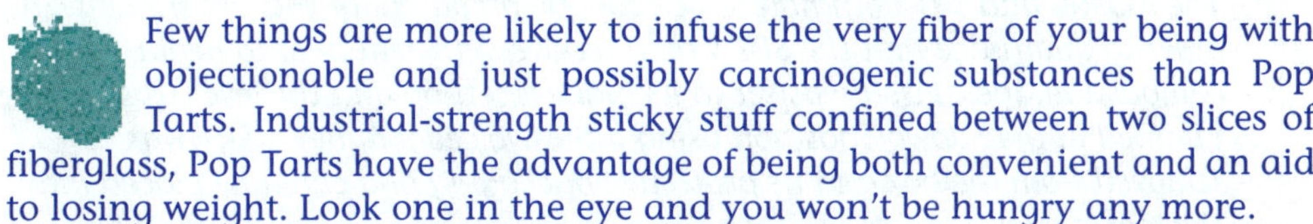

Few things are more likely to infuse the very fiber of your being with objectionable and just possibly carcinogenic substances than Pop Tarts. Industrial-strength sticky stuff confined between two slices of fiberglass, Pop Tarts have the advantage of being both convenient and an aid to losing weight. Look one in the eye and you won't be hungry any more.

Many of the ingredients in Pop Tarts can't be pronounced correctly unless you have a degree in biochemistry. Rumor has it exposing Pop Tarts to long-wave ultraviolet radiation will cause them to become temporary doorways into an alternate universe where everyone is comprised of pure energy and polysorbate 80.

Much of the foregoing is somewhat speculative, of course. The Strawberry Pop-Tart Blow-Torches Web page deals only with pure fact and scientific method. It outlines a simple experiment you can perform in your own home using nothing more than a toaster and some strawberry Pop Tarts. The page begins:

> *Strawberry Pop Tarts can be a cheap and inexpensive source of incendiary devices. Toasters that fail to eject Pop Tarts cause the Pop Tarts to emit flames 10-18 inches in height.*
>
> ***Introduction***
>
> *Last year, an article by well-known newspaper columnist Dave Barry noted that Kellogg's Strawberry Pop Tarts (SPTs) could be made to emit flames "like a blow torch" if left in a toaster too long. Given previous work in the field of food entertainment . . . it was obvious that this was a new frontier that requires further exploration. The present work describes our independent verification and experience with SPT-based combustion.*
>
> ***Materials Used***
>
> *Only two basic materials are needed to cause SPT-combustion: a (hopefully inexpensive) toaster and some strawberry Pop Tarts. In this work, the authors used Kellogg's Strawberry Pop Tarts with real Smucker's fruit. SPTs can be obtained either with or without frosting; the nonfrosted variety were used for this experiment.*
>
> *In addition to the basic materials, a number of safety-related items were needed to conduct this experiment. First, a suitable location for the experiment was required, it being expected that the kitchen was not the appropriate place for blow- torching SPTs. The author's driveway was chosen as a suitable site. Second, an appropriate means for extinguishing the SPTs would be needed; a research assistant brought along some baking soda for the purpose.*
>
> ***Experiment Preparation***
>
> *The toaster and SPT both had to be properly prepared for this experiment. In order to guarantee that the SPT would receive sufficient heat to begin combustion, the toaster was set to its highest setting and the lever was jammed in the "down" position using adhesive cellophane. A SPT was removed from the box and its protective packaging and carefully placed into the toaster slot.*

Written in a lucid, well-documented format that would make most high-school physics teachers grow tearful less than halfway through the work, this page is well worth browsing. Try not to do it when anyone who had breakfast this morning is near by—unless, of course, they had Pop Tarts.

This page also includes a link to the authors' earlier work, which discusses the pyrotechnic effects possible through the use of grapes and a microwave oven.

Sumo Wrestling

http://akebono.stanford.edu/users/jerry/sumo/

It's hard to know what to think of sumo wrestling—perhaps the Japanese habitually shake their heads and say the same thing about monster trucks and bungee jumping. I imagine that it's something you have to want to do very, very badly. I'm not obsessive about my feet, but I would like to be able to see them every so often without the use of a periscope.

The Sumo Wrestling page is impressively complete—aside from the fair bit of Sumo lore it maintains, it's heavy with links to other Sumo resources. Perhaps *heavy* is a poor choice of words.

You can download pictures of world-famous Sumo wrestlers, learn the rules and nuances of this ancient sport, and check out the official Japanese terms for Sumo moves, the various participants in a Sumo match, and some of the paraphernalia involved. You probably didn't know that a *dohyo* was a wrestling mat or that the winner of a Sumo match is paid *kenshoukin*, prize money. Don't be embarrassed—I can't say that I did either 'til I linked to this page.

I confess that having become so enlightened I'm none the less highly unlikely to immerse myself in Sumo culture. My jeans feel tight enough as it is.

Tag Lines

http://www.brandonu.ca/~ennsnr/Tags/

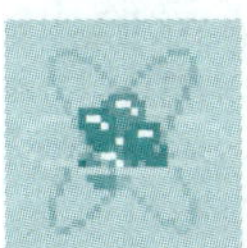

One of the grand traditions of electronic mail is having something witty to stick at the ends of your messages. These "tag lines" are almost an art form in themselves. After a while, software appeared to collect them. Now and again you'll see files with several dozen of the best of them so you can swipe a few for yourself.

The Tag Lines page is a continually updated interactive tag-line database. As of this writing it offered 49,423 distinct tag lines, classified alphabetically, as well as several lists of special-purpose tag lines. Some of these are almost Zen-like. Consider the following:

- A beer always goes down easy.
- MARS PROBE ERROR: A)bort R)etry T)ell 'em where I am?
- A penny saved is a congressional oversight.
- Save your country! Vote the tax and spend Democrats out of Congress!
- MAN: Make Animal Noises.
- Mixed emotions is when your kid gets an "A" in sex class.
- S & M: You always hurt the one you love.
- News flash—dyslexic sells his soul to Santa.
- Rabbit of Borg: No, Pooh. That's not how to assimilate someone.

Of course, if you don't like these you can choose from among 49,414 others. You can also submit tag lines of your own to the author of the page. The Tag Lines page offers the following disclaimer:

> *Warning! Some of you politically correct type people might find something that offends you here. Tough.*

Finally, it notes that the correct term for a collection of tag lines is a *boring*.

Tank Girl

http://www.mgmua.com/tankgirl/

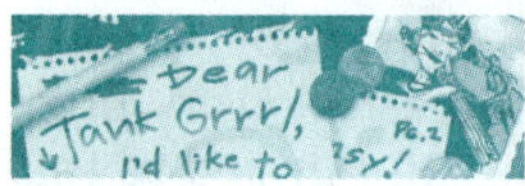

Well, I thought it was a fantastic flick. It played for about three days out here, and the night we went to see it there was a real fight for seats. Actually, that's not quite true—there was no one else in the theater and we had to go argue with the guy out front to get him to roll the film. If you missed it, check out the Tank Girl Web page. It says:

> *Come inside—help me save the world, etc., get pissed, get laid, get bent! I gotta GET KESSLEE and put things to rights in time to get home and quaff a few with my posse, the RIPPERS. And only YOU can help me! How? (Read the phucking MANUAL, scrotum child!)*

One of the better movie pages, Tank Girl offers all sorts of bits to read about the movie itself, and QuickTime files to download and look at. If you were unfortunate enough to miss Tank Girl in the theaters—with a three-day run this probably wouldn't have been difficult—you can get a feel for it here and check it out on tape or disc. There's a lot of Tank Girl narration at the page, too—for example:

> *Flattered, I'm sure.*

This you know: My parents died when a huge comet smashed into Earth 15 years ago. It hasn't rained since, and I get off stealing water from Water & Power. Some other things that move me:

- *I love green eggs and ham*
- *The annual Barney's of New York sale is a total rip-off*
- *I hate it when I get sand in my underwear*
- *I can do amazing things with vacuum attachments*
- *Believe it or not, I do my own hair*
- *And I love a good spanking. Use a spatula. It leaves a cool design.*

But that's not why you came all this way, is it . . . You want to see me naked.

Totally negatory. If you really need to, though, you can see me taking a shower. Just look around this freaky site for the showers after you get inside the tank.

Something of a virtual comic book, the Tank Girl page is agreeably vulgar and vastly entertaining. Check out the online puzzle, the tank manual, and the e-mail option to send Tank Girl a letter.

One of the best bits about the Tank Girl page is a whole seething vat of behind-the-scenes details and insights into how the movie was made and what some of the people involved thought. It begins:

Enter Rebecca Buck, a.k.a. Tank Girl. A spiky-haired, bawdy, clever, insolent, beer-chugging, cigarette-dragging, renegade smartass, she's the Water and Power's worst nightmare. The perfect post-apocalypse heroine. Only Tank Girl has the balls to take them on. Her weapons are charm, wit, impudence, sexuality, and an independent tank. Her army: a cadre of feared, underground special forces known as the Rippers. Her mission: to defeat the twisted Kesslee, to liberate the water supply, to recklessly right wrongs, and to have an immense blast. Not necessarily in that order. Never underestimate the power of a Girl and her Tank.

If you really liked Forrest Gump and thought it deserved all those Oscars, you'll probably think this page ought to be deleted.

Transient Images

http://www.cais.com/jpadgett/www/home.html

Transient Images might well become as essential to the operation of your television set as a remote control or the cable bill. It's a singularly well done source of insider gossip, news of upcoming television programs and movies, and numerous other bits of video lore.

Updated more or less weekly, it's well written, well edited, and thoroughly enjoyable. Here's one of the items in Transient Images as I write this:

> *STAR TREK: GENERATIONS News. Now with the film coming to an end of its theatrical run, RICK BERMAN reports that he has begun discussions with Paramount as to the next TREK film, and that the 2nd film is earmarked for late 1996 release. "I think everyone in the NEXT GENERATION cast has deals to make the next movie, with the exception of PATRICK STEWART and BRENT SPINER," said BERMAN. But he doesn't think getting the two actors will be a problem. "They're just deals that have yet to be made." [Hollywood Column, N.Y. Daily News dated 1/11/95]*

In addition to news about television, there's a weekly ratings page. While not quite as thorough as the Neilsons, it surveys several hundred viewers.

As I write this, Transient Images is the work of Alex Agostini and Jol Padgett. In addition to its World Wide Web manifestation, it's available as a mailing list. You can have the text of its articles sent directly to your e-mail address. It also features a list of links to other television Web sites. On a scale of one to ten, Transient Images deserves a twelve.

U.S. National Parks and Preserves Resource List

http://www.gorp.com/gorp/resource/US_national_park/main.htm

If you spend enough time in cyberspace, your biomolecular cohesion will begin to degrade and the dimension stability of your cerebrospatial matrix might become extradimensional. You can laugh at this if you like, but I've seen it happen. The next time you're clipping along the information superhighway at the speed of infinity^2, check out those dark areas just past the virtual street lamps. They aren't oil slicks, jack—they're the lost generation of virtual reality unstuck and formless in the Net.

You can avoid this arguably unpleasant fate by leaving cyberspace for real space now and again. One of the best sorts of real space going is the kind with trees and grass. That's real trees, rather than fractal trees, by the way—check 'em out if you haven't seen one before.

The U.S. National Parks and Preserves Resource List Web page will let you browse and search through a large and growing list of national parks. Most of them include links to more detailed descriptions of the parks in question, with information about the terrain and facilities available, the sort of clothing and other gear you'll probably want along, and the nearest towns. There are also directions to help you find the parks in question—unlike cyberspace, real space doesn't include hyperlinks.

Urban Desires

http://desires.com/index.html

One of the really superb online publications, Urban Desires covers a broad range of topics. It includes movie reviews, provocative articles about burning social issues, and less than burning high-tech toys—and a lot of the sort of thing the Internet's getting really infamous for. It goes where *Time* and *Newsweek* would certainly fear to tread without extensive disclaimers.

Here's a selection of items from the contents page of the current issue of Urban Desires as I write this:

> ***THE WRITTEN WORD***
>
> *REVIEWS: The Inferno of Dante and an Anthropologist From Mars—Reviewers Judith Van Buren and Peter Selgin explore Hell and insanity in a whirlwind of words.*
>
> *THE RANT: Rantings of a Mad-Fan—Resident spew-master Brian Dykstra is in a good mood this time. It's a happy, wonderful, ball-catching, base-stealing, fly-hitting time of year, and Brian tells you (once again) how he feels about it.*
>
> ***ART***
>
> *RANDOLFO ROCHA: Black and White—Welcome to our gallery. Turn off your underlined links option. Use Netscape 1.1N. Words by Eleanor Heartney. Interactive curating by the crew at AGENCY.COM.*
>
> *NINA GLASER: From the Earth We Come—A.D. Coleman provides the framework on which we hang the chilling photography of Ms. Glaser.*
>
> ***TECHNOLOGY AND TOYS***
>
> *I Fought the Law—Resident technologist Mike Peck uses the Simpsons to help put this whole censorship issue in order. And you know what . . . it works!*
>
> *High-Tech Sex: You'll be shocked to learn what you've been missing. Richard Greenfield jumps a few electron states in the name of erotic journalism.*
>
> ***SEX***
>
> *RAIN: Zane Rivera gets a little wet in the pursuit of one of the baser pleasures.*

S&M: Take Me There Master Jim!—David Levine gets a personal tour of the S&M scene with an upstanding member of the infamous Eulenspiegel Society.

MUSIC

REVIEW: The Band, Across the Great Divide—A 3-CD compilation of their best tunes, reviewed by David Levine. (Do we pay him for one review or three?)

PERFORMANCE

INTERVIEW: John Leguizamo—After having just wrapped To Wong Foo, Thanks For Everything, Julie Newmar, John Leguizamo hangs up his heels. Deborah Gregory spends some time talking to the lipstick-laden actor.

Three Movie Reviews: Jackson Armaly sets his eyes loose on three offerings of the Springtime movie frenzy: Basketball Diaries, Crumb, and Exotica await his lucid opinion.

FOOD

Late Nite Bites: Okay, you've been dancing for hours. The overpriced meal—where you were treated like the scum that the waiter thinks you are—is a distant memory and, gosh darn it, you're feeling a bit peckish. What to do? Sarah Bragaw and Peter Cassel lend a helping hand to the night noshers.

Chinese Tea Ceremony: Paulette Licitra journeys to the Lower (Far) East side and is greeted with a ritual where the tea is the thing.

STYLE

Lounge Bars: Curl up on the velvet and steel sofa, pretend you're reading Nietzsche, and see who you can impress. The eighties are over and have been replaced with a hipness a touch too relaxed. Amelia Dallas shares the secret of cool.

Designer Cynthia Rowley: Bart Boehlert talks high fashion and roof-top trampolines with hyper-designer Rowley.

Unlike some of the magazines that have appeared on the Web, Urban Desires is really well written and edited. Its articles run just long enough to be engaging—and manage to get down to the "return to contents page" icon well before they get long-winded and tedious. There's a surprising amount to read in an issue. The Web page also features access to back issues.

Vanuatu

http://www.clark.net/pub/kiaman/vanuatu.html

Here's a pop quiz—which of the following best describes Vanuatu?

- A portion of the female anatomy located just to the left of the G-spot, which when touched will send any woman screaming into paroxysms of ecstasy until she has to be peeled off the ceiling.
- A long-polymer dimethyl pseudo-styrene plastic that combines the elastic properties of rayon with the high cohesion, low bulk, and moderate electrostatic resistance of the uroformaldyhydes.
- A fifteenth-century mystic writer from Tuscany whose prophesies included the invention of television, the popularity of the Beatles, and a cure for liberal tendencies.
- A small place in the south Pacific.

Now, I would have chosen the first answer, myself—not because it seems likely to be right, but just because it's more fun than the other three. In fact, the correct answer is the fourth.

All I knew about the island of Vanuatu prior to encountering its Web page was that you can buy postcards of topless girls in grass skirts there in just about any shop. I would have said that was enough to keep the place interesting, but there does prove to be a great deal more to say about a nation that many would have ascribed to a printing defect on most maps.

Until 1980, Vanuatu was called the New Hebrides. It actually consists of 66 tiny islands in a cluster some 1,200 miles northwest of Australia. It's home to about 146,000 people who speak over 130 languages—typically not all at the same time. It has the distinction of having been screwed up by both French and British colonial administrations simultaneously for several hundred years.

Having ditched its colonial parents, Vanuatu became a really splendid place—or so says its Web page—with stunning beaches, friendly people, and pretty reasonable weather. Actually, the weather was reasonable back when the place was still the New Hebrides, but no one really cared because they were too busy being oppressed. There are lots of pictures in the Vanuatu Web page illustrating the foregoing beaches, people, and weather, and bits of descriptive text like this:

> *Vanuatu's indigenous people (formally called ni-Vanuatu, colloquially called ni-Vans) are, generally speaking, among the nicest in the world. The capital (Port Vila, if you're French, just Vila if you're not) rates a 10 on the*

friendliness scale. Not at all like, say, the relatively nearby Port Moresby, Papua New Guinea, where the sane think twice before walking down the main streets in broad daylight.

The Vanuatu Web page also offers links to several other South Pacific pages—and some sound bites from the local radio station.

I should note that one thing Vanuatu doesn't appear to have at the moment is Internet connectivity—its Web page is maintained on a server in the United States. Of all its alluring features, this is certainly one of the best.

Venusian Uterus

http://www.eskimo.com/~gnosis/

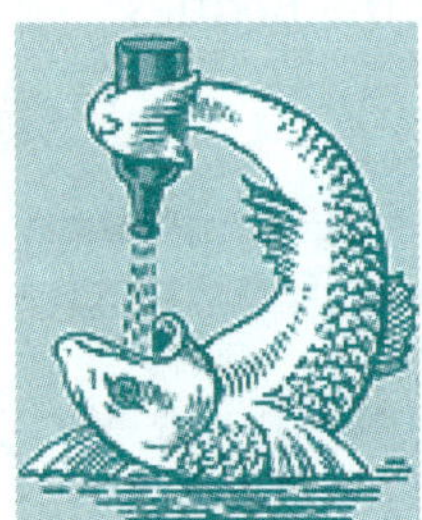

A highly selective link to a variety of Web pages that are pretty far into the depth of the netherworld, Venusian Uterus will illuminate you about things like ambient music, Christ-O-Matic, the Loompatics book catalog, and all sorts of other things that defy easy description. It also offers a selection of useful Web searching tools. The derivation of its name remains unexplained.

Vibe On Line

http://www.pathfinder.com/@@bAQYIwAAAAAAK7O/vibe/VibeOnline!.html (Home Page)

http://www.timeinc.com/vibe/vibeline/open.html (Vibe Line)

Vibe magazine is something of an acquired taste, and not really one I've acquired. Sort of like *Time* for people with loud stereos, it offers up-to-the-minute information about popular music and ads on every other page. The online version isn't much different—as I was writing this, there was a plug for 1-800-COLLECT on its home page, and the Vibe's Promotions and Give-Aways page was a subscription advertisement.

The one aspect of Vibe On Line that can be genuinely interesting is the Vibe Line. This is a page with links to dozens of sound bites from recently released albums. The sounds are stored in WAV and AU format. Technically well sampled and long enough to be representative of the albums they're standing in for in most cases, they allow you to preview discs you might want to buy. As I was writing this, all the discs in the Vibe Line came from Atlantic and Polygram. Prince and Madonna were well represented, as were several fairly synthetic studio bands. None of the samples I downloaded could be said to have been hanging out over the leading edge of contemporary music.

If you like AM radio but can't be bothered with all the intros and commercials, the Vibe Line is a fairly quick way to keep up with what's current. Many sound players will also play the samples backward, allowing you to see if any of them include the devil speaking in middle English or still more plugs for 1-800-COLLECT.

Vicarage Jaguars

http://www.satelnet.org/jaguars/

My favorite cars are not made in Detroit—they come from a factory in Coventry. Mind, they're controlled from Detroit—Jaguar is a subsidiary of Ford now. The latest redesign of the XJ-6 Jaguar looks like a fusion of a Ford Torus and a BMW after a mishap on the Autobahn.

The Vicarage Jaguars page is a shrine of sorts—it offers a tour through the Jags that were. Maintained by a firm in England that specializes in restoring classic Jaguars, it includes graphics of E-types, Mark II's, pre-Ford XJ-6's and the XJ-13, which was reputedly capable of burying its speedometer at over 200 miles an hour.

In the days when the earth was flat, before air bags, emission controls, shoulder belts, crush zones, photo radar, passenger side environment controls, factory installed compact disc players and all-wheel drive. . . they built cars.

Visa

http://www.visa.com/visa/

The people who brought you and the next three generations of your descendants limitless plastic credit and indentured servitude have a page on the Web. Credit cards have probably changed the way we do business to a greater degree than any of the business toys bought with them. Consider that it's no longer necessary to have money in order to buy things, to go to a shop to do some shopping, or to bother your bank manager when you need a loan.

A lot of the Visa page is the usual sort of corporate posturing and advertisements for things Visa will do for you other than empty your bank account. However, there are a few interesting and genuinely useful features of this page, including an international ATM locator and information about dealing with lost or stolen cards.

One of the slogans of the Visa empire is "one world, one currency"—an interesting outgrowth of credit cards that are accepted everywhere. You don't even have to know what the local currency is when you travel abroad if you have plastic. Alternately, if you think you might need some real money, it's worth noting that ATM machines in most parts of the world can be accessed with any Visa card.

Web Museum

http://www.oir.ucf.edu/louvre/
(University of Central Florida)

http://sunsite.unc.edu/louvre/
(SunSITE University of North Carolina)

http://www.emf.net/louvre/
(Berkeley, California)

http://cutl.city.unisa.edu.au/louvre/
(University of South Australia)

http://SunSITE.sut.ac.jp/louvre/
(SunSITE Science University of Tokyo)

http://sunsite.nus.sg/louvre/
(SunSITE National University of Singapore)

http://cair-archive.kaist.ac.kr/louvre/
(CAIR, Korea Advanced Institute of Science and Technology, Daejon)

http://www.cnam.fr/louvre/
(Conservatoire National des Arts et Mitiers, Paris)

http://www.cineca.it/louvre/
(INECA-Interuniversity Computing Center, Italy)

http://oak.ece.ul.ie/louvre/
(University of Limerick, Ireland)

Experience a museum on the Internet. While it lacks an admission fee, a gift shop, queues, tourists, signs warning you of prompt flogging if you're caught with a camera, and guards with discreetly carried Kalashnikovs, the Web Museum page allows you to enjoy the diversity and splendor of a French museum from the comfort of your own monitor. It features links to numerous paintings and other works of art scanned into GIF files. Each picture is included as a thumbnail, which you can click on for a larger image if you're interested in the subject.

The exhibits change periodically, and the diversity of subjects is impressive. As I was writing this, the Web Museum page included:

- An exhibit on Paul Cezanne, including selected paintings and an extensive text biography.
- *Les tres riches heures,* du Duc de Berry. This is one of the most ornate of the medieval books of hours to have survived. It's presently at the Chantilly museum, but not available for viewing.
- An extensive list of famous painters, with links to selected artists.
- A virtual tour of Paris. You can walk around on your own, enjoy a guided tour, or grope about in the catacombs. Of the latter, the tour page says "This unique bone collection of 5 to 6 million people covers a surface of 11,000 square meters, a tiny portion of the 300 km of old mine corridors. Galleries are an average of 2.3 meters high, and the temperature is a constant 11°C during summer and winter. 148,970 visitors visited the place in 1993."
- An opportunity to win a bottle of French champagne by predicting the winner of the upcoming French elections. This is real champagne, too—not the stuff from California with bubbles painted on the sides of the bottles.

You can access the Web Museum through a variety of links, as listed at the beginning of this section. Choose the one closest to you.

What Snooz

http://www.digimark.net/mfu/whatsnoo.html

Should you really get into the Web, you'll no doubt become familiar with the What's New page, as discussed in chapter 5 of this book. Impeccably executed and essential for keeping up with new links on the Web, it's about as indispensable as air is to poodles.

Needless to say, nothing this vital to the continued survival of western civilization could go unsatirized on the Internet for very long. For a brilliant send-up of What's New, link to What Snooz. Cosmetically similar to What's New but perhaps a more accurate reflection of the true nature of the World Wide Web, What Snooz offers several pages of bogus listings. All the links work—sort of. That is, they link to real pages, but you could make a fortune selling swamp land in Florida to anyone who believes what they find there. The introduction to What Snooz says:

> *This page contains a list of links to the hundreds of thousands of new Web pages that have been created and announced in the last ten minutes. The list is updated each eleven minutes, and the previous listings (now ancient history) are immediately removed and placed on our inaccessible archives server.*
>
> - *Submit your listing*
> - *Attempt to access our always busy archives server*
> - *Search for a way to search for search engines*
> - *About C/3F's What Snooze page*
> - *Readers, keep it to yourselves!*

If some of the entries at What Snooz seem distantly familiar, you might have been browsing some of the more pretentious What's New listings a bit too avidly. For example:

> ***Trenton Quarantino's Home Page***
> ***New Britain, CT, US***
> *The hot young director of the films Pulp Dogs and Pulp People—about living organisms being reduced to, well, pulp—now has his own Web site, with hundreds of thousands of pages of dialog taken straight from his past films. Though you'll be bored to tears by this stuff, just when you're ready to give up on it, your monitor will lean forward and cut off your ear—just to keep you interested. (Requires Netscape 2.2.6b3 with VVRML extensions.)*

Or consider this next one. If everyone who'd ever written an incomprehensible book or paper and announced it in What's New as the next quantum leap in human understanding were marched four abreast into the sea, they'd all be dead. Think about it.

> *Why Things Must Suck by Nan Doorman*
> *Quadrupleday Books, NY, NY, US*
> *In this stunning new exegesis, Professor Doorman explains, in layman's terms, just why exactly it is that everything really MUST suck. You know, REALLY SUCK. Illustrated. 455pgs., online, free at:*
>
> *http://quad_day.com/whymustitsuck/ohyeahpleaspleas/tellme/why.html*

I think this next one was my favorite as I was writing this. I confess that I find the best thing about sports on television is the mute button.

> ***Drawbridge Racers Page***
> ***Philadelphia, PA, US***
>
> *The new sport that's sweeping the nation. Results of recent games. Pictures of all your favorite racers and their families. Stats, history, schedule of upcoming games, standings, predictions, full-color pix of the world's fastest drawbridges half-open, more.*
>
> *http://www.bridge.com/draw.html*

If you were to delete the word "f**k" from What's Snooze, the page would get a third smaller, but ignoring this it's genuinely amusing. Some of the pages linked to by the main list have nothing at all to do with the subjects that got you there—a bit like What's New, actually.

I should probably mention that What's Snooze was actually a link from What's New as I was writing this.

Why Ask Why?

`http://www.eng.auburn.edu/~rudolmc/why.html`

Some things really stop making sense if you think about them. This page is a list of them. It's a collection of rhetorical questions, piquant inquiries, and the ponderings of gods. For example:

*Why isn't *phonetic* spelled the way it sounds?*

Why are there interstate highways in Hawaii?

*Why do *fat chance* and *slim chance* mean the same thing?*

Do you need a silencer if you're going to shoot a mime?

Have you ever imagined a world with no hypothetical situations?

If Seven-Elevens are open 24 hours a day, 365 days a year, why are there locks on the doors?

If a cow laughed, would milk come out its nose?

Why do they put Braille dots on the keypad of the drive-up ATM?

*Why isn't *palindrome* spelled the same way backwards?*

Why do we drive on parkways and park on driveways?

*Why is it that when you transport something by car, it's called a *shipment*, but when you transport something by ship, it's called *cargo*?*

*Why do they call them *apartments* when they're all stuck together?*

*Shouldn't there be a shorter word for *monosyllabic*?*

These are the things that have riven the minds of the wisest of men.

WIPE: The Worldwide Institute for the Preservation of Everything

http://www.dungeon.com:80/~weaver/

The dangerous thing about WIPE is that there are some really intense souls who will link to it, read all the articles offered by its home page, and take it very, very seriously. It sounds like it could almost be real. To be sure, it sounds a lot less flaky than some genuine environmental groups—you won't find WIPE out on the high seas threatening to ram a factory trawler with an inflatable raft. Of itself, WIPE says:

> *Welcome to the cozy world of WIPE, tireless campaigners for the eradication of decay, in all of its unholy and degenerate forms.*

The WIPE page features a respectable list of very authentic-sounding scientific papers and articles about the decay of all sorts of things and its prevention. For example, here's the beginning of an especially learned piece—I should note that the original paper was replete with hypertext links to further explain some of its more technical aspects.

> ***A Polymer Coating for the Planet***
>
> *Our guest speaker, Professor Shimpling Chadacre, brought us up to date on the advances being made in the ever-expanding and contracting world of polymers. His charming assistant, Miss Madeira Rockfish, operated the slide projector.*
>
> *The word *polymer* comes from the Greek, *polumeres* meaning *many mothers*. The Greeks were in the habit of indulging in a yearly ritual that involved them imbibing copious quantities of hallucinogenic mushrooms. During these festivals, the great scientists of the day would take their portion of the intoxicant, go off into the surrounding fields, and theorize.*
>
> *During one of these sessions, Polygamy, the renowned mathematician, envisaged a reality consisting entirely of pregnant women, of various sizes and hues, spinning around each other in a perpetual dance of energy. This "Dance of the Mothers," as it came to be known, was the basis for modern chemistry.*
>
> *If you think of a row of 50 pregnant women all holding hands with each other, then you have some idea of what a polymer looks like. But it's not just a polymer's appearance that excites us scientists, it's its properties: some are strong and stiff, as if they all had rigor mortis, while others are fluid, as if they were all laying down and rolling over each other.*

Now that we've covered the background, I'll tell you about some of the more recent developments in polymer coatings, and how they relate to your field of interest. I'd just like to say, at this point, that I share the heartfelt compassion that you all feel, most especially since I lost my Dwarf Gourami to Dropsy, the terrible "inflating fish" disease.

The paper went on for quite a while longer and never really got to the point—as well it probably shouldn't have done. Imagine trying to drive on a planet with a polymer coating. It doesn't bear thinking about. The WIPE page also says of itself:

The Institute was established in 1995 to recognize and coordinate the growing concern over all forms of decay, destruction, disintegration and devolution. Mawkish sentimentality has been derided for far too long. In this high-speed world of information technology, few people have the time to fully recognize man's many great achievements. While global culture rushes heedlessly ahead into the next millennium, who will preserve the world cherished by our fathers, and our fathers' fathers? Our founder, the late Dame Eris of Brocklebank, summed up the Institute's raison d'etre most elegantly during her speech at our first Annual General Meeting:

"What a crying shame it would be if even the most meager morsel of man's creative effort should ever be lost. Everything is connected. When we feel loss, it hurts. I don't want any more pain. It's time to stop. You're all going too fast."

Attendees of the meeting will remember clearly how Dame Eris selflessly demonstrated the "loss equals pain" theory by expiring midway through her inaugural speech, leading to a period of intense public mourning. No one who was present will ever forget the sight of her robust figure as it crashed forwards into the front row, still clutching the lectern with a white-knuckled vice-like grip, or the hollow sound of breaking shins.

The remaining board members would like to take this opportunity to thank the Emergency Services for their sensitive handling of the incident, and to wish those who are still in hospital a thorough and speedy recovery.

Actually, the WIPE page says a lot more of itself—like most institutes and committees, it's a lot more concerned about what it is than what it's supposed to be doing. This seems to lend it a particular sense of authenticity.

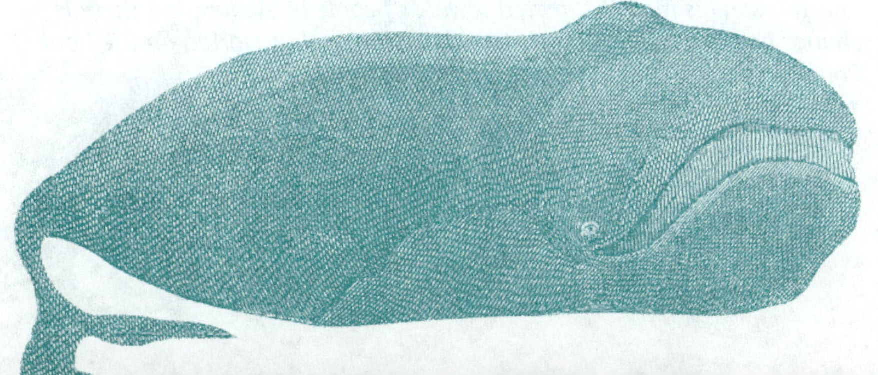

World Wide Cats

http://www.xs4all.nl/~dmuller/wwc.html

When I wrote the first *Planet Internet* book, I thought that whatever negative feedback they might engender would have been on the grounds of the art director's self-portrait wearing nothing but a bowler hat, the section about satanists in New Zealand, or the picture of the president of the United States with an arrow through his head. Actually, none of this came to pass—there were only two nasty letters. Both of them were from people who objected to my observation that cats probably taste like chicken, and that the exotic ones probably taste like really good chicken.

I've never actually eaten a cat, so I couldn't say for sure. However, Murphy, my 150-pound Labrador retriever, really likes chicken and he lunches out on cats just as readily, which lends some credence to the observation for me. Mind, he doesn't like to pin chickens to the ground and flap them around 'til their necks break. Damn but I love that dog.

The World Wide Cats page is maintained by people who probably think Murphy ought to be taken out back and shot. It's a link to dozens of other cat resources on the net, including no small number of home pages ostensibly set up and maintained by cats. These are identified as Otis the cat, Naomi the cat, Mr. Puddy the cat, Clio the cat, and so on. Most include pictures of the cats in question. Sadly, most of them seem to have been alive when they were photographed.

Included in the list of links as I was writing this were several pages for lost cats. Here's one of them:

OUR CAT IS MISSING

Rocky was lost in Sydney, Nova Scotia, Canada in November of 1994. We have searched the area quite thoroughly and had no luck finding him. We know he wasn't run over by a car because he is terrified of them and runs every time he sees one. He is a very friendly cat, and will always run up to unfamiliar people. This had led us to one of two conclusions:

- *He is living in someone's house*
- *He got on a cruise ship that comes to Sydney every year*

This message is mainly directed towards people in Sydney, but there is a chance he could have made it to either Montreal or Florida on the boat! Pretty good for a one-year-old cat, eh? He has:

- *orange fur*
- *orange eyes*
- *a strange liking for bottle caps*

- *wrestling talents*
- *a white teardrop marking on the left side of his nose*

If you love cats you'll unquestionably love this page. If you like the way they always land on their feet after the fifth or sixth bounce, you might find a bit of vicarious amusement here, perhaps along the lines of what a cat does with a mouse—or a Labrador retriever does with a cat.

World Wide Glide

http://www.halcyon.com/zipgun/wwg/wwg.html

The distinctive sound of a Harley can't even be approached by other bikes. Costing as much as a good car but quite a bit easier to park, Harleys aren't intended to be ridden by dilettantes or weekend warriors. They're as much a culture as a way to get around.

The World Wide Glide page is maintained by the owner of a Harley bike, rather than by the Harley Davidson Motor Company. The author identifies himself as Zipgun Beauregard.

Rich with both technical information about owning, riding, and maintaining a Harley and with all sorts of anecdotes and unique Harley graphics, World Wide Glide offers numerous links to its own dependent pages and to other motorcycle resources on the net. The list as I was writing this included:

- The Harley Alphabet Soup Revealed
- Bike Designations
- Performance Books
- A Few Words on Pipes
- The Gospel on Plugs
- Factory Recalls (at Harley Digest site)
- What's a CV Carburetor?
- Toolkit for The Road
- A Word on Jets
- Seat-of-the-Pants Timing
- My Grandaddy was a Knucklehead! (Engine pictorial.)
- The Harley Digest. Plus some of its members' bikes.
- Which states are limiting our freedom to ride?
- Harley-Davidson on the Net?
- H-D related Daytona results.
- The 1995 Bikes (no pictures)
- The Future of Motorcycling?
- The Terminator jumping his Fatboy into a drainage canal (627KB)
- And you think Bikers are scum?

- Welcome to the brave new Media-Blitz(tm) of Harley. . .
- Motorcycle-Related Internet Resources

One of the unfortunate aspersions of Harleys is that suits think only bikers ride 'em. Most suits don't have much to say about bikers that would be repeatable in polite company—breathing polyester fumes for 20 years probably does that to you. However, the last graphic in the Harley Davidson page probably defines the issue in clearer terms. It says:

FREEDOM = RESPONSIBILITY

Internet access providers

The following is a short list of commercial Internet access providers. As was discussed earlier in this book, a lot more of these companies are appearing.

a2i communications
Modem: 408-293-9010 (v.32, v.32 bis) or 408-293-9020 (PEP)
Login as guest
Voice mail: 408-293-8078

Aimnet Corporation
20410 Town Center Lane, Suite 290
Cupertino, California 95014
Modem: 408-366-9000
Login as guest at the prompt and register online. No password is required.
Voice: 408-257-0900
Fax: 408-257-5452

RainDrop Laboratories
Modem: 503-293-1772 (2400) 503-293-2059 (v.32, v.32 bis)
Login as apply

Anomaly (Rhode Island's Gateway to the Internet)
Modem: 401-331-3706 (v.32) or 401-455-0347 (PEP)
Voice: 401-273-4669

Ariadne (Greek Academic and Research Network)
Modem: +301 65-48-800 (1200 to 9600 bps)
Voice: +301 65-13-392
Fax: +301 6532910

Communications Accessibles Montreal
Modem: 514-281-5601 (v.32 bis, HST) 514-738-3664 (PEP), 514-923-2103 (ZyXeL 19.2K), 514-466-0592 (v.32)
Voice: 514-923-2102

CAPCON Library Network
Modem: contact for number
Voice: 202-331-5771
Fax: 202-797-7719

Cooperative Library Agency for Systems and Services
Modem: contact for number
Voice: 800-488-4559
Fax: 408-453-5379

Community News Service
Modem: 719-520-1700
ID: new, password: newuser
Voice: 719-579-9120

CONCERT-CONNECT
Modem: contact for number
Voice: 919-248-1999

connect.com.au pty ltd
Modem: contact for number
Voice: +61 3 5282239
Fax: +61 3 5285887

CTS Network Services (CTSNET)
Modem: 619-593-6400 HST, 619-593-7300 V.32bis, 619-593-9500 PEP
Login as help
Voice: 619-593-9597
Fax: 619-444-9247

CR Laboratories Dialup Internet Access
Modem: 415-389-UNIX
Voice: 415-381-2800

Colorado SuperNet, Inc.
Modem: contact for number
Voice: 303-273-3471
Fax: 303-273-3475

The Cyberspace Station
Modem: 619-634-1376
Login as guest
Voice: n/a

Demon Internet Systems (DIS)
Modem: +44 (0)81 343 4848
Voice: +44 (0)81 349 0063

DIAL n' CERF or DIAL n' CERF AYC
Modem: contact for number
Voice: 800-876-2373 or 619-455-3900

DIAL n' CERF USA
Modem: contact for number
Voice: 800-876-2373 or 619-455-3900

The Direct Connection
Modem: +44 (0)81 317 2222
Voice: +44 (0)81 317 0100
Fax: +44 (0)81 317 0100

Eskimo North
Modem: 206-367-3837 300-2400 bps, 206-362-6731 for 9600/14.4K,
206-742-1150 World Blazer
Voice: 206-367-7457

Express Access (Online Communications Service)
Modem: 301-220-0462, 410-766-1855, 908-937-9481
Login as new
Voice: 800-546-2010, 301-220-2020

genesis, MCSNet
Modem: (312) 248-0900 V.32, 0970 V.32bis, 6295 (PEP)
Follow prompts
Voice: (312) 248-UNIX

Grebyn Corporation
Modem: 703-281-7997
Login as apply
Voice: 703-281-2194

Halcyon
Modem: 206-382-6245, 8N1
Login as new
Voice: 206-955-1050

Institute for Global Communications/IGC Networks
(PeaceNet, EcoNet, ConflictNet, LaborNet, HomeoNet)
Modem: 415-322-0284 (N-8-1)
Login as new
Voice: 415-442-0220

HoloNet
Modem: 510-704-1058
Voice: 510-704-0160

UK PC User Group
Modem: +44 (0)81 863 6646
Voice: +44 (0)81 863 6646

The IDS World Network
Modem: 401-884-9002, 401-785-1067
Voice: 401-884-7856

The John von Neumann Computer Network (Tiger Mail and Dialin' Terminal)
Modem: contact for number
Voice: 800-35-TIGER, 609-258-2400

The John von Neumann Computer Network (Dialin' Tiger)
Modem: contact for number
Voice: 800-35-TIGER, 609-258-2400

Maestro
Modem: (212) 240-9700
Login as newuser
Voice: 212-240-9600

Texas Metronet
Modem: 214-705-2902 9600bps, 214-705-2917 2400bps
Login as info or signup
Voice: 214-401-2800
Fax: 214-401-2802 (8am-5pm CST weekdays)

Merit Network, Inc. (MichNet project)
Modem: contact for number
Voice: 313-764-9430

MindVOX
Modem: 212-989-4141
Login as mindvox or guest
Voice: 212-989-2418

MSen
Modem: contact for number
Voice: 313-998-4562
Fax: 313-998-4563

MV Communications, Inc.
Modem: contact for numbers
Voice: 603-429-2223

NEARnet
Modem: contact for numbers
Voice: 617-873-8730

Netcom Online Communication Services
Modem: 206-527-5992, 214-753-0045, 310-842-8835, 408-241-9760, 408-459-9851, 415-328-9940, 415-985-5650, 503-626-6833, 510-426-6610, 510-865-9004, 619-234-0524, 714-708-3800, 916-965-1371
Voice: 408-554-UNIX

North Shore Access
Modem: 617-593-5774 (v.32, PEP)
Login as guest
Voice mail: 617-593-3110

NovaLink
Modem: 800 937-7644, 508-754-4009 2400 (14400)
Login as new or info
Voice: 800-274-2814

Northwest Nexus Inc.
Modem: contact for numbers
Voice: 206-455-3505

OARnet
Modem: send e-mail to nic@oar.net
Voice: 614-292-8100
Fax: 614-292-7168

Old Colorado City Communications
Modem: 719-632-4111
Login as newuser
Voice: 719-632-4848, 719-593-7575, 719-636-2040
Fax: 719-593-7521

PANIX Public Access Unix
Modem: 212-787-3100
Login as newuser
Voice: 212-877-4854 (Alexis Rosen), 212-691-1526 (Jim Baumbach)

The Portal System
Modem: 408-973-8091 high-speed, 408-725-0561 2400bps
Login as info
Voice: 408-973-9111

PREPnet
Modem: contact for numbers
Voice: 412-268-7870
Fax: 412-268-7875

PUCnet Computer Connections
Modem: 403-484-5640 (v.32 bis)
Login as guest
Voice: 403-448-1901
Fax: 403-484-7103

NeoSoft's Sugar Land Unix
Modem: 713-684-5900
Voice: 713-438-4964

Telerama Public Access Internet
Modem: 412-481-5302 (2400)
Login as new
Voice: 412-481-3505

The Meta Network
Modem: contact for numbers
Voice: 703-243-6622

UUnorth
Modem: contact for numbers
Voice: 416-225-8649
Fax: 416-225-0525

Vnet Internet Access, Inc.
Modem: 704-347-8839
Login as new
Voice: 704-374-0779

The Whole Earth 'Lectronic Link
Modem: 415-332-6106
Login as newuser
Voice: 415-332-4335

APK-Public Access UNI*Site
Modem: 216-481-9436 (2400), 216-481-9425 (V.32bis, SuperPEP)
Voice: 216-481-9428

The World
Modem: 617-739-9753
Login as new
Voice: 617-739-0202

Wyvern Technologies, Inc.
Modem: (804) 627-1828 Norfolk, (804) 886-0662 (Peninsula)
Voice: 804-622-4289
Fax: 804-622-7158

B FTP sites

Some of these entries have been derived from Perry Rovers' FTP listing. This is a tiny sampling of the available FTP sites on the Internet; most sites support fairly technical matters, and aren't all that interesting if you're looking for something to browse. Like other things on the Net, FTP sites will move and even close down from time to time. This list was accurate when I assembled it.

ames.arc.nasa.gov
This site is located in the United States, and is supported by NASA. It includes space images and several other archives. Look in the directories /pub/SPACE/GIF and /pub/SPACE/JPEG.

archie.au
This site is located in Australia, and is supported by the Australian Academic and Research Network. It offers a lot of shareware for popular platforms, such as Windows and Macintosh systems.

archive.nevada.edu
This site is located in the United States, and is supported by the University of Nevada. It includes the U.S. constitution and relevant documents, and some religious texts.

c.scs.uiuc.edu
This site is located in the United States, and is supported by the University of Illinois. It includes some astronomy graphics.

cathouse.aiss.uiuc.edu
cathouse.org
This site is located in the United States, and is supported by the University of Illinois. It includes Rush Limbaugh transcripts, Monty Python sketches, all sorts of humorous files, song lyrics, movie scripts, and a lot more. This is a wonderful archive.

ccphys.nsu.nsk.su
This site is located in Russia, and is supported by Novosibirsk State University. It has a lot of files related to games and simulations.

cdrom.com
This site is located in the United States, and is supported by the Walnut Creek CD-ROM company. It offers files related to CD-ROMs.

cs.stmarys.ca
This site is located in Canada, and is supported by Saint Mary's College. It offers graphics and music files.

cs.wm.edu
This site is located in the United States. It offers files related to animal rights.

elbereth.rutgers.edu
This site is located in the United States, and is supported by Rutgers University. It offers buckets of files on science fiction.

explorer.arc.nasa.gov
This site is located in the United States, and is supported by NASA. It includes images from various space probes, such as Viking, Voyager, and Magellan.

ftp.apple.com
This site is located in the United States, and is supported by Apple Computer. It includes software and product information about Apple's computers . . . and perhaps a list of who's being sued this week.

ftp.brad.ac.uk
This site is located in the United Kingdom, and is supported by the University of Bradford. It includes sound files, quite a few graphics, and an ongoing program guide for "Married . . . with Children."

ftp.cc.umanitoba.ca
This site is located in Canada, and is supported by the University of Manitoba. It offers extensive travel information.

ftp.cis.ksu.edu
This site is located in the United States, and is supported by the Kansas State University. It includes an archive of original Star Trek stories . . . pretty weird stuff, some of it.

ftp.crs4.it
This site is located in Italy, and is supported by Centro di Ricerca, Sviluppo e Studi Superiori. It offers a selection of MPEG movies.

ftp.cs.colorado.edu
This site is located in the United States, and is supported by the University of Colorado. It includes documents pertaining to Esperanto.

ftp.cs.ruu.nl
This site is located in the Netherlands, and is supported by Utrecht University. It includes an archive of aircraft images.

ftp.cwru.edu
This site is located in the United States, and is supported by Case Western Reserve University. It includes an archive of U.S. supreme court rulings.

ftp.sys.utoronto.ca
This site is located in Canada, and is supported by the University of Toronto. It includes archives of anime, comics, and eclectic music.

ftp.uwp.edu
This site is located in the United States, and is supported by the University of Wisconsin. It includes a lot of files related to music, including lyrics, discographies, artists pictures, and press kits.

gatekeeper.dec.com
This site is located in the United States, and is supported by Digital Equipment Corporation. It offers zillions of recipes. It's unclear how big a zillion is, but it's somewhat greater than "quite a few."

ftp.hab-weimar.de
This site is located in Germany. It offers a selection of graphics and digitized sounds.

ftp.mantis.co.uk
This site is located in the United Kingdom, and is supported by Mantis Consultants Ltd. It includes archives of several engagingly weird newsgroups, including alt.angst and alt.atheism.

ftp.nevada.edu
This site is located in the United States, and is supported by the University of Nevada. It offers a selection of resources for guitarists.

ftp.spies.com
This archive is located in the United States. It's the ultimate archive for text documents on absolutely everything. Its contents range from the scholarly to the exceedingly weird. Don't miss it.

uunorth.north.net
This archive is located in Canada. It offers downloads of the Graphic Workshop software discussed in this book.

Index

A

B

C

D

E

F

H

I

J

K

L

M

Q

R

S

U

V

W

INDEX

About the author*

Steve Rimmer lives in rural central Ontario with his wife Megan, three dogs, and a variety of unusual cars. All his neighbors are cows. He is the president of Alchemy Mindworks Inc., a small software company that creates graphics applications. He has written over a dozen books about computer-related topics and several novels about witchcraft and pagan magic. His computer books include *Planet Internet*, *Return to Planet Internet*, *Bitmapped Graphics*, and *Windows Multimedia Programming*, all published by McGraw-Hill. His most recent works of fiction include *The Order* and *Wyccad*, published by Jam Ink Books. His hobbies include archery and playing celtic music with a local band.

*Mostly true

123...

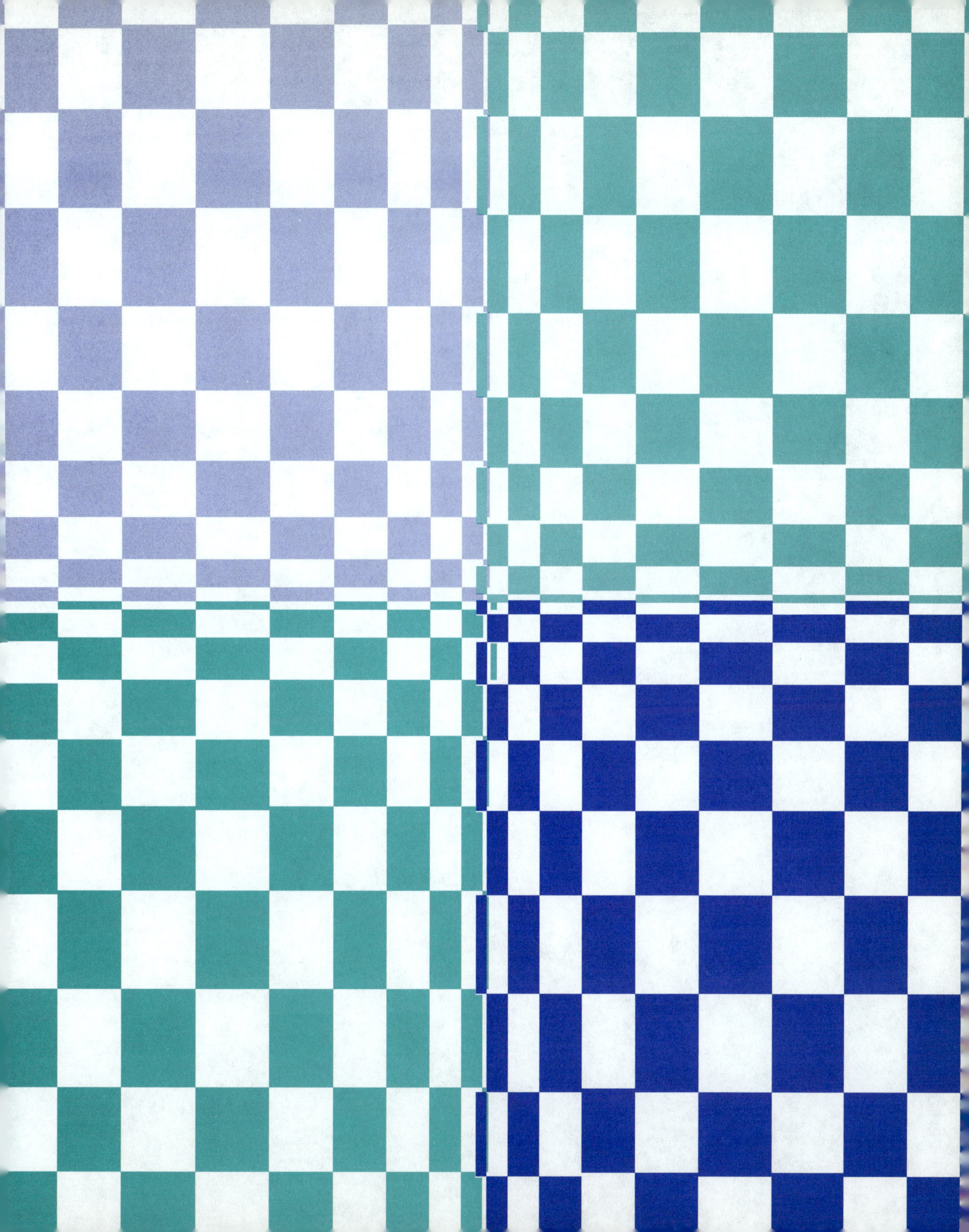

...abc